Thinking Riding Book 2
"IN GOOD FORM"

Thinking Riding Book 2
"IN GOOD FORM"

MOLLY SIVEWRIGHT
F.I.H., F.B.H.S., F.A.B.R.S.

Illustrations by the author

J. A. Allen

British Library Cataloguing in Publication Data
A catalogue record for this book is available from the British Library

First edition published 1984
Reprinted 1986
Reprinted 1989
Reprinted 1993

Published in Great Britain by
J. A. Allen & Company Limited
1 Lower Grosvenor Place
London SW1W 0EL

ISBN 0-85131-378-7

Book production Bill Ireson

Printed in Great Britain by St Edmundsbury Press Limited, Bury St Edmunds, Suffolk

Contents

Introduction

The main purpose of this book is to give practical guidance to young and inexperienced instructors. Such guidance will help them to apply their teaching so that their own, and their pupils', confidence and competence improve with each lesson and they and their horses obtain maximum satisfaction and enjoyment from their work together. Its secondary purpose is to help the intermediate instructor to progress in his or her chosen career; to rearrange, or even re-seed, some of the more experienced instructors' ideas and systems.

The term or title "riding instructor" has been used and abused for countless centuries. During the early Chinese dynasties and in Xenophon's time, 400 B C, the riding instructor was a very important person indeed. The victories of the generals of those days and of the armies under their command were largely attributable to the country's chief riding instructor, for on his equestrian knowledge and expertise and the skill with which he imparted that knowledge to his pupils, depended the prowess and strength of that nation's cavalry. Superior horsemanship coupled with willing, obedient, well-balanced and fit horses were the components of a fighting force which had superior speed, stamina and manoeuvrability, which could "conquer all before it" – and did!

Later, when kings and queens had both the need and the time to learn and to patronise the art of horsemanship, the court riding instructor was held in high regard, often as a counsellor and friend as well as a master of his art.

Unfortunately in more modern times the title of riding instructor has been abused, by its being conferred upon or sometimes assumed by persons who have received little or no training. Sometimes this has been due to lack of understanding of how much training and how many years of diligent study and application are required before an instructor can be worthy of the title. However, it would be grossly unfair to belittle the value of proven qualified instructors because of a few whose shallow perception of the training of riders and horses is revealed in their use of short cuts and gadgets, and the resultant tension and inconsistency in their pupils' performances.

Fortunately, there are a number of gifted horsemen who have both the desire and the ability to teach. They should not be deterred by the foregoing paragraph, they should rather regard it as a constructive incentive to their joining the list of the nation's qualified instructors.

Studying and training for such a qualification can bring immeasurable benefits and enjoyment to the student, of whatever age. Obtaining the instructor's certificate will provide confidence-giving proof of his competence, both to the instructor himself and his pupils, as well as giving positive support to the nation's equestrian federation.

The equitation instructor can only become qualified and respected when he has learned the techniques of his craft and has applied and practised those techniques over a period of years. Providing that he retains a degree of humility he will appreciate that there is far more to learn than ever he can assimilate in a lifetime; he will remain staunchly interested, undaunted by the mighty task ahead, and eventually he may develop his craft into an art. If this should happen to him then he will not only increase his own store of knowledge so that he has more to give, but will be repaid a thousandfold, not by the size of his bank balance but in the less tangible and greater rewards found in his human and equine pupils' improvement. Their success and their appreciation of his efforts, and his own joy in being able to give will be his reward. "Giving", that surely is what instructing is all about. Giving, helping, caring and learning how to achieve the highest possible standard in all aspects of riding, of horse care and of teaching others to become equally proficient, so that the craft of horsemanship is preserved, improved and even, by some, developed into an art.

Author's Note

Whilst this book is a companion volume to Thinking Riding, Book 1, it is, and can be used as, a completely separate entity. However, in preparing this work I have occasionally referred the reader to Book 1 and also sometimes quoted extracts from it. The two books are intended to be a continuing training course for student riders and instructors.

1 The Meaning of "In Good Form"

The horseman's usage of the word *form*, with regard to his horse, was explained briefly in Book 1. It is an important distinction and will bear repetition here:

> The word "form" is translated from the Swedish, where it means not only the horse's outline and his being correctly on the bit, but also the way in which the horse goes as a whole, mentally and physically; how he moves, and what he feels like to sit on, as a ride, in all his gaits. It is a small, simple word with a large and complex meaning.

In this book we shall develop the meaning of form and then put it into practice.

Good Form

The meaning of good form should be studied in greater depth, for it has many different meanings each of which implies and assumes a vast number of highly desirable qualities. The word "form" itself can conjure up a wide variety of pictures, all of which enhance the horseman's interpretation and may even provoke an extra thought or two. When put together all the different aspects will help thinking riders to gain a deeper concept of "form" and to understand more fully the meaning of this vital little word.

Let us look at these aspects in more detail.

EMOTIONAL

Being "in good form" is synonymous with feeling positively optimistic, creative, in high spirits – the sky is blue, the sun shines, the birds sing, the riders and horses are going well (in good form, of course), and "everything is fine – just fine!"

FORM, OR OUTLINE

When used in the context of an object good form means that the proportions of the object in question have a balance and symmetry. Whereas the word "outline" is often used in relation to the horse, it is only a small part of the whole. For example, "That horse has a good novice outline" can be taken correctly to mean that the horse has a well developed top-line, or incorrectly that he is rather "cresty", with the nose tucked in and nothing happening behind the saddle, or incorrectly again, that he is on his forehand leaning on the bit as though the rider should provide him with a fifth leg.

From these inconsistencies, the lessons can be learned that riders, as well as would-be instructors and judges, must know as much as possible about the horse's outline – his conformation when he is stationary and when in action. They must develop X-ray eyes to see how the horse moves, which muscles he employs to move which bone, and whether he flexes the main joints as he should. Instructors and judges should also train their eyes, brains and hearts to assess the rider's form – whether he is

Adjusting stirrups...

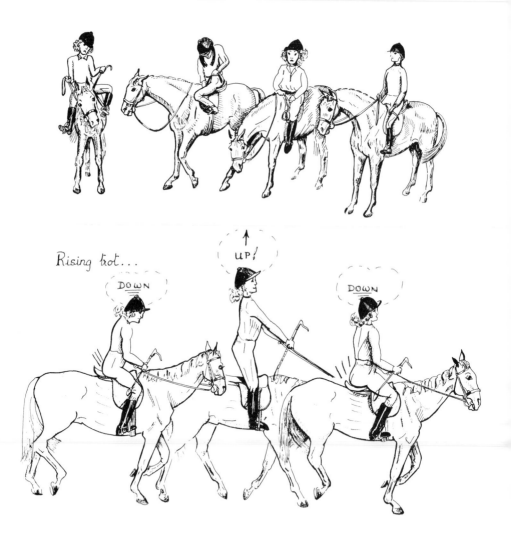

Rising trot...

Untrained, thoughtless riders (spot one correct rider.)

in perfect balance, straight, level and poised yet without constraint and whether he is a good leading partner for his horse. Then, and only then, will these horse-persons be able to discern good form from bad form, with regard to the horse and rider's combined outline or silhouette.

FORM, OR BENCH

Made of timber with stout legs at either end and possibly having an equally stout central support. It is stable and strong enough to withstand the balancings and bouncings of several gyrating gymnasts without turning a splinter.

Certainly some riders seem to imagine that a horse's back is just as stout, stable, strong and unfeeling as a wooden form or they would not bang and wriggle about on the saddle as they do when mounting, altering stirrup leathers or girths, when rising to the trot, or when watching a friend's round over show jumps – or on many other thoughtless occasions.

In fact, the horse bears no resemblance to this type of form: his skeletal structure is far too fragile. However, instructors must appreciate that if children have not been brought up riding sturdy ponies and, later, larger cobby types, it is not surprising if they imagine a horse's back to be indestructible, perhaps even a small relation of the Giant's Table at the Badminton Horse Trials. Due to the layers of fat they may not even realise that he has a spine! Rarely have beginners ever given the matter a thought – instructors must introduce anatomical landmarks, one by one, at an early stage if they are to produce good horsemen.

The number preceding the word "form" as used in schools denotes the standard at which a pupil is working. The younger, weaker and less advanced pupils work together at the lower end of the form scale, while the older, stronger, more advanced pupils work together in a higher form. So it is with riders and horses: novice pupils and horses must not be expected to work at too severe demands until they are prepared, established and ready – mentally and physically. The form must match the form.

Good form – good taste, impeccable manners and wise judgement – can mean a good record, with regard to the horse's performance on the racecourse or in competition. Good form will lead to good form.

Both the rider and his horse should show good form at all times; they should be a pleasure to look at when standing still and when on the move. Together they should make a strong appeal to the onlooker's aesthetic sense.

The Horse's Form

The horse's form will be good if:

- He is submissive and calm yet bold; he is confident and trusting yet respectful; he is happy in his work – with no sign of worry or excess tension.
- He has a natural balance, waiting on reasonably good conformation – without any major fault.
- He is sound.
- He is in good condition, being fit for the work required of him.
- He is seen and felt to have three true basic gaits; extravagant action is not essential, even for a competition horse – every horse's action will improve with correct training.
- He gives a rider a good ride, being safe and a pleasure to sit on at all gaits and in every circumstance, on the flat and over fences or rough terrain.
- He accepts the rider and follows his aids with a ready response.
- He carries the rider with efficient co-ordination and ease.
- He is straight and supple (laterally and longitudinally).
- He is willing, thinking of moving forwards – even when working backwards!
- His feet tread upon the ground evenly, in a correct sequence, his steps being light yet secure.
- He is of a suitable type and size for his rider – the last is a bonus rather than an essential.

The Rider's Form

The rider's form will be good if:

- He is generous, warm-hearted and fair-minded.

- He is in a good mood and is capable of creating a quick and obvious rapport with the horses he rides.
- He has one correct mental approach, a thoughtfulness in all that he does, an indefatigable desire to improve the training standards of himself and of his horses. With regard to the latter, a degree of humility ensures that he does not blame his horse for faults which are in truth of his own making. It also enriches his sympathy enabling him to search for the easiest way to ask his horse to carry out suitable movements in as good a form as is reasonable at his present standard of training. Although quick-witted, he is also calm and in complete control of his emotions and temper.
- He is a thinking rider whose theoretical knowledge matches his practical experience and who has belief and confidence in the methods he uses.
- He understands the mental and physical problems of horses and knows how to ride all types of horses to improvement.
- He understands how to organise and control with ease the movements of each part of his own body, due to a basic knowledge of human anatomy. He is extremely careful not to impede or oppose his horse's movement by an inadvertent movement of muscle or bone.
- He has learned sufficient facts concerning the horse's anatomy and physiology so that the demands he makes will be fair, improving and enhancing.
- He influences his horse with soft, smooth and (most usually) invisible aids, measuring the degrees and the timing with infinite care.
- He understands with a clear single-mindedness the prime importance of his thought and weight aids.
- He is well aware of the dangers of forceful, hurried, unjust or otherwise incorrect training.
- He has an elegant poise based on a correct, supple and balanced position; he is a natural horseman with no hint of awkwardness or constraint, for whom all horses go kindly and well.

Good riding enhances nature – it never offends it. As with the horse, the rider's form must never be forced into one set pattern to comply with the whim of a nation, school or instructor. He must "do his own thing" naturally and easily, whilst following correct principles to the best of his ability.

A small expansion of detail is added here in an endeavour to help new riders and not-so-new riders whose horses always seem to be uncooperative if not downright awkward and obtuse. In fact, by nature horses are born kind, honest and generous creatures and the majority display an earnest desire to please. Unfortunately in this present age of stress and haste there is an increasing number of riders who fail to appreciate that there is much more to learning how to ride than meets the eye – much more!

Nowadays too few riders are being taught how to use their thought and weight aids carefully and correctly. Consequently, they do not ride their horses well. These most important aids have been omitted from their education. Without them riders can never achieve equestrian tact and a nice degree of mental and physical harmony with every horse they ride. The faults for which the horses are unjustly blamed and the lack of form should be laid fairly and squarely at their riders' feet: the horses' awkwardness and seeming stupidity or obstinacy is a reflection of their riders' bad horsemanship. Much of the blame should be put back one stage further to the riders' instructors who failed to teach their pupils adequately, perhaps omitting all mention of thought and weight aids in their lessons.

To my astonishment, in my travels at home and abroad, I have come across a small number of instructors who have never thought, given credit to or taught their pupils anything concerning these two most obvious and practical aids. Some have even been taught themselves that any mention of the weight as an aid could be dangerous, and this illogical nonsense they pass on to their ever-trusting pupils who accept the theory without question, sliding (literally) into very bad practices. A few of these instructors have carried out a little research: they have realised that all the equestrian masters' books mention the use and shifting of the rider's weight or of his seat. These few instructors may then venture a shy mention of "the rider's seat and back" but that is usually followed by the phrase, "this may be used, occasionally, later". Is it surprising that their pupils perch precariously, ineffectively and uncomfortably on their forks, trying not to use what Nature gave them to sit on ... until ... later?

It must be said, in fact, that "the boot is on the other foot": this negative attitude is incorrect, illogical and – yes, you've got it – *dangerous*!

That such thinking, or lack of it, is entirely illogical is easy to explain and for the sake of the riders of the future and even more, for their horses, explained it must be.

Every pupil must be taught, from his first lesson, that riding is all about *communication* and *influence* – the rider with and on his horse.

The instructor must not just teach his pupils to sit on their horses in what to him is a pleasing position, for then it will be a miracle if they ever develop into horsemen. The instructor must explain that the rider's *thought aids* commence as he approaches the horse and that the *weight aids* commence the instant the rider sits on his horse's back. Immediately, he must be aware of the positioning not only of his weight but of every bone and sinew in his body. The rider must learn to "tune" his mental and physical powers to gain the best possible reception and response from his horse from the first moment that he mounts.

As explained in Book 1, the rider's thought aids work in three main directions – forethought (preparations), mind to mind (telepathy), and general awareness (of the rider himself and of his environment). Of these

"The Thought Aid commences..."

three the second is the most obscure. The mental vibrations of unspoken communication between a man and his horse can be developed into the very strong influence of willpower providing that its presence is recognised and appreciated. Thought aids are based on the natural love of animals which itself promotes a bond of sincerity and trust as well as engendering an intense interest. This bond is usually strongest in purity, truth and directness in child pupils: the young mind is untrammelled by the complex worries of the adult world. Instructors must preserve and cultivate this gift, for by ignoring its existence they can easily extinguish the flame. I feel very sorry for any rider who has not opened his mind to the possibility that he and his horse are able to meet on the same mental wavelength, with even a weak ray of communication between them. I do not wish to sound condescending – I do feel sorry for them, most sincerely so, for such riders miss one of the most exciting joys of riding, that of rapport with the horse which is the very essence of horsemanship. Given a little open-minded willingness, it is easy for every rider to train his mind to tune into his horse's mind and thus to direct his thinking and reactions.

The instructor should give this teaching top priority, so that all his pupils understand these simple, basic facts upon which may be built the mental and physical partnership between the rider and his horse. To help young instructors, two imaginary situations are outlined below.

The tree

The *rider* sees a tree, standing in the path straight ahead of him. As its

The tree...

branches are a little lower on the left hand side he decides to pass to the right of it. That seems simple enough but the *horse* sees the same tree and develops his own ideas about it. He may think, if he is a simple horse with a high regard for his tummy, "I wonder if its bark tastes good?" Alternatively, "I can fit my head under the branches quite easily whichever side I go – hum, I think I'll go to the left" – or "I wonder if a wolf or some dangerous 'thing' is hiding behind that tree – perhaps it would be safer not to go anywhere near it!"

The *solution* is for the rider to retain a confidence-giving contact with the horse's mind from his own brain, and through his body by means of his seat. In plenty of time he should think and plan which side of the tree they will go and he should shift his weight to the right to invite the horse to take that direction. Only in this way will he be fair to his partner and will the horse develop confidence in his rider.

"He won't go on the bit!"

This is a most common complaint . . . "he" being the rider's horse. The *rider* has heard that, if only to please the dressage judge, his horse should be on the bit. The main requirement of this desirable quality, as this novice rider understands it, is that the horse's nose should be tucked in so that the front line of the face is more or less vertical with the ground. So . . . the rider pulls on the reins with ever-increasing pressure until the horse brings his head into the required position in an endeavour to avoid the pain being inflicted upon him by the bit in his mouth.

There is a fair chance that the horse will come into and remain in this position if the rider's seat is stable and supple. If however, the opposite is the case, he will bump on the horse's back, the horse will hollow away from the pain, raise his head and stick his nose out, whereupon the rider will resort to even more force (even to a cruel gadget), and a thoroughly vicious circle results.

The *horse* feels a tugging on the reins and thinks, "My rider often does that when he wants me to stop." How wrong the horse was he soon realises as his sides are belaboured with heels, spurs and whip. "My goodness how extraordinary he is – 'stop' and 'go' at the same time!" "Ouch, the pain in my mouth – why must he stiffen and jump up and down on my back – if this is dressage I only hope it finishes soon."

The *solution* is for the rider to realise that it is he who needs the correction and the reschooling – the horse deserves a medal for long suffering. The rider must appreciate that he himself does not yet know or understand nearly enough. It would, of course, be totally unfair to reprimand him for lack of knowledge. Instead the instructor must lead the rider to accept the true situation – to understand that only by building on correct foundations can a rider be so called.

Story-making, where the pupil is encouraged to imagine what the horse thinks and feels is of very real value to all instructors. Through intelligent use of their imagination they can help their pupils to under-

A Vicious Circle. (Pity the horse.)

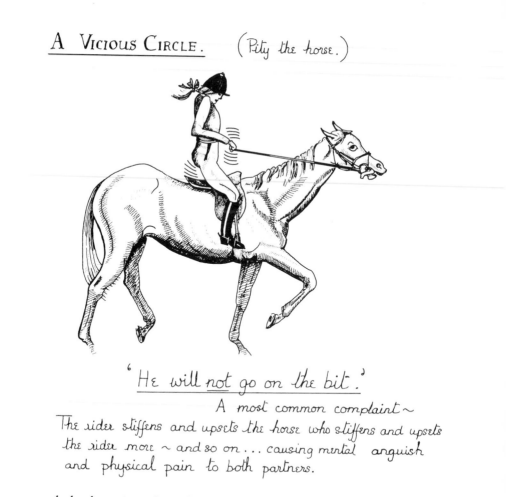

'He will **not** go on the bit.'

A most common complaint ~
The rider stiffens and upsets the horse who stiffens and upsets
the rider more ~ and so on ... causing mental anguish
and physical pain to both partners.

stand the horse's point of view in the many (to the horse), peculiar situations into which man takes him. This may be on the racecourse or over the cross-country course, the trotting track, the show jumping or dressage arena, or even hacking down a busy thoroughfare. At all times the rider must help his horse to understand his wishes as he rides or drives him as part of his chosen sport. The horse has no choice in the matter, often he has little joy, but instead is forced to endure unnecessary degrees of anguish, discomfort and even pain. Riders must learn how to influence their horses kindly, in plenty of time for them to make their own considerable readjustments, to demand only that which is reasonable, and to use aids which are simple, clear, natural and nearly invisible. No human has the right to abuse any horse – that is the moral aspect. Commercially speaking, a horse will only appreciate in value if he puts his heart into his work in an honest, trusting, way – if he enjoys it; he will then become more beautiful, his performance will improve, his working life will be extended and he will give his rider countless hours of pleasure as a wonderfully elating and uncomplaining companion.

THE SOLUTION ~ First cure the rider ~
improve UNDERSTANDING, POSITION and INFLUENCES (AIDS.).

The weight aids

Instructors must be equally clear and painstaking in their explanations and teaching of the rider's weight aids. They are not mysterious, rough or dangerous, in fact, the opposite is the case. Weight aids used correctly are utterly natural and logical and, when blended with thought and feel, the combination of all three can appear to be quite magical!

As soon as the rider rests the weight of his whole body on the horse's back he applies weight aids – "for better or for worse". Unless the rider is trained from his earliest lessons to be aware of how his weight and any movement of his body affects the horse he will not achieve a correct seat for the horse, and his weight will disrupt the horse's balance and hamper his movement rather than being "with" him or inviting him into new directions or movements. Any pupil who is kept in ignorance of the strong influence of the weight aids will use them very badly more often than not. He will not know any better. Therefore the pupil will then have to counteract his incorrect weight aids by overacting forcefully with his hands and legs in order to countermand the loss of balance (and bewil-

BAD RIDING ~

The wrong way to turn to the right.

dered misunderstanding) to his horse, caused by his own lack of training in this respect.

Inadequate education and failure to appreciate the simple logic of the rider's weight as an aid is the most common cause of a very low standard of horsemanship, roughness and cruelty replacing the desirable properties of good form in the equestrian events and in the riding and training of horses in these present times.

Concerning the weight aids, let us be entirely practical and logical. The very fact that the rider sits on the horse's back presents the rider with a weight aid like it or lump it – ask the horse! From the first instant that the rider settles into the saddle, the horse is only too aware that the rider is there, on his back. Immediately he has to stand and move more carefully; his balance is upset, for there is now even more weight to carry on his already massive forehand and he must use more muscle power and energy to carry himself and his rider over the ground. He feels a burden which can either be in perfect balance and thus relatively easy for him to carry, or his rider may be an awkward, unbalancing burden who disrupts his every move. The rider's weight aids can be only of two possibilities – they can be right or they can be wrong. Every rider must be trained to place, shift and poise his whole body correctly, safely and subtly, from the very first riding lesson, and to work at and improve this technique for the rest of his riding life.

The rider should think and feel for and with his horse at all times. There are so many people who ride their horses without any thought or consideration because they have never been taught otherwise – their instructor failed in his most important duty. In too many instances riders' motives are selfish: they ride to "keep up with the Joneses" or because they have a keen competitive drive and are attracted by the additional excitement and glamour which the horse presents to the participant in any horse sport.

Riding does not just "happen" – riders are not born miraculously to the sport or art of horsemanship, they cannot be trained to a high degree unless they have acquired a good posture and continue to maintain, if not improve it, all day and every day.

This cannot be stressed too much and, as quoted in Book 1, we should follow the advice of W. E. Tucker, CVO, MBE, TD, MA, MB, BCh, FRCS, the famous orthopaedic surgeon and consultant:

> Correct upright posture is the consequence of a particular attitude of the mind towards the body; one which promotes both mental and physical poise. Once the principles have been accepted and mastered, the various positions can be held unconsciously with little exertion. There will be no sign of tension and no wasted effort. It is a balanced posture, and therefore, is a form of continuous isometric exercise, since the muscles on one side of the body are constantly working against those of the opposite side. Childhood is the best time to learn but it is a simple matter for older people also to master the correct upright posture and derive physical benefit as a result. (*Home Treatment and Posture*)

Mr. Tucker's advice should be copied out and placed above every rider's bedroom door – on the inside, to remind the rider to carry out a simple programme of exercises when he gets out of bed, and to walk and sit (run, skip and jog) with a good posture all day.

Whenever a human being sits down he is supported by and balances on his two seat bones, which are the lower prominences of his two hip bones. That is an undeniable anatomical fact. There is no way that a rider can turn into an airy-fairy Peter Pan person every time he wishes to mount a horse: fantastic though that transformation might be, he must remain a mere mortal. Thus it follows that whenever the rider mounts and sits on his horse's back, the not inconsiderable weight of his entire body rests straight, supple and poised, upon the two prominences at the bottom of his two hip bones: his weight aid is in position, he must use it with the deference it deserves.

Unless a rider can control and organise the two to three hundred bones in his body how can he possibly organise those of his horse as well?

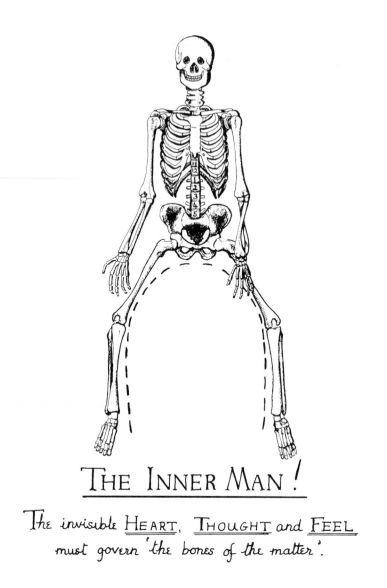

THE INNER MAN!

The invisible HEART, THOUGHT and FEEL must govern 'the bones of the matter'.

Riders must be taught dismounted, then mounted at halt and later at walk, how their own muscles can be called on to act, for example, to move a bone or alter the angle of a joint, in order that they may use these tiny movements simply and tactfully to influence the horses they ride. From these interesting, logical and easy beginnings, the rider will soon learn how to poise and balance his body so that he can adjust it to shift his weight imperceptibly exactly when and where necessary.

Instructors must not be afraid to teach their pupils about their weight aids, to give them simple exercises to carry out and to understand the method and the effects for themselves in the earliest lessons. "Using weight aids" does not mean leaning to one side or the other or hardening the muscles in the riders' backs. Heaven forbid! Quite the reverse, the riders must learn to shift their weight softly and subtly so that they can be exactly in balance – even when riding the smallest circle the axis of their hips and shoulders must be level. Riders should never harden their backs against their horses' backs.

Pupils must be given the chance to learn, time, feel and refine their shiftings and adjustings until these become spontaneous and instantaneous natural habits – minute movements which aid their horse partners and which are invisible to all but the most trained and perceptive eyes.

Some riders may argue that "the rider's seat has no means of direct communication with the horse, there is a thick saddle with all its padding and a numnah between the rider and the horse's back – anyway his back is fat and muscly so he won't feel much even if he could, which he can't! So why all this concern over the rider's seat bones?"

If an instructor is asked this question he should feel delighted that he has a thinking pupil. He should show enthusiastic pleasure and ask the

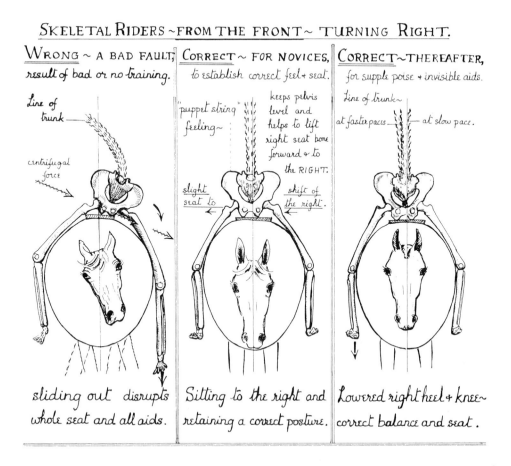

SKELETAL RIDERS ~ FROM THE FRONT ~ TURNING RIGHT.

WRONG ~ A BAD FAULT, result of bad or no training.

Line of trunk

centrifugal force

sliding out disrupts whole seat and all aids.

CORRECT ~ FOR NOVICES, to establish correct feel + seat.

"puppet string" feeling~

keeps pelvis level and helps to lift right seat bone forward + to the RIGHT.

slight seat to — shift of the right.

Sitting to the right and retaining a correct posture.

CORRECT ~ THEREAFTER, for supple poise + invisible aids.

Line of trunk~

at faster paces — at slow pace.

Lowered right heel + knee~ correct balance and seat.

pupil to dismount and to remove his saddle. If the instructor stands by the horse's left shoulder facing the front and places his right hand just behind the withers, his right thumb on the left side of the horse's spine and the first two fingers on the far side, and runs his thumb and fingers backwards, with quite a marked press, on either side of the horse's spine, the horse will show very convincingly whether he feels pressure on and through his muscles or not. Then, the instructor can ask the pupil to stand on the far side of the horse, with his hand resting flat on the horse's back just behind where the seat of the saddle would come, while he gives "the magic spot" a prod unseen by the pupil who can then *feel* the result. These are two most useful "eye-openers" for pupils which awaken their interest in the horse's physique and in his point of view as a whole. With an important dimension added to his understanding, the pupil can then be told to re-mount.

It is absolutely essential that the rider understands how much his weight can influence his horse and that he must place, adjust and move his seat bones, together with every part of his body, with the utmost thoughtfulness, care and precision. This must be thought about, discussed and taught from the earliest riding lessons so that, due to correct training initially, this placing and positioning of the rider's whole seat can be combined carefully with either one or many of the hundreds of possible nuances of movement within his body. In this way young riders will grow up with easy, subconsciously correct, riding habits. It must be remembered that bad, thoughtless habits are comparatively difficult to eradicate. Just as the rider's seat upon his horse is the foundation of his horsemanship, so logically must his weight aids be accorded primary importance.

Whereas a good form of horse and rider together is the ultimate aim, a rider can have a good form on a great variety of horses, but the quality of the horse's form is entirely dependent on the skill of the trainer and the rider. This will be most easily understood by, for example, those readers who were fortunate enough to see Granat in his youth, or when he was resting in the collecting ring, looking as if he knew more about moving a hay-wagon than dressage, and can contrast that picture with the transformation which occurred when his diminutive rider organised him into a good form. Can you ever forget the majesty of Granat's half-passes at trot or his piaffe and passage? There is the proof of the rider's ability to create and develop good form in the horse.

Riders must be led to think more, much more, of their horses' form whenever they ride. To this end, instructors must never tire of seeking new ways to explain this desirable "happening" and how it can (must) be achieved.

When an instructor sees that a new pupil obviously has not the slightest clue about riding his horse in a good form, the instructor must be kindly patient, understanding and diligent (as ever!); he must give the pupil clues to work on for himself. One small correction, idea or clue carefully explained and demonstrated at each question-time and followed thereafter by practice, feel, and thought, in constant repetition, are the best ways to solve problems, to advance equestrian education and to build up a genuine understanding.

If ever the instructor is faced with a pupil who has already been taught that "to use the seat too early is a bad and dangerous thing", the instructor must never be impatient. He must try to discover exactly how and why the pupil believes this. Perhaps the original "instructor" imagined or misinterpreted the "use of the seat" to mean an inclination of the rider's upper body backwards, behind the vertical, while sitting heavily and stiffly on the horse's back with the muscles over-tensed in what is sometimes falsely called "the driving seat". Or perhaps the instructor thought that use of the seat implied that the rider should wriggle the small of his back or his pelvis, as though he was wearing a grass skirt, rather than sitting on a horse. Such a pupil will relax considerably if his concern or interpretation problem is discovered and, more, if it is understood. It is important that by tactful questioning the instructor finds out the cause of the pupil's "hang-up" about his seat, for only then will he be able to establish a rapport and create in his pupil the receptive mental state which is primed for learning.

The instructor must be sure that his pupils do not have a restricted seat-area in their minds. They must understand that the whole term has a much broader meaning, that "the seat" refers to *the whole of the rider's body*; the major portion is above his two seat bones when the rider is sitting in an upright position but his legs too are part of the whole seat, and all parts must combine to give a wide variety of weight aids. When the rider is inclined forward with a light seat then it is patently obvious that his weight aids are supplied by the whole of his body, from his toes to the top of his head, for there is little if any weight then on his seat bones.

The rider's weight aids can only be one of two things – they can be right or they can be wrong.

In order to be able to give weight aids – or any other aids for that matter – which are consistently correct, the rider must be trained to sit straight and level, soft and supple, and above all, thoughtfully. All his points and joints which come in pairs must be carried at a level height and he must be in perfect balance with his horse. The rider must prepare well for all transitions and changes of direction, the latter should be invited by a thoughtful shifting of his weight a little in advance of the intended turn. This shifting should be felt clearly by the horse but should be imperceptible to the onlooker due to the speed, accuracy and controlled lightness of the shifting and the levelness of the rider's horizontal axis before, during and after the turn.

Conclusions

Although the rider wishes to alter the horse's skeletal shape to accommodate and carry the rider-burden he has placed upon the horse's back,

i

Half-halt,

and plan...

THOUGHT!

ii

Shift weight
to right...

(keep body
upright
and level.)

Do this
early enough
to invite him round
and to enable the
horse to make _his_ adjustments.

WEIGHT!

Memo:

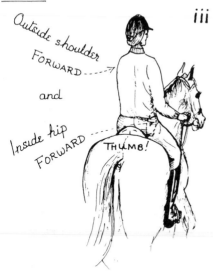

Outside shoulder
FORWARD

and

Inside hip
FORWARD

THUMB!

iii

Head conveys thought plan
and its turning co-ordinates all aids.
Both legs — lift up his middlepart...
(right 'puppet string' taut ~ up and forward)
Both legs maintain impulsion and form;
inner leg pushes into corner and asks for bend,
the outer leg also controls hindquarters.
Inner thumb leads with an open rein.
Outer hand gives to allow the horse
to stretch his outer side and to bend
round the rider's inner leg.

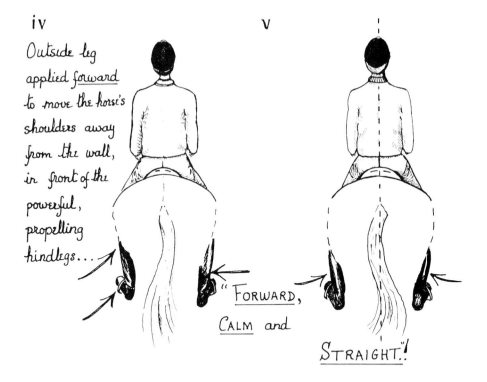

iv

Outside leg applied forward to move the horse's shoulders away from the wall, in front of the powerful, propelling hindlegs...

v

"FORWARD, CALM and STRAIGHT."

the rider cannot bend the horse's hindlegs himself nor, physically can he lift up the front end of the axial spine and the horse's trunk. However, what he can and should do is to encourage the horse to employ his own muscles in order to better his shape, balance, carriage, action, strength and carrying ability under his well-balanced, poised and "leading" rider.

All riders must understand that the whole of the rider influences the whole of the horse. Then, together and happily, they will have good form as they move in perfect harmony, the rider leading the partnership with aids which are thoughtfully timed and measured, clear, soft and smooth and almost impossible to see.

While it is true that "form is a small, simple word" it is equally true to say that it has "a large and complex meaning". However, its use is valueless if the full complexity of the word is not appreciated by those who use it.

Unfortunately, due to the bustle of our modern times and to the shortage of trained instructors, only a small minority of riders have been taught the true meaning of riding their horses well – so that the horse's form is not only good, it is improving during every moment he is ridden and so that horse and rider are happy with each other.

If this serious vacuum in equestrian training is to be filled (think positive!), it is essential that the instructors themselves understand

The rider cannot "bend the horse's hindlegs" ~

nor can he "lighten the horse's forehand" by lifting it!

The road is long,

many hours in many years of thoughtful and enjoyable work together ~

will turn a duckling

into

a swan!

thoroughly the importance of all horses being ridden in a good form, being happy and improving in their work. Only then can instructors pass on this information with the necessary degree of sincerity and urgency to their pupils and only then can those pupils learn a correct feel and the joy of a real "togetherness" with their horses. It is up to all instructors to encourage (veiled insistence!) every pupil they teach to grasp a true understanding of the term "in good form".

I hope the reader will find that the mists of misunderstanding are lifting, that instructors will have made one or two mental half-halts and will understand more clearly that children and beginner adults must be taught to be in perfect mental and physical balance and harmony for the sake of the pony or horse carrying them, from their first riding lesson. Then they will think for and of their horses in a much more realistic and caring way. Immediately they will have a worthwhile purpose in striving for a classically correct position, to sit in balance, straight and level with an easy poise, and they will use their weight aids correctly and naturally, from those early lessons onwards. From all of this will blossom a whole field of efficient, sympathetic and elegant riders.

I hope that more experienced riders also may have been given some food for thought and that these introductory explanations may ensure that their riding will be accomplished with even less visible aids, and that they and their horses will develop the increasingly good form which gives both partners great joy and perhaps . . . improving competition success. Although, with regard to the last of these, the love of the trophy or the rosette must never be allowed to outweigh the love of the horse.

The rider must be *with* his horse's movement . . .

Lack of thought

results in discord,

loss of balance, and of confidence.

Thoughtful riding ~ in balance, light, smooth aids ~ Horse and rider form a happy and successful PARTNERSHIP.

Feel

Feel is the intangible quality that makes possible this timing and refinement of the riders' aids. It has been said that feel is a God-given gift and that those lucky enough to be born with feel will make horsemen while those who lack feel will never make riders. Personally, I prefer to teach a different, albeit more optimistic approach. I believe that the majority of people are born with feel but that in some it is in a state of hibernation! Very often seemingly unfeeling people do grow into riders and instructors of more than average sensitivity, and one of the best developers of the necessary self-confidence of this quality can be the horse himself.

There is a widespread theory that, "Feel is born – it cannot be taught" which is bolstered up by remarks such as, "Whereas it is quite possible for a rider who is without feel to become a very good rider and trainer, that same person with 'feel' added to his makeup could then be an artist with a horse."

Feel is complex: it is composed of many ingredients, such as a mental balance which works closely with physical balance, patience, natural sympathy and love of horses and people, an awakened interest and an acute perception, complementary degrees of trust, understanding, generosity, confidence and humility, bonded together with intuition and compassion. Feel enables the rider truly to get under the skin and into the minds and hearts of the horses he rides, and the instructor to do the same for the pupils and horses he trains. The instructor should have a certain tactful drive, an inner energy to help others reach higher goals.

How then can feel be awakened? Firstly, by the parents in the home. I believe that feel blossoms best in a country environment where there is an added responsibility towards and communication with wild and domestic animals and where there is room for the eyes and mind to make connection and to appreciate fully.

School teachers should provide the next stepping-stone but alas, in these highly pressurised times, they rarely have the time to do so. So, next comes the riding instructor with every possible opportunity to get his pupils to understand the wide-ranging use and value of feel. For he has contact with pupils all of whom are following a hard but chosen path. They are working with horses whom they love.

Desperate as the instructor may become with some pupil whose attitude seems dour, dreary and unhelpful to the point of being anti-social and "agin the government", he must remember that feel can never be driven into a person by aggressive or forceful methods. He must carry out some tactful research, for the pupil may have personal worries such as problems at home, fear of jumping, a clash of personalities between fellow students or another instructor or perhaps against himself. Above all the instructor must be positive in his attitude for, in these seemingly most unlikely cases, a little extra attention and encouragement will work wonders and as confidence, trust and interest replace the pupil's defensive attitude, the latent quality of feel will also rise to the fore, often in a most amazing and rewarding way.

If riders can be led to understand about their thought and weight aids and can apply these with an ever-increasing knowledge and feel then talented riders will abound, fewer horses will be abused or wasted and horsemanship in general must rise to new heights of mutual benefit and enjoyment.

Now we will venture further afield, covering ground which already is familiar and also delving a little deeper to make some new discoveries. I hope that the following chapters will help riders of all standards to ride their horses with even greater understanding, interest, pleasure and success.

2 Modern Trends – Bad and Good

Bad trends first, to analyse the problems of the present situation. A look at standards and then, to finish on a high note, the good trends.

Bad Trends

To sum them up in one word – superficiality. Too little depth of knowledge will lead to bad trends.

A rider should have, or set about acquiring, a good knowledge of:

Human psychology

How to inspire positive thinking; how to lead; how to correct; how to encourage; how to develop and employ willpower – in the right way; how to produce thinking riders and thinking instructors.

Human physiology

Basic skeletal facts – epitomised by the old negro spiritual which plays on "the hip-bone is connected to the thigh-bone" and so on! Basic myology – the study of the human muscular structure and function. Basic neurology – (main roads only!).

Equine psychology

Understanding how the horse "ticks" and how to use that knowledge when training horses so that they carry out increasingly demanding work willingly and without constraint or stress.

Equine physiology

Facts and figures of the horse's skeletal, muscular and neural systems, how these are inconvenienced by the rider's weight – especially if he is a bad horseman! – and how correct and patient training can minimise the encumbrance and can even improve the beauty of the horse's form as well as his performance.

The craft of instructing

How to use the tools of the craft correctly, with imagination and to the best advantage.

Too often the knowledge is scant and the methods slipshod. Combined with the above shortcomings there are the following modern hazards:

New owners

There are innumerable new horse owners with scant knowledge of riding or of horse care.

Lack of understanding

There are riders who lack understanding of their responsibility towards the comparatively helpless dumb creatures in their care.

Ignorance

Riders are sometimes ignorant of how much there is to learn, and of the rewards which such learning will bring to all riders, from the beginner to those competing at international level. Ignorance also of country life in general and of horses in particular.

Competitive ambition and hunting

The lure of prizes, limelight, or the thrills of the chase often over-shadow the first priority, the need to learn how to ride well first. Riders are too inclined to think that they know all there is to know about "horseback riding" as soon as they can ride over a few fences or after a polo ball without falling off. In truth they are still novices and their lack of horsemanship often causes anguish and pain to their horses who are worn out before they have even reached their prime.

Declining standards

Where there is a breakdown of law and order, theft and vandalism of property, stock and gear will follow. Decline in standards leads to an escalation of the risk of cruelty due to ignorance, and of accidents involving horses and traffic.

Lack of government support

It is difficult for a nation's riders to hold their own when they have to compete against nations whose equestrians are supported by state funds, sometimes of huge amounts. True, we retain our individuality and the right to ride our own horses, but a little financial encouragement from the state would be welcomed as tangible recognition of the service the horse world renders to the country's education, citizenship and industry. Meanwhile our thanks to the splendid efforts of British Equestrian Pro-motions, whose generous sponsorship provides injections of much-needed hard cash into many equestrian veins – figuratively speaking, of course!

Lack of animal sense

Although man's remarkable brain should make him vastly superior in intelligence, this gift is unfortunately often allowed to remain quite dormant when he meets and handles animals. Untrained riders are often amazingly unimaginative, unsympathetic and even downright stupid to the point of cruelty in their dealings with horses. It is not reasonable to expect that all would-be riders will have natural flair in their relationships with animals, especially if they live in a town environment. Instructors must therefore take every available opportunity to explain how to manage horses in a firm but kindly way. They must never weary of passing on this knowledge because it is one of their foremost responsibilities to ensure that the craft of horsemanship is perpetuated.

Low level of instruction

The chief reason for poor standards of riding and of horse care must be that the level of instruction for beginners and less experienced riders just is not good enough. These early lessons often fail on five counts:

(i)   The instructor himself may have insufficient knowledge, training or interest – or "spark". A shortage of any one of these will bring the quality of the lessons tumbling below standard.

(ii)   The horses are unsuitable: they may be too lively, or stale, slothful, obstinate or cunning. They may be short-striding or "hefty" animals. None of these are conducive to good riding. I believe, most sincerely, that a correct feel can only be taught on horses who are willing, interested and happy in their work, who move well, in a good form having been trained to answer their rider's aids and to go on the bit – from their two hind heels, *forwards*!

(iii) The instructor fails to teach the early lessons well enough; he does not appreciate the interest they should arouse.

(iv) The instructor has forgotten, or has insufficient compassion to understand, how bewildered and frightened a novice rider can feel when the demand is too much for him. Going too fast can be the most terrifying of all riding experiences. The mistake of trying to run before they can

Beginners' lessons may not be good enough. . . .

RIDING IS A HIGH RISK SPORT.

walk creates many bad riding faults in beginner riders, such as being taught rising trot before having learned correct technique at walk and sitting trot.

(v) The instructor has too small a store of lesson plans; he runs out of ideas for teaching his pupils at slow gaits, so before (or after) a dreary note of dullness pervades the lesson he enlivens it in the only way he knows, a faster gait and perhaps even "a jump or two", long before his pupils are ready, willing and able.

Insufficient anatomical knowledge

Immediately after the beginner stage there is another dangerous gap – an anatomical void. Few present-day riders know how their bodies and those of their horses are constructed, how they move and may be moved, and how much they may be stretched for development and improvement before the ogres of injury and damage rear their ugly heads.

This anatomical void is caused by the overriding *temptation* of the practical side of riding horses – the thrills and even the spills!

Economics

As the cost of keeping horses rises ever higher, riders feel they must "get by" without lessons to improve their horsemanship, the main aim being to keep their horses housed, fed, shod and generally well maintained. A few might buy a ticket for a horseman's quiz, the hunt ball or for some similar, light-hearted form of social entertainment, but no organiser in his right mind would think of advertising "An Evening on Anatomy" – the hall would remain chillsome and uneconomically empty.

Lectures

Although their desk-diaries may be full of the riding lessons they are due to give, few instructors are asked to give even one lecture on human or horse psychology or anatomy; the subjects are considered by most horsemen to be dull, too technical and complicated and probably "quite unnecessary" as well, an opinion which is often shared by the instructors themselves.

Schools of equitation

Whereas military cavalry schools did include anatomy as an important subject in their curriculum this is not the case with the majority of modern riding schools. Easily it could be and I would recommend strongly that it should be.

After all, the subjects of basic psychology and of physiology should be as important and as interesting as a hunting map is to a hunting man. He must know the bridle-paths, level crossings, tunnels and fords, because he has learned them from his map – he cannot take off his gloves and pull his map out of his pocket after every fence he clears – he must know the

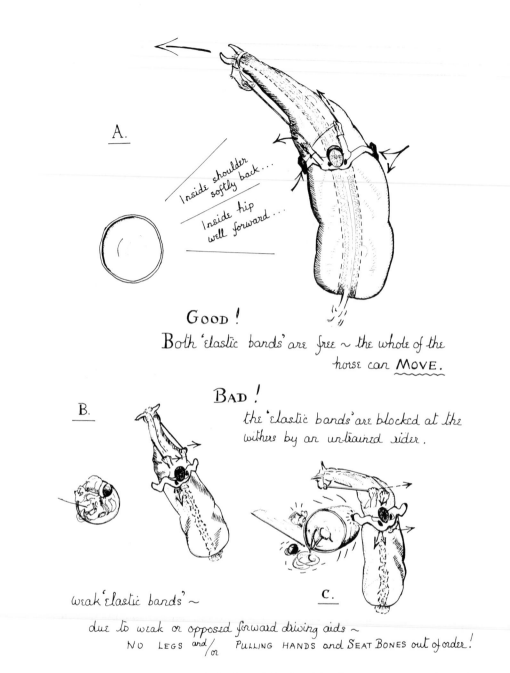

A.

Inside shoulder softly back...

Inside hip well forward...

GOOD !
Both 'elastic bands' are free ~ the whole of the
horse can MOVE.

BAD !

B.

the 'elastic bands' are blocked at the
withers by an untrained rider.

weak 'elastic bands' ~

C.

due to weak or opposed forward driving aids ~
NO LEGS and/or PULLING HANDS and SEAT BONES out of order!

highways and byways and the lie of the land by heart. So must the rider know which bone lies where, which muscle moves it and which other muscles are brought into play. This he must know about his own body as well as that of his horse, for only if he has this knowledge can he feel and think and think and feel – and ride his horses *forward* with tact and skill born of understanding, so that the horse comes on the bit, from his two hind heels, through the whole of his supple body, thus ensuring that horse and rider can move together in good form and perfect harmony.

However, rather than risking a deepening depression, if not a "slough of despond", a change of scene is indicated.

Good Trends

With the advent of the 1980s there came a universal upsurge in the quest for knowledge, an awareness that deeper research brings forth greater satisfaction and richer rewards. This trend is evident in many other present day aspects of life as well as in the horse world. Annually, new discoveries are being made while ancient myths, methods and medicines are re-discovered and many found to have factual foundations. So it is with riding: instructors, examiners, judges – the elders and the "youngers" – are becoming more interested, more aware of the horizons yet to be explored and of the compelling need to learn, and for instructors of the future to be well trained in order to perpetuate the knowledge, the craft and, hopefully, the art of horsemanship.

My own awareness of this upsurge in interest was most obvious when I was travelling abroad in 1980, in South Africa in January and in Australia in April. In both countries, in addition to the normal duties of judging dressage and of helping riders with their horses, there was a strong appeal for help from instructors.

In Australia, a two-day conference held at the Victorian Equestrian Centre outside Melbourne was attended by over four hundred people, most of whom were actual or aspiring instructors. The centre and the demonstration riders, recruited from the Victorian Pony Club, were immaculately turned out and the latter had obviously been particularly well instructed. The conference was the brain-child of Miss Kay Irving, MBE, an institution in herself, respected and beloved by all Australian Pony Clubbers, young and old. It was one of the most inspiring conferences I have ever run because all the participants were so genuinely and keenly interested. Their questions were of a practical, intelligent nature, not carping or cunningly critical, and I knew that the facts and exercises I taught them were assimilated, accepted and would be practised long after I had left.

A postscript caught up with me when I had moved to Adelaide to judge at the inter-state Expo '80 Dressage Championships in the distinguished company of Colonel Gustaf Nyblaeus and Major Burman, the newly appointed Australian national equestrian coach. Together with two pairs of Australian deer-skin roping gloves, a horse-brass commemorating the Victorian Pony Club's 25th anniversary and a mini public address system built into a cough-lozenge tin, I received a little message, "Do tell Mrs. Sivewright that we really *do* believe her but that when we went out for a ride in the bush two days ago we thought '*trot*' and absolutely *nothing* happened – and we had imagined that telepathy would work particularly

41

well in the bush!" Then, "Seriously, the horses do tune in to our thoughts, its most exciting, the course was fabulous, you have given us so much to work on – do come back soon!"

Following such tours abroad, I have been delighted to realise that would-be instructors are questing after knowledge with similar enthusiasm in Great Britain too. This surely must be the major good trend: one can but hope that the thirsting will be assuaged by the attaining of knowledge and skill as well as qualifications – certificates 100 per cent proof!

3 The Tools of the Craft

Knowledge

The quest must be ceaseless for the store is inexhaustible! The instructor must add to his own knowledge daily by means of tireless enquiry, observation, research and confirmation. It is only possible to teach that which you know yourself. He must also inspire his pupils with an urgent need to accumulate knowledge for themselves.

The Assistant Instructor

The instructor must do his utmost to produce assistant instructors who are worthy of the name. Not only must he train his assistants to ride and care for all the school's horses and pupils with intelligence and diligence – but he must also encourage them to become better and better and to match up to the qualities listed in Book 1. The instructor should use and stretch his own mind, increasing his knowledge, using his imagination and senses of perception and of humour to inspire his pupils to maximum improvement. Above all, he must kindle the fire of self-motivation within his assistants so that they exert themselves, both mentally and physically, with common sense, diligent application and reasoned attention to detail.

The instructor must work hard himself, showing clear examples of dedication and devotion to duty. He must project the maximum amount of his own enthusiasm, interest and education into each of the pupils in the classes, throughout every lesson period. During the day he must reward his assistants, not only by praise for work well done, but also with instruction. In these ways he will create an invigorating, loyal team spirit with a good learning atmosphere and an assurance that his assistants will teach their pupils the same methods in a similar manner when their turn comes.

The assistant instructor must be shown the correct attitude towards the horses he rides and cares for, as well as appreciating the need to inspire a similar attitude in the pupils with whom he works. He must understand that all members of the equine species are sensitive, have feelings and wonderful memories. In fact, he should teach his pupils all the facts regarding attitude as outlined in Book 1.

Instructors must remind their assistants regularly that most new riders look upon a pony or a horse as a kind of mobile pram or a bicycle, and that the foundations and future of equitation truly do lie to a great extent in the hands of the assistant instructors.

The beginner is taught the points of the horse, but too often that is

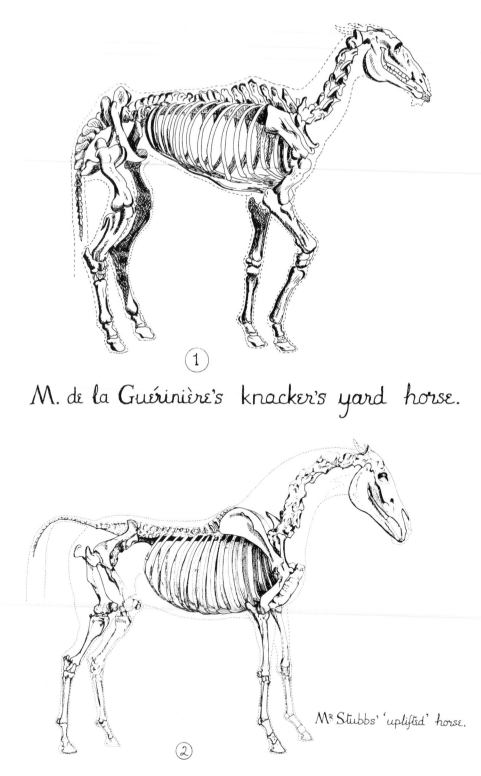

1

M. de la Guérinière's knacker's yard horse.

Mr Stubbs' 'uplifted' horse.

2

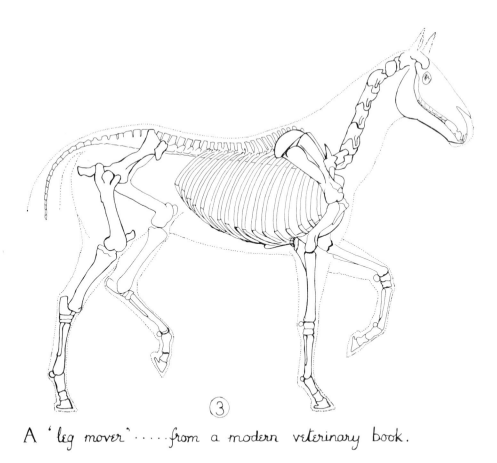

A 'leg mover'.....from a modern veterinary book.

where an important subject begins and ends. As a result, even quite experienced riders have little or no knowledge of the good and bad points of a horse's conformation or even of his basic anatomy or of the mechanics of his balance and movement. Without this knowledge, it is small wonder that many good horses are spoiled by incorrect riding caused by bad or insufficient training.

All riders must be encouraged to study anatomy and equine posture and movement. Three illustrations will help here. The first is of the sorrowful skeleton, which illustrates a book by M. de la Guérinière. The second shows the marvellous posture depicted by Stubbs. The third illustration is from a modern book, and shows a "leg mover". This last is typical of many horses of today whose owners think they have a trained horse. A careful look at his lack of muscle and of his self-carriage reveals that he has not been trained correctly to work truly through his back and to develop a rider-carrying posture and musculature to match. There is no "lightening of the forehand", "engagement of the haunches" or "ease of movement" – instead there is an obedient trudging which is far removed from the desired qualities of an equine athlete.

The horse's memory is extremely retentive but it is not selective. He cannot differentiate between what he should remember from a good rider, and what he should not remember from a bad rider – he simply remembers the lot! If a rider treats his horse as if he were specially created as a convenient mode of transport for human beings – as if the horse had two or four wheels, handle-bars, an engine and a hand-brake – then it is not surprising if that horse's mouth, legs and gaits deteriorate beyond redemption, and if he loses condition because he is so miserable.

Junior students, training to become assistant instructors learned how to sit correctly on horses who were on the bit and moved well in a reasonably good form. Now they must learn how to improve a horse's form making him work correctly, and later still how to train spoiled, problem horses. The students must be taught carefully so that they can bring about these improvements by their own good horsemanship and thus will never have to resort to over-forceful riding or to gadgets of any sort. They must be encouraged to study, and be taught to think of, the mechanics of the horse in action, of the long bones, joints and muscles and of how the latter can be stretched, made supple and developed by correct work in various simple exercises. Such thought must reach deep, to brain and bone, and the exercises must be based on principles which are logical and suitable for the present standard of the class, for the improvement and enjoyment, if not elation, of all horses and riders.

The Horses

The development of a correct attitude towards the riding horse must take top priority in every aspiring or experienced horseman's requirement list. When the rider himself is first taught to ride, when he embarks on a career as an instructor, and later, when he trains his own pupils, the love of horses must remain foremost in his heart and mind.

All horses' brains become trained to receive and act upon their riders' thoughts with ever-improving sensitivity. High-class polo ponies and gymkhana ponies provide excellent evidence of this and the trainers and riders who work with their minds are always "the tops". If the school horses are to maintain a high, or even rising standard of training, it is essential that every pupil who rides those horses is started off on the right foot – they must be quizzed and instructed regularly and frequently with regard to the aids they use – "Thought, weight, legs, rein aids and voice". Their hands must be confidence-giving and light, passing on smooth rein aids which start from and are supported by the rider's shoulder-girdle, his back and pelvis, the joints and muscles of which are pliant, and unconstrained yet controlled. All pupils must be encouraged to be more and more aware and to *think* with and for the horses they ride. The school horses' mental state is just as important as their physical fitness and health – they *must be kept happy* in their work.

All horses are in reality two different horses:

The indoor horse

Has less natural impulsion and has to be ridden forward more energetically; often it is so much less fun for him to be indoors or in a restricted area.

The outdoor horse

Has much more natural impulsion. When he is being ridden out of doors he often has to be slowed down, he may even be over-exuberant, especially if he is being ridden in company with other horses – high spirits are infectious.

This knowledge can be used to great advantage for everyone concerned if the fun and stimulus provided by working together in company is brought into the majority of schooling sessions conducted in a restricted area.

The class lesson can make good use of a horse's natural gregariousness. Because horses enjoy working in company they move forward in all their gaits through the school figures and movements with a natural forward urge, responding readily to their riders' influences. For their part, the riders do not have to use their forward-driving aids as markedly as they would have to when working a single horse in a lonely state, on his own. Thus, in a class lesson, riders can be more subtle with their aids and they have a better opportunity to think and feel – and to feel and think.

The horses used for teaching riders must be good movers; a variety of temperament and of training standard is an advantage. The reforming of difficult or "impossible" equine characters is an essential part of every horseman's further education.

Horses on which novice pupils will be taught must be suitable in every way. They must be willing and kept that way so that they enjoy their work – a sour pony invariably produces a sour rider. Beginners' horses should be free-going but not highly strung or too quick in their movements or reactions. They should be reasonably good movers and not stiff or hard in their backs or mouths. Temperamentally they must be kind, stable and reliable.

In conformation school horses should not be too wide or heavy in front – in fact their shape and action should be as near perfect as the pocket will allow, so that they have a natural ease and balance, and will give their riders a good feel.

I am convinced that it is incorrect to use short-striding horses to teach pupils to ride. By this I do not mean that the horses have to be expensive animals of show quality. Reliable utility horses can be found who are not expensive; they may have a superficial blemish or a bad habit, but if they move well that is a most important quality for a riding school horse.

Schoolwork – Indoors and Outdoors

School figures, gymnastic exercises and movements should be carefully

The Indoor Horse.

The Outdoor Horse.

taught and used in all work periods, with a combination of logic, knowledge, training and inspiration to improve riders and horses in their work indoors, out of doors, on the flat and over fences. Dressage was the name re-chosen by the late Colonel and Mrs. V. D. S. Williams during the 1950s. They felt that the terms "breaking horses" and "rough rider"

However, the most angelic pony...

The Indoor Pony.

... may become a demon!

The Outdoor Pony.

should be replaced by "training" and "trainer". However, these terms had already been adopted by the racing fraternity and the Williamses found themselves continually approached for advice on racing and racehorses rather than as hitherto on lungeing young horses!

The verb "to dress" may mean "to train" when applied to animals. The

Duke of Newcastle used the expression in this sense for the title of his second book *A New Method to Dress Horses*, published in 1667. As "dressage" means a way of training an animal, this was the term chosen eventually for referring to the training of the general purpose riding horse; thus training tests became dressage tests. Low-school dressage does and should include jumping small to medium fences as well as work on the flat. One complements the other. If, at a later stage of his training, a horse shows an above-average talent for work on the flat, then he may be trained to the higher school of dressage, or he may advance up more than one ladder of the three riding horse disciplines. Why not? He needs to be a well-trained athlete in order to perform creditably in top-class competition. There are two cautionary provisos: he must not be worn out, mentally or physically, nor must he be injured.

Training or dressage objectives

The horse should be trained to be free-going, willing, honest, calm and brave – all depending on implicit confidence in and respect for his rider. When ridden, the horse moves with a good form, carrying his rider with assurance, ease and grace.

His appearance, carriage and action are improved by his training, which also leads to a conservation of energy – maximum result from minimum effort. Due to the development of his mental and physical powers his value is increased and his working life is prolonged.

The horse becomes a good, comfortable and reliable ride – he may even become elated – as he thinks and moves *forward*.

His general suppleness, balance, co-ordination and ability are improved, and his natural talents are developed to their fullest realisation.

Lesson Plans

The format and general principles have been described fully in Book 1. These procedures, which are taught to student instructors when they commence their training remain as the basic framework on which they will build their lessons throughout their careers, although each instructor will develop an individual and personal flavour in his techniques as confidence, experience and the passage of time allow.

PREPARATIONS

Must always be made. They must suit the pupils, their numbers, standards and aims, the venue and the time available. Preparations must also include personal turnout and "props", for example the public address system, music, markers.

INTRODUCTION

Must include class involvement in a test of the pupils' knowledge of doctrine, for example, position, the aids (especially those of thought and weight), and the rider's influence on his horse (how? when? where? in

The Horses' Natural Reactions.

5. TRACK RIGHT (OR LEFT)

4. HALF HALT

3. FORWARD ← PUSH 3.

2. HALF HALT

1. STRAIGHT (after TURN)

what quantity and mixture and *why*?). However good or advanced a rider may be the foundation stones must always be taught or tested. Basic knowledge must *never* be assumed.

NEW WORK

Must always be explained and demonstrated while the pupil or class is halted. It should be taught, thought about and tried at the walk, with minimal rein aids, before pupils are allowed to attempt the new work at the trot or canter.

CLASS AND PRIVATE LESSONS

Both have their place in every instructor's "tool box". Whilst riding in a group has many advantages, teaching a class lesson well requires a high level of training and skill. More about this later!

REMINDER OF THE BASIC PLAN

Preparation; explanation; demonstration; execution; interrogation; repetition.

Training Areas

These must be safe for horses and riders, having good, sound footing and fencing. They should provide variety and educational scope combined with genuine usefulness. While there should be room for mental and physical expansion, there should be at least one smaller enclosure on level ground, for more organised riding on the flat and for riding over fences.

Although a "skeleton" marked out and lettered dressage arena is not essential, it does have many advantages. All fences should be jumpable and cross-country fences should have smaller, alternative sections whenever possible. It is advantageous to have some undulating ground

With the ride halted on the centre line.....

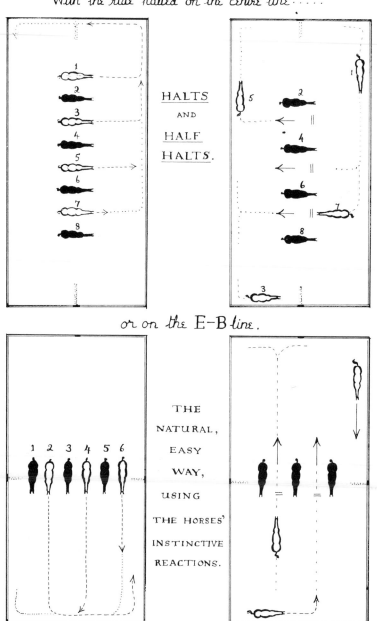

HALTS

AND

HALF

HALTS.

or on the E-B line.

THE

NATURAL,

EASY

WAY,

USING

THE HORSES'

INSTINCTIVE

REACTIONS.

Treading in – making good
at the end of a cross-country schooling session.

and a few well-constructed permanent fences, such as banks and ditches of various sizes, steps, a corner fence or two and a "coffin". All fences and their footing must receive regular inspection and repair. Refusals are always damaging to the surface on the take-off side of the fence. Riders should replace the divots and make good before they leave the area.

Lectures

The lecture is often an underestimated "tool". Forewarning of a lecture can cause pupils' hearts to rise or sink. Of course, it is a lecture which produces the first reaction that is of value.

For a lecture to succeed it must be well prepared and well delivered, full of interesting material and followed up with some form of questioning for confirmation.

The instructor must use his imagination and tax his enthusiasm to the full if his lectures are to be successful. Not only must his audience be interested, they must learn something new and they must enjoy learning it.

Apart from their value as a means of dispensing information or provoking thought, lectures on riding or horse care can offer additional less obvious benefits.
• The pupils can concentrate; they can take notes.
• They can ease and refresh muscles which have been made weary by riding – especially if the pupils are unfit, or are of novice standard.
• The horses have a rest; their energies are conserved for the riding sessions.

Lectures should be related to the overall present and future work programme. The subject matter can be chosen to clarify or emphasise certain facts, rules or methods and to aid practical lessons. If the work to be covered is new or complex, the speaker must be a good, if not inspiring, lecturer.

Student instructors should be encouraged to give low-key, informal lectures, on simple subjects, to help them gain confidence, to encourage them to learn their work thoroughly and to become more articulate.

Lecturers of all standards should become proficient at using the more common visual aids. However, just as it is essential to know when to call in the veterinary surgeon, so, similarly, it is wise to ask for a trained projectionist if a 16 millimetre film with sound is to be shown.

Detailed advice on delivering a lecture was given in Book 1.

Diagrams

These could be called the writer's means of demonstration. Often diagrams convey the message far more clearly than does the written word, for instance in the all-important shape of the tracks of an exercise. Diagrams are easy to understand and "photograph" well into the brain's memory. For these reasons diagrams serve a most useful purpose as a prop in a lecture; in all instances, it is obviously essential that they are accurately drawn.

I feel that there are far too many inaccurate diagrams in the majority of today's horse books: by their very inaccuracy they are not only misleading, they actually teach wrong methods. Sometimes it is possible that the artist has been misinformed by the text, or perhaps he has taken it upon himself to be extra artistic: what should have been an exercise based on classical equitation lines bears a far closer resemblance to a bow on a gift-wrapped Christmas present! Neither pupils, riders nor horses can learn from slip-shod school figures, for every figure is especially designed to fulfil a training objective; exercises based on school figures can only achieve miracles if they are correctly ridden. Good ground-plans can only be followed by good riders on horses who have a good form.

Similarly, diagrams concerned with human or equine anatomy must be carefully researched and accurately drawn. I am not recommending that students or their instructors should become body-snatchers or visit the morgue or abattoir as did artists of olden times, but I am suggesting that they should make their researches in recognised anatomical text-books, use X-ray plates and sketch from actual skeletons. The latter particularly will prove several drawings of good repute to be impossibly inaccurate.

Instructors must be meticulous when drawing diagrams for their pupils, and when checking homework in students' notebooks, so that they pass on correct techniques to the next generation of riders.

4 Revision

At whatever standard the instructor himself or his pupils are working, it is imperative that he constantly awakens, refreshes and adds to his store of knowledge, for only by so doing will he keep his teaching alive and inspiring.

With the gaining of a qualification, the assistant or the intermediate instructor is always put at risk: either people will ask and expect too much of him, or he will ask too much of his pupils. His explanations, demonstrations, or the lessons themselves may become too complicated or too demanding. If he tumbles into any of these pitfalls his pupils will become tense, they will not enjoy their riding and there may even be an accident.

As has already been stated in Book 1 – the aims for all early lessons must be safety, confidence, fun and improvement. All four words are chosen with great care, none more so than the last. "Improvement" is selected in preference to "progress" because a mistaken interpretation or over-emphasis of the word "progress" can lead to the obliteration of all four aims in one blow.

To illustrate the hidden danger of using "progress" as an aim for early lessons I will recount a true story.

"Victoire's Histoire"

An instructor was teaching a class on the first morning of their course. She found that the parents of one pupil had over-estimated their daughter's ability on their application form and that, "Quite experienced, has had riding lessons for two years", meant in reality a very nervous eleven-year-old who had never been off a lunge-line. The instructor enlisted the aid of a newly-qualified assistant to give the pupil individual coaching. For half an hour all went well, and the child, Victoire, the pony and the assistant instructor, Diana, were getting on together excellently. It soon became obvious that during her previous lessons Victoire had been taught how to shorten her reins and that she must do this whenever she and her pony contemplated a faster gait. Victoire was an excellent pupil: as soon as the pony gathered himself together to change his gait programme from the one-two-three-four of his walk to that of one-two for a slow trot, the reins were shortened with amazing alacrity until Victoire's hands were a bare 23 centimetres from the bit.

Quite correctly Diana had spotted this habit and it was nipped in the bud during the first half hour. Then Diana, realising that she had a keen and intelligent pupil on her hands who was longing to progress as far as possible, and whose confidence was growing from strength to strength, also realised about half an hour had passed.

"Finish on a high note!" she thought. "Right, we'll try a canter."

Victoire was obviously delighted at the prospect so Diana held the pony's bridle, leading him for safety's sake and the trio embarked on the next step of the big adventure. The following few minutes were entirely safe but also highly frustrating for all three parties. Because of the excitement of the moment, Victoire's old habit reappeared: the more madly active her legs became, the further her hands rushed up the reins – had her arms been longer she would have been holding the bit itself. Diana was nearly at blood-vessel bursting pitch from trying to make the bewildered pony canter. Fortunately, generously, he produced three canter strides after which everyone ground to a halt while breath and wits were recovered.

At this point the instructor, who had sized up the situation, gave her group of pupils a simple exercise to ride and think about at the walk, while she joined Diana to support her just when she needed it. She asked Victoire about the rein-shortening habit and explained how uncomfortable the last few minutes had been for the pony.

"He was so worried and his poor mouth must be awfully sore" (exaggerating the reality for emphasis). "Now I want you to learn to ride really well and with Diana's help you can become a true *rider*. She will teach you how to guide your pony, how to ask him to walk just where and how you want him to, on long reins, without pulling on his mouth at all."

A look of genuine interest came into Victoire's face and from then on she made remarkable improvement and progress. The progress was little by little, slow but sure – the only way to learn to ride.

Each day that week, Diana conferred with the instructor, reporting Victoire's progress and asking for guidance on the next day's programme. The instructor gave her many different plans and exercises all of which gave Victoire a chance to practise improving her position without getting stiff, to guide and influence her pony with nearly invisible aids, "Thought, weight and turn your thumb away", or "Think halt, straighten your shoulders and he will stand still". Victoire and the pony quickly built up an excellent rapport and confidence in each other, and best of all was the thrill she experienced when she succeeded.

Perhaps the greatest impact of "Victoire's histoire" was felt by a very senior instructor-examiner who happened to witness the first day's tussle and who then watched the final lesson of the week's course five days later. She just could not believe what Diana had managed to achieve in so short a time, as Victoire rode the pony as a member of the class lesson executing the school figures and transitions confidently and competently as the instructor commanded. The senior instructor-examiner could hardly believe that Diana had been able to achieve such a transformation – and through this she found a renewed and strengthened belief in the doctrine and the exercises which Diana had learned herself and had passed on to her pupil.

The reason for relating Victoire's histoire is that this incident and many similar ones proved to me that there is a real *need* for a book which newly-qualified assistant instructors can use as a text-book to guide them through the first years of their careers and help them towards their next qualification. Whereas Book 1 will be their reference book I hope that this one will not only help them with the practical application of their lessons, but also the many riders who ride together in groups or who school their horses on their own, with only occasional opportunities for tuition.

Revision

An important facet of study, revision may consist of a re-reading of the original text, or reading or listening to identical facts and ideas couched in different terms. Both forms of revision are invaluable to the understanding of information and to realisation of how to put the theory into practice: as with a cow chewing the cud, redigestion of the matter improves the nourishing qualities of the meal.

Revision and research should complement each other. Whereas revision is comparatively easy, provided the books are listed and ready, the pupils self-motivated and the lessons absorbed, research is more difficult. For research to be of real value the pupils must receive trained guidance. This applies to research in general but to riders in particular in order that they waste neither their horse's potential nor time from their all-too-short lives. They must be guided to understand the simple facts, and they must be guided again when they practise what has been "preached"!

Trusting that riders and instructors will give themselves regular shots of revision from Book 1 now is the time to broaden horizons and find pastures new. In fact, the pastures are not new. As with old water meadows, good riding rules have changed but little over the past thousands of years. Many riders may have heard odd phrases bandied about in the saddle room, over a cup of tea, in the members' tent or wherever horse-talk abounds, but they have not understood what was meant. The number of new riders who would like to know more is increasing rapidly and I hope this book will help them in their explorations, researches and their understanding of the horses they ride.

5 Further Explorations

Training Through the Ages

As an introduction to this chapter I would like the reader to contemplate two parallel historical lines. These are: training the horse and rider; training the gymnast and the dancer.

The inclusion of gymnast and dancer might seem odd in a book about riding, but a few minutes spent on the background of gymnastic training could provoke interesting comparisons and ideas.

The earliest known evidence of the methods applied in these disciplines was recorded thousands of years B C in the East. Then their raison d'être was for transport and war. From those ancient times, the lulls between wars were spent in improving fitness, skill and artistry and these sports and arts gradually spread westwards. The earliest Olympic games, held in Greece, contained several gymnastic contests.

During the Middle Ages both groups continued to retain an existence through carousels, jousting, fencing and troupes of tumblers and dancers. In those days their true form was concealed and encumbered by the addition of spectacular, sometimes to us ridiculous, costumes, in the struggle to "keep their ends up", to retain recognition and make greater impact.

The clouds of war rolled over Europe in gathering strength during the 18th and 19th centuries, so that manoeuvrability and stamina in mounted troops and transport became essential factors in every European country's thoughts and work. Physical training became an important aspect of the education of civilian and military personnel.

In the latter part of the 18th century two outstanding educational leaders were born, one in Sweden and one in Germany. The two great men, Peter Henrik Ling (1776–1839) of Sweden and Friedrich Ludwig Jahn (1778–1839) of Germany revolutionised the thinking behind the training of the human body – they could be called the fathers of modern gymnastics as we know them today.

Communication and exchange of ideas between countries, especially those divided by sea, could not have been easy in the 18th and early 19th centuries, so although it is surprising that these two were both driven towards the same goal, "perfection of the physical education of man", in such far separated countries, it is not surprising that their approaches differed slightly.

Ling put particular emphasis on freedom of movement, considering fluent physical expression to be the essence of physical education. Jahn liked to develop the gymnast and test his accuracy with the fixed gymnasium apparatus such as the vaulting horse, the box, bars and rings. It is fair to say that these same differences were reflected again in these two countries in their methods and aims of training horses and riders. The internationally comprised Dressage Bureau of the Fédération Equestre International, or F.E.I. as we more commonly know it, has achieved much in the way of pooling and unifying ideas and rules for riders and has encouraged training methods based on their collective knowledge combined with a love of the horse, but still differences do exist. For example, when lungeing the horse, the Swedish trainer will rarely resort to using side reins for he believes in the horse developing natural forward movement and expression and that he can improve the horse's form best by building it through his own forward driving and restraining aids. "If you do not lunge well enough you may need to use side reins" (Boltenstern). Most German trainers, however, believe that side reins are an essential part of the lungeing equipment – unless they are lungeing over fences.

However, to return to the gymnast. His preparation, training and performance have similar requirements to those of the horseman: mental and physical fitness and balance, strength, stamina, poise and confidence, all combined with the *suppleness* essential for the achievement of a maximum range of thought and movement and of nuances within that range; and *control* by means of purposeful discipline of the muscles of the pelvis, legs, back, stomach, shoulders, neck and arms. These muscles may be trying to hold the body's poise or they may be exerted with full power should a wayward horse require extra strong restraint or driving.

Having had a "hack-out" or mind-stretching peep into the world of the gymnast, it is worth considering the purpose of such a jaunt, for purpose there is, of course. The main objective of gymnastics, dancing and physical education is to improve the working of the human body by learning the basic structure and mechanics, the techniques of movement and, additionally for riders, their influences and the effects these may have on the horses they ride, all of which sounds a frighteningly vast and complicated subject. As with the anatomy of the horse, most of the names of the human's muscles are complex and are most easily retained by Latin scholars. However, I am convinced that, firstly, too many riders know too little about their seat (the basic riding position) and how it should be organised, secondly that they can be led to understand the basics with the aid of some diagrams and, thirdly, that this fundamental knowledge is "a must" for all horsemen.

The Rider's Conformation

Be they riders, trainers or instructors, all horsemen must know how to make the maximum use of their mental and physical powers in order to ride and train their horses with minimum confusion and effort to all concerned.

Posture, poise, balance, suppleness and co-ordination are agreed to be some of the essential "invisible" ingredients of a good riding position.

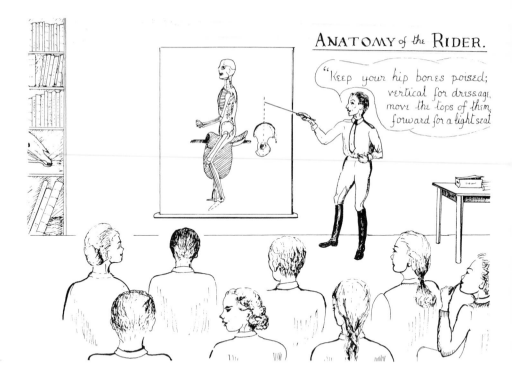

ANATOMY of the RIDER.

"Keep your hip bones poised; vertical for dressage, move the tops of them forward for a light seat"

The horseman must use his brain and his feel in order to employ only those muscles . . .

which are necessary to retain the poise of his seat and of his horse, or to exert the extra power required to control a wayward horse.

They are all produced and governed by the rider's brain power. It is of great assistance to that brain if its owner understands at least the basics of his own physical structure.

Whereas the human's two feet form the base of support for most of his activities and sports, the horseman's base of support is his two seat bones, or the lower end of his two hip bones. To be slightly more technical, the weight of the rider's body rests on the medial and lower parts of the ischial tuberosities.

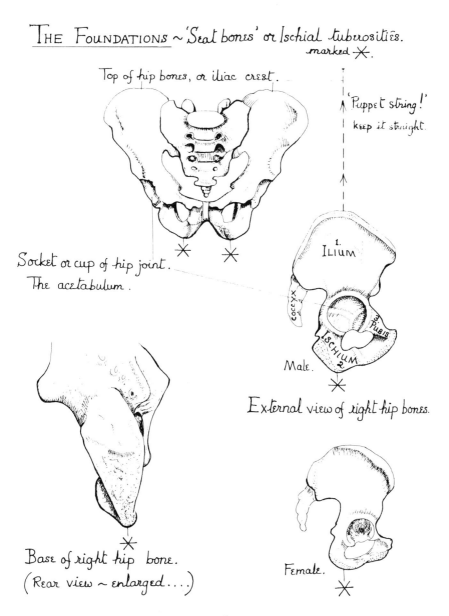

THE FOUNDATIONS ~ 'Seat bones' or Ischial tuberosities.
marked ✗.

Top of hip bones, or iliac crest.

'Puppet string!'
keep it straight.

1.
ILIUM

Socket or cup of hip joint.
The acetabulum.

COCCYX

3. PUBIS

ISCHIUM
2.

Male.

External view of right hip bones.

Base of right hip bone.
(Rear view ~ enlarged....)

Female.

THE RIDER'S BACK.

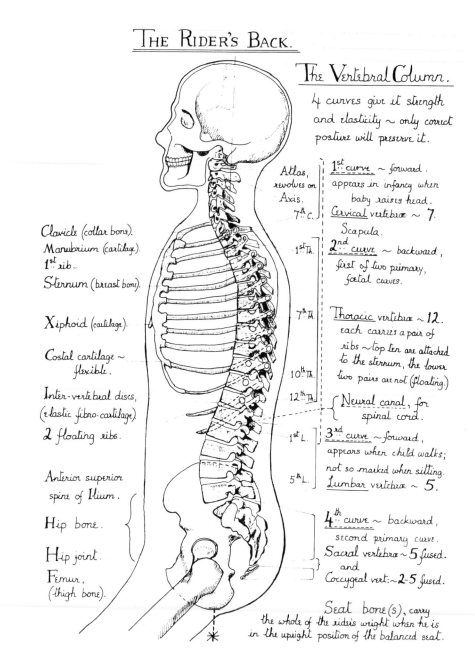

The Vertebral Column.

4 curves give it strength and elasticity ~ only correct posture will preserve it.

Atlas, revolves on Axis.
7ᵗʰ C.

1ˢᵗ curve ~ forward. appears in infancy when baby raises head.
Cervical vertebræ ~ 7.
Scapula.

1ˢᵗ Th.

2ⁿᵈ curve ~ backward, first of two primary, foetal curves.

7ᵗʰ Th.

10ᵗʰ Th.

12ᵗʰ Th.

Thoracic vertebræ ~ 12. each carries a pair of ribs ~ top ten are attached to the sternum, the lower two pairs are not (floating.)

{ Neural canal, for spinal cord.

1ˢᵗ L.

3ʳᵈ curve ~ forward, appears when child walks; not so marked when sitting.

5ᵗʰ L.

Lumbar vertebræ ~ 5.

4ᵗʰ curve ~ backward, second primary curve.
Sacral vertebræ ~ 5 fused.
and
Coccygeal vert: ~ 2-5 fused.

Seat bone (s), carry the whole of the rider's weight when he is in the upright position of the balanced seat.

Clavicle (collar bone).
Manubrium (cartilage).
1ˢᵗ rib ~
Sternum (breast bone).

Xiphoid (cartilage).

Costal cartilage ~ flexible.

Inter-vertebral discs, (elastic fibro-cartilage)
2 floating ribs.

Anterior superior spine of Ilium.

Hip bone.

Hip joint.

Femur, (thigh bone).

If riders can be encouraged to spend some time and thought considering anatomically how they sit on the backs of their horses, and how they can organise their bodies to obtain the best effect on and result from the body of the horse beneath them, their riding of horses and the sports in which they are involved will be much more beneficial and enjoyable for all participants. Some short study periods, combined with genuine interest, thought and practical application can help to dispel the "aggro" and despondency caused by poor performances, replacing them with the therapy of correct physical exercise for horse and rider, and a sense of well being and contentment arising from "a job well done".

The whole of the rider influences the whole of the horse; in this way, together, they may have *good form.*

To be a good horseman a rider must have perfect balance, co-ordination and complete mental and physical control governing every part of his body. As the human skeleton consists of over two to three hundred bones, the rider can truly be said to have a Herculean task on his hands – or rather, on his seat bones!

The evolution of man has seen to it that he now walks erect and balances himself either on his two feet when standing, or on his two seat bones (the lower edges of his hip bones) when he sits without any other support. The latter situation is of particular interest to riders.

Whenever man sits on an animated support he can only retain an easy posture and perfect balance if he is sufficiently confident, poised yet supple in all his joints. Constraint, even of the slightest degree, mental or physical, is the arch enemy of aspiring horsemen. Imagine how unattractive and unsuccessful would be a stiff dancer, juggler, skier, gymnast or high-wire artiste – all of whom must have perfect control of each of the approximately seven hundred muscles of the body combined with a good sense of rhythm and timing, and a feel for movement.

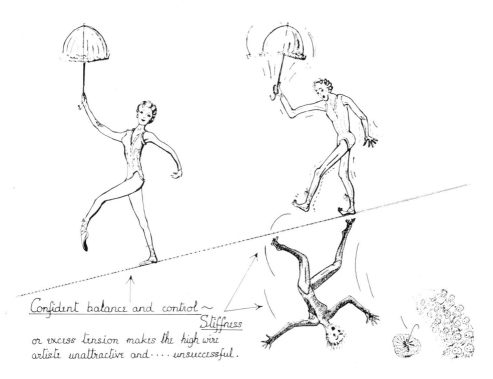

Confident balance and control ~
Stiffness
or excess tension makes the high wire
artiste unattractive and···· unsuccessful.

HORSE AND RIDER PARTNERS ~

compare their skeletal structures.

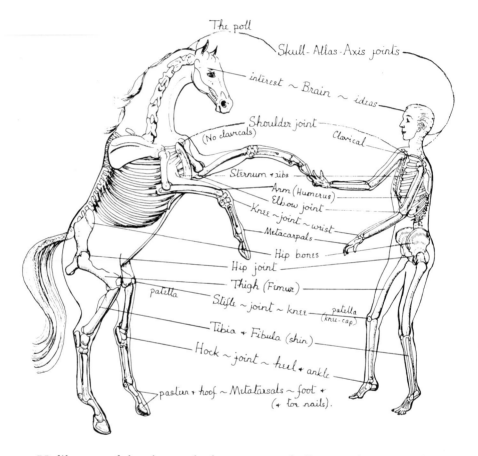

The poll

Skull - Atlas - Axis joints

interest ~ Brain ~ ideas

Shoulder joint

(No clavicals)

Clavical

Sternum + ribs

Arm (Humerus)

Elbow joint

Knee ~joint ~ wrist

Metacarpals

Hip bones

Hip joint

Thigh (Femur)

patella

Stifle ~ joint ~ knee

patella (knee-cap)

Tibia + Fibula (shin)

Hock ~ joint ~ heel + ankle

pastern + hoof ~ Metatarsals ~ foot + (+ toe nails).

Unlike any of the above, the horseman's challenge is far greater for he does not "go it alone": his enjoyment and success are entirely dependent on skills extended beyond the training of his own body to those of riding and training his equine partners. Thus all lessons, from the earliest given on a leading rein, to those for more experienced riders, must be:
- Easy to understand and to accomplish – step by step.
- Interesting and educational – teaching correct techniques and following a logical progression.
- Utterly *safe*.
- Fair in their demands – never setting too ambitious a target.
- *Fun* – based on enlightenment, spiced with reasonable adventure.

The Horse's Conformation

Moving on to the horse: after millions of years the horse has evolved from a fox-sized animal into a beautiful creature who, in his natural state would roam the plains searching for and relying on water and herbage for his survival and on his swiftness to escape from marauding predators – but then along came man and leaped on to the horse's back, disrupting his balance and his lifestyle.

As will be shown the horse's structure is complicated and cumbersome enough without having to support an ungainly and unbalancing rider burden. This last statement is made, not to dissuade riders from riding but to persuade them to learn to ride well!

6 The Rider's Physiology

All riders need to understand their own physiology and that of their horses. To do so will enable the rider to become the finely tuned instrument he needs to be to ride his horse.

As the practical rider reads he must not skid impatiently over the text and spare mere cursory glances for the accompanying illustrations: he must feel as he reads. The outlines of the main bones and muscles must be discovered and charted and their respective actions should be studied and understood before a rider can be expected to retain a correct, supple posture and to remain in perfect balance while sitting on a horse. This knowledge and understanding will enable him to time and use unseen movements of his body to influence his horse effectively, tactfully and thus with the maximum chance of success. As new technical names are read and spoken, the illustrations will help to give an impression of the size, shape and action of each member part; the reader can also trace on his own body the outline and workings of many of the bones, joints and muscles for himself and he will surely become more familiar with and less frightened of their names.

This research is vital to the rider's basic education. He must do a great deal of thinking combined with logical practical application. Every rider must work hard – the art of horsemanship will not fall into his lap like a ripe, juicy peach. A good instructor can be a tremendous help; he can guide and correct his pupil's work, he may even inspire, but it is the rider himself who has to apply himself with remarkable tenacity and dedication if he is to become a really good horseman. The rider has to learn – from his instructor, from his studies and from his horse. The recognition of the latter aspect can be hard for many ambitious riders to accept. They must be humble enough to realise that most of the horse's faults stem from habitually faulty riding, for example, "He won't go on the bit" is a common complaint which riders make about their horses. If, whenever he is ridden, the horse receives a barrage of bangs on the saddle from his rider's hard back or tightened hips while simultaneously the tender bars of his mouth are being knocked about by rough, unsteady hands, to name but two of the most common rider faults, then it is hardly surprising that he is not on the bit!

It is in order that the rider shall be able to organise, arrange and use the bones, joints and muscles of his body to influence his horse easily, that the following notes have been made. Pupils have to be corrected at regular intervals and they have to work at obliterating their faults and improving their riding for themselves. Corrections are always made more readily and completely if both the fault and the reason for the correction are fully understood. Only if he knows the following basic facts, combined with practical experience, sensitivity and feel can the rider achieve the required split-second timing and fine measures of his aids to lead his horse to an ever-improving partnership.

The explicit details of the composition of the human body will have been learned in school or can be found in the many books on human physiology. As some readers may not have given their full attention to, or have forgotten, those early lessons, and other readers may have had neither the time nor the inclination to acquire and peruse the necessary books, the following is a précis of the one subject a knowledge of which is most essential for any enthusiast interested in improving his prowess at any of the active sports, crafts or arts.

Of all the wide range of sportsmen, riders have the greatest incentive to explore the subject of physiology, for such learning will benefit both themselves and their living partners. Also, there are many bones and muscles which are common to both the human and the equine species: this lessens the load for the memory and adds much to the interest and the understanding as we shall see.

The reader will double his benefit from this work if, in his mind, he applies it to the horse as well as to himself. If he compares the illustrations of the horse's skeleton and muscles with those of the human and relates the muscle work to the horse as he reads, he will derive twice as much value from the text of this chapter; if then he applies these theories to his practical work he will find that his researches will produce "treasures" which hitherto were buried.

Geographical Terms

Before looking in detail at the human body, we need to establish in our minds where its various parts are located.

We call these geographical terms, and describe them thus:
- Anterior or ventral – near or facing the front (or the horse's head).
- Posterior or dorsal – near or facing the back end.
- Internal or medial – near to the middle line of the body.
- External or lateral – away from the middle line.
- Superior – high or above.
- Inferior – low or below.
- Proximal or upper – on limbs, near to attachment of limb to trunk.
- Distal or lower – on limbs, more distant or further away from the attachment of limb to trunk.

All the facts and many of the details which follow are equally applicable to horses and humans. The reader should compare these details and relate them to the accompanying illustrations.

As mentioned earlier, there are approximately two to three hundred bones and seven hundred muscles in one human body, plus the joints, ligaments and so on. It is not intended therefore to list them all! The

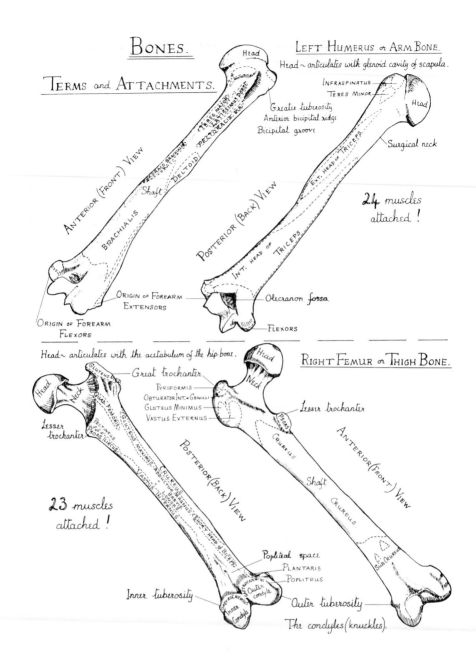

BONES.

TERMS and ATTACHMENTS.

LEFT HUMERUS or ARM BONE.

Head ~ articulates with glenoid cavity of scapula.

Head

Greater tuberosity
Anterior bicipital ridge
Bicipital groove

INFRASPINATUS
TERES MINOR
Head

Surgical neck

24 muscles attached!

ANTERIOR (FRONT) VIEW

TERES MAJOR
LATISSIMUS DORSI
PECTORALIS MAJ.
CORACO-BRACHIALIS

DELTOID
Shaft

BRACHIALIS

POSTERIOR (BACK) VIEW

EXT. HEAD of TRICEPS

INT. HEAD of TRICEPS

ORIGIN OF FOREARM EXTENSORS

Olecranon fossa

ORIGIN of FOREARM FLEXORS

FLEXORS

Head ~ articulates with the acetabulum of the hip-bone.

RIGHT FEMUR or THIGH BONE.

Head
Neck

Great trochanter

GLUTEUS MED.
QUAD. FEM. ORIS.

PYRIFORMIS
OBTURATOR INT. & GEMELLI
GLUTEUS MINIMUS
VASTUS EXTERNUS

Lesser trochanter
PSOAS
CRUREUS

Lesser trochanter

PECTINEUS
PSOAS-ILIACUS

POSTERIOR (BACK) VIEW

ANTERIOR (FRONT) VIEW

CRUREUS
Shaft

23 muscles attached!

Popliteal space
PLANTARIS
POPLITEUS

Inner tuberosity

Outer condyle
Inner condyle

Outer tuberosity

The condyles (knuckles).

following text describes a few of the most interesting and relevant parts together with their respective actions.

For the sake of simplicity we will group them initially under two headings, the *skeleton* and the *muscles*, with a joint or two thrown in where necessary.

The Skeleton

The bony framework is sub-divided into the *axial* skeleton, that is the head and trunk, and the *appendicular* skeleton, that is the upper and lower limbs. We shall discuss these sub-divisions in more detail later.

There are five types of bone – long, short, flat, irregular and sesamoid. Some terms used to describe them are listed below.

Parts of bones

- Process – a projection from a bone.
- Tuberosity, or trochanter – a broad, rough process. For example, tuberosity of the humerus, trochanter of the femur.
- Tubercle – a small process.
- Condyle – a large rounded eminence or end of a bone.
- Spine – a sharp, pointed eminence.
- Crest – a ridge on a bone.
- Groove – a furrow on a bone.
- Fossa – a hollow or depression.
- Foramen – a hole through a bone.

The Muscles

Muscles are tissues which have the power of contraction. Without muscles there can be no movement. Muscle tissue is composed of 75 per cent water and 25 per cent solids. Approximately 18 per cent of the solids consist of protein, while the remainder is made up of fats, gelatine and salts. Muscles are sub-divided into the following groups:

VOLUNTARY
Striped or striated. Under direct or remote control of the will, for example the skeletal muscles.

INVOLUNTARY
Plain or unstriped. Not controlled by the will, for example the muscles of the digestive tract.

CARDIAC
Slightly striated. Have special, automatic, rhythmic contractions, for example the heart muscles.

Muscle tone is a state of readiness and of fitness. Muscles are never completely at rest, they are always alert, ready to respond to stimuli.

The speed with which muscles respond will depend on a variety of factors:
- The strength of the stimulus.
- The weight the muscle is required to move.
- The temperature: warm muscles respond quickly, cold muscles may become sluggish.
- The development or fitness of the muscle.
- The training of the operator to work that particular muscle efficiently.
- Fatigue – makes muscle reaction sluggish and the muscle itself vulnerable to injury.

Muscles are attached to bone, cartilage, ligaments and the skin. They are named according to their shape, the direction in which their fibres lie, their position, attachment and function and to the number of their parts, for example, biceps and triceps, which mean having two and three heads respectively.

Some useful muscular terms

THE ORIGIN
The more fixed of the two points of attachment.

THE INSERTION
The other, more movable point.

The above are often interchangeable.

FLEXORS
The muscles which cause a joint to bend inwards.

EXTENSORS
Muscles which straighten a joint.

ADDUCTORS
Move parts (limbs) in towards the body's midline.

ABDUCTORS
Move parts away from the midline.

These two groups of pairs oppose each other and one is then referred to as the other group's *antagonist*.

LATERAL FLEXION
Sideways flexion of the head, neck and trunk.

FIXATION MUSCLES
Stabilise one part of a limb while other parts are being moved.

SYNERGISTS
Steady one joint while another joint moves.

TENDONS
White glistening, inelastic fibrous bands which bind muscle to bone.

LIGAMENTS
Similar to tendons but they bind bones together.

APONEUROSES
Flatter than tendons but having the same function.

FASCIA
The outer muscle layer which lies immediately under the skin (superficial), or the next layer down (deep). The superficial fascia wraps up, binds down and generally protects the soft structures of the body, the deep fascia is made of stronger material and forms muscle.

Having established these references, we can now turn to the skeleton and examine it in more detail. It is essential that the reader looks carefully at the accompanying illustrations when reading the text – as well as feeling his own body to identify the various parts mentioned.

As we saw, the skeleton is divided into the axial and the appendicular and these are described below, beginning with the head and working down the body.

The Axial Skeleton

The axial skeleton controls the head and the trunk and its movement and muscles.

The head

Perhaps the three most important facts about the head are:

- It contains the brain – that most vital component of *thinking riding*.
- It is comparatively very heavy; thus any weaknesses of posture, awkward movements, habitual inclinations, noddings or stiffenings in the atlanto-occipital or the atlanto-axial joints between the skull and the head-bearing vertebrae at the top of the neck always have an adverse effect on both the rider and his horse.
- The head is very vulnerable – terrible injuries can result from brain damage caused by a blow from a hard substance such as a road, rock or hoof when the rider's hard hat comes off during a riding accident.

FRONT VIEW.

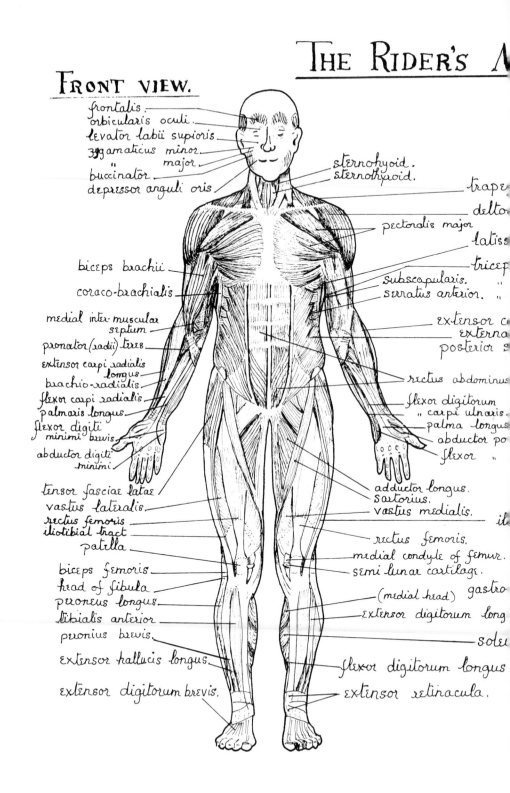

frontalis.
orbicularis oculi.
levator labii supioris.
zygamaticus minor.
   "   major.
buccinator.
depressor anguli oris.

sternohyoid.
sternothyroid.

trape
delto
pectoralis major
latiss
tricep

biceps brachii
coraco-brachialis.

subscapularis.
serratus anterior.   "

medial inter-muscular
   septum.
pronator (radii) teres.
extensor carpi radialis
   longus.
brachio-radialis.
flexor carpi radialis.
palmaris longus.
flexor digiti
   minimi brevis.
abductor digiti
   minimi.

extensor c
externa
posterior s

rectus abdominus

flexor digitorum
   " carpi ulnaris.
palma longus
abductor po
flexor   "

tensor fasciae latae
vastus lateralis.
rectus femoris
iliotibial tract
patella.

adductor longus.
sartorius.
vastus medialis.

il

biceps femoris.
head of fibula
peroneus longus.
tibialis anterior
peronius brevis.

extensor hallucis longus.

extensor digitorum brevis.

rectus femoris.
medial condyle of femur.
semi lunar cartilage.
(medial head) gastro
extensor digitorum long
soleu
flexor digitorum longus
extensor retinacula.

72

CLES.

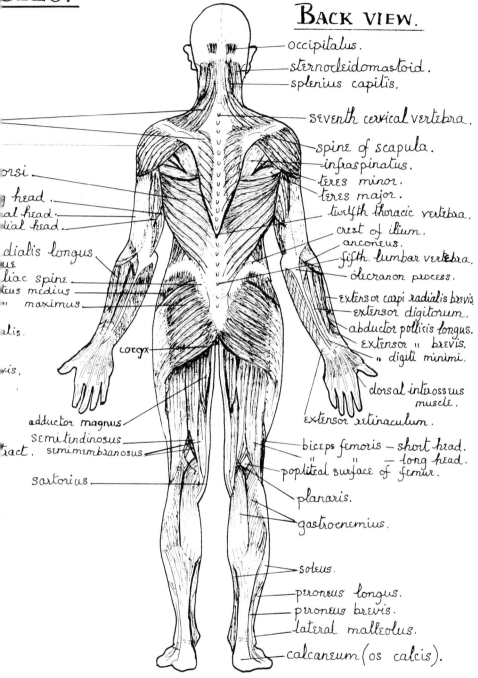

occipitalus.
sternocleidomastoid.
splenius capitis.

seventh cervical vertebra.

spine of scapula.
infraspinatus.
teres minor.
teres major.
twelfth thoracic vertebra.
crest of ilium.
anconeus.
fifth lumbar vertebra.
olecranon process.

extensor carpi radialis brevis.
extensor digitorum.
abductor pollicis longus.
extensor „ brevis.
„ digiti minimi.

dorsal interosseus
          muscle.
extensor retinaculum.

biceps femoris — short head.
„   „   — long head.
popliteal surface of femur.

planaris.

gastrocnemius.

soleus.

proneus longus.
proneus brevis.
lateral malleolus.

calcaneum (os calcis).

orsi.
head.
al head.
dial head.

dialis longus.
us
liac spine.
teus medius
„   maximus.

alis.

vis.

coccyx

adductor magnus.
semitendinosus
tact. semimembranosus.

sartorius.

73

THE PRECIOUS CONTENTS OF THE HEAD.

THE BRAIN.
{ Develop it with knowledge and understanding ~
USE it for THINKING ... in many ways.

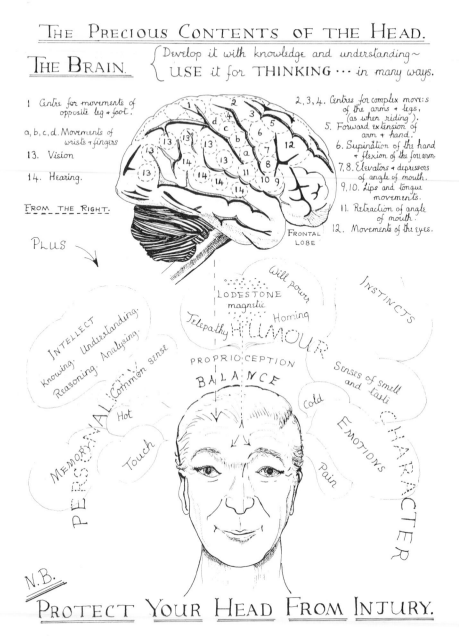

1 Centre for movements of opposite leg + foot.

a, b, c, d. Movements of wrists + fingers

13. Vision

14. Hearing.

FROM THE RIGHT.

PLUS

2,3,4. Centres for complex move:s of the arms + legs, (as when riding).
5. Forward extension of arm + hand.
6. Supination of the hand + flexion of the forearm.
7, 8. Elevators + depressors of angle of mouth.
9,10. Lips and tongue movements.
11. Retraction of angle of mouth
12. Movements of the eyes.

FRONTAL LOBE

LODESTONE magnetic
Will power
Telepathy
Homing
HUMOUR
INSTINCTS
INTELLECT
Knowing. Understanding. Reasoning. Analysing.
Common sense
PROPRIOCEPTION
BALANCE
Senses of smell and taste
MEMORY
PERSONAL
Hot
Touch
Cold
Pain
EMOTIONS
CHARACTER

N.B.

PROTECT YOUR HEAD FROM INJURY.

Muscles of the head

TEMPORAL

At the side of the head. Its *action* raises the lower jaw.

MASSETER

At the side of the face beneath the parotid gland. Its *action* is seen in mastication. (When a horse chews on the bit it massages a parotid gland encouraging saliva. This produces a creamy, wet mouth.)

74

From the cheek to the angle of the mouth. Its *action* retains food between the molars. It controls the whistling muscle (the latter does not apply to the horse!)

Movement of the head and neck

The main ligament and muscles involved when the head and neck are moved are:

FLEXION

Tilting forwards – longus capitus and the muscles depressing the fixed mandible (lower jaw); flexion is also aided by gravity – hence the term, "nodding off".

EXTENSION

Stretching and leaning back – the many postvertebral muscles.

LATERAL FLEXION

Tilting sideways – the sterno-mastoid and trapezius muscles.

ROTATION

Turning to face one side or the other – the sternomastoid, trapezius, splenius capitis and inferior oblique muscles.

(The horse sometimes uses a combination of the last two head movements when he uses the weight of his head to counter-balance his rider's awkwardly placed seat. The horse is often reprimanded for "head-tilting" whereas it is the rider who should be corrected).

Two riders causing their horses to tilt their heads in an endeavour to compensate for their riders' lack of posture and balance.

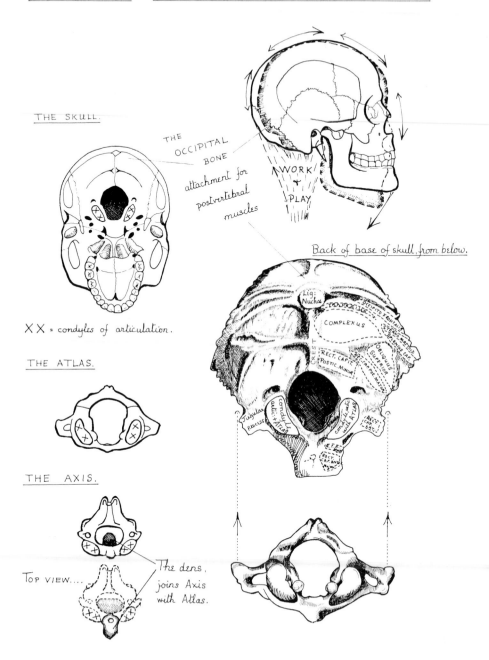

THE SKULL.

THE OCCIPITAL BONE attachment for postvertebral muscles

WORK + PLAY

XX = condyles of articulation.

THE ATLAS.

THE AXIS.

TOP VIEW....

The dens, joins Axis with Atlas.

Back of base of skull, from below.

Lig: Nuchæ

COMPLEXUS

CREST

RECT. CAPIT POSTIC. MINOR

OBLIQUUS SUPERIOR

Jugular Process

Condyle articles with ATLAS

Condyle article with ATLAS

RECT. CAPIT LAT.

The Head ~
Poise and
use it well.

The Muscles
Through them
the rider can use
effect the working

OF THE NECK.
the weight of his head to
of the rest of his body.

Lower jaw ──────
Stylo hyoid ──────
Hyoid or tongue bone ──
Omo hyoid ──────
Sterno hyoid ──────
Sterno cleido mastoid ──
  { sternal origin ───
  { clavicular origin ──
Pectoralis ~ connecting with sternum
  and muscles of front of trunk.

Mastoid process
Splenius
Levator anguli scapulæ
Scalenus posticus
Scalenus anticus
Clavicle or collar bone
Trapezius ~ connecting with back.
Deltoid + muscles of arm.

77

To the question, "Where is the ligamentum nuchae?" I have received a wide variety of answers including, "In your heel or the horse's hock"; "It runs down the horse's tail – we only have a little one"; "Is it to do with the toes?"

Occasionally I hear the answer I hope for. "The ligamentum nuchae is a very strong ligament at the back of the neck."

In man it is a rudimentary remnant of the important elastic ligament which in the horse is situated at the top of the neck, just under the crest. In both cases the ligamentum nuchae extends from the base of the skull to the spine of the seventh cervical vertebra where it joins and is continuous with the supraspinus and interspinus ligaments which run down the remainder of the spine to the sacrum. The main body of the ligamentum nuchae is similar to a length of slightly elasticated and very strong rope, the front (or lower) border of which is extended into a fibrous lamina. The ends of the lamina are attached to the occipital crest, the posterior tubercle of the atlas and the spinous process of each of the cervical vertebrae. Thus the lamina provides a partition to the muscles at the back (top) of the neck and "guy ropes" or "stays" from the cervical vertebrae to the sturdy main body of the ligamentum nuchae at the top of the neck. This structure is more clearly developed in the horse.

If the rider knows this, it is easy for him to understand that thoughtful encouragement of the correct use of the ligamentum nuchae will have an increasingly excellent effect on the skeletal core of the neck – and of the whole of the horse's balance and form in general. The reader can easily

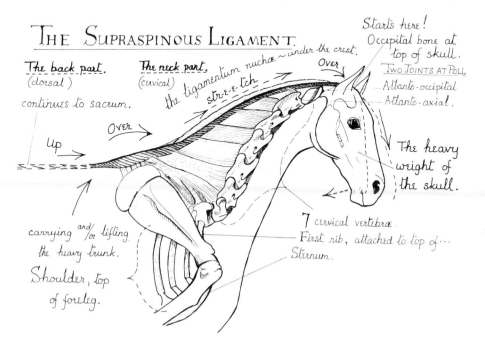

THE SUPRASPINOUS LIGAMENT.

Starts here! Occipital bone at top of skull.

The back part. (dorsal)

The neck part. (cervical)

the ligamentum nuchae ~ under the crest.

Over

TWO JOINTS AT POLL
Atlanto-occipital
Atlanto-axial.

continues to sacrum.

the ligamentum str-e-e-tch

Over

Up

The heavy weight of the skull.

7 cervical vertebrae.
First rib, attached to top of...
Sternum.

carrying and/or lifting the heavy trunk.

Shoulder, top of foreleg.

feel for himself the stretching, lifting movement he can give to the back of his neck – a feeling of "growing tall ears" as he inclines his neck forward. Frequent daily practice of this exercise will prove to be extremely beneficial for his posture and health as it will stretch, strengthen and supple his spine and all its supporting muscles which will retard spinal deterioration. In addition to all these good things, he can feel it for his horse and each practice will remind him how he should encourage his horse to use and develop the muscles which fill out and strengthen the top line of his neck and of the body behind it.

THE STERNO-CLEIDO-MASTOID

The main neck muscle. It originates from the sternum and the clavicle, runs obliquely up each side of the neck and inserts into the mastoid process of the temporal bone. If one side only acts it flexes the head sideways and rotates the face to the opposite side. If both sides act the head is flexed towards the chest.

This muscle is often referred to simply as the sterno-mastoid. It is the equivalent to two well-developed and important muscles in the horse, namely the sterno-cephalicus and the brachiocephalicus.

There are a considerable number of strong muscles in the neck, many of which have their greater part and function in the trunk area so they will be described later.

The sterno-cleido-mastoid, the deep scaleus muscles and those attached to the hyoid (tongue bone) are of further interest when their action is related to the horse. The lower ends of these muscles are attached to the strong first rib which, in turn, is attached to the sternum (breast bone). When these three groups of muscles are employed they lift up the thorax (chest, rib-cage) which is important for the rider's carriage and is absolutely vital for the horse's form. In both cases these muscles, together with the ligamentum nuchae, can only be employed and developed to their full uplifting strength if the rider understands their action and if the horse's poll and lower jaw is supple.

It is so important that this poll-area is finely tuned in both partners in order that the respective skills may be used as counter-weights to play and work all the muscles throughout the combined bodies. Both partners must have good head-carriage and supple polls!

The vertebral or spinal column

The thirty-three vertebrae and their intervening cartilaginous discs form a flexible pillar which is united by ligaments and supported and strengthened by a network of muscles. Each vertebra is a marvel of construction: not only does it support the human being, his head and upper limbs in an upright posture but also it withstands the stress and exertions put upon it by movement, lifting, carrying, pushing, pulling heavy weights and of concussion. The vertebrae are not like strong solid bricks, each one has a weakening hole in the middle, forming a connec-

THE 'CORE' OF THE RIDER'S BACK ~ HIS SPINE.

As seen from :—

in front   the left side   behind

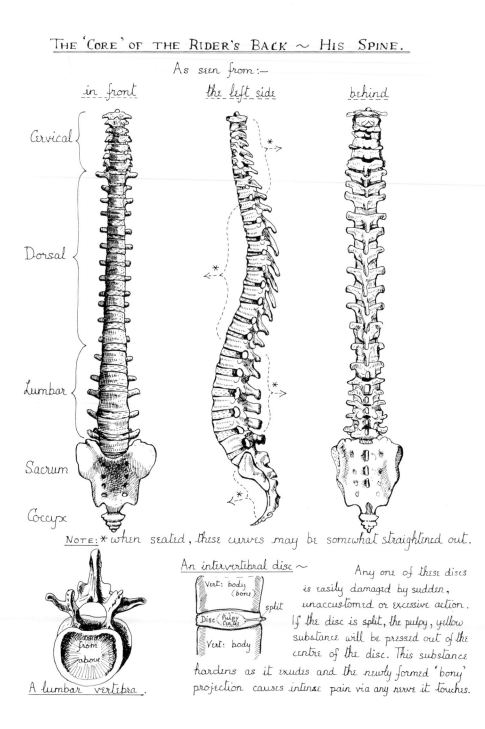

Cervical

Dorsal

Lumbar

Sacrum

Coccyx

NOTE: * when seated, these curves may be somewhat straightened out.

A lumbar vertebra.

An intervertebral disc ~

Vert: body (bone)

split

Disc (Pulpy centre)

Vert: body

Any one of these discs is easily damaged by sudden, unaccustomed or excessive action. If the disc is split, the pulpy, yellow substance will be pressed out of the centre of the disc. This substance hardens as it exudes and the newly formed 'bony' projection causes intense pain via any nerve it touches.

tion tunnel which surrounds the bony, ligamentous spinal canal. This canal contains and protects the dural sac which encloses the spinal cord, spinal nerves and cerebrospinal fluid. The dural sac is protected from the harsh surface of the canal wall by a fat-filled extra-dural space in which lie the lowest spinal nerves and the internal vertebral venous plexus.

SPINAL CURVES

The primary curvature is that in which the spine is flexed throughout its length; it is the first and only curve in the human spine before birth. This original flexion is changed after birth when two secondary, opposite curvatures develop; extension of the cervical (neck) region is produced by the muscles which raise the head, while the extension of the lumbar region is produced by the muscles which support the erect posture. The thoracic (chest) and sacral (pelvic) regions retain their primary curvatures. These four curves and the intervertebral discs give the vertebral column a certain resilience as well as some built-in shock-absorbers.

It is interesting to note that the human spine has a slight lateral curve, being fractionally concave on the left side if the person is right-handed and vice versa. Thus human and horse spines have concave and convex sides: one-sidedness and "his stiff side" are physiological facts and not a recalcitrant horse's misdemeanours – although a rider who lacks understanding may imagine them to be misdemeanours or may cause them to be so.

Movement of the vertebral column

Although there is only slight movement between any two adjacent vertebrae, when these slight movements are combined throughout the length of the spine, the total movement of the vertebral column is extensive. The spine is capable of the following movements.

FLEXION
Bending forwards; most extensive in the cervical region.

EXTENSION
Bending backwards; free in the cervical and lumbar regions, extension is restricted in the thoracic region.

LATERAL FLEXION
Bending to one side and the other; although possible to some degree through the spine, lateral flexion is more extensive in the cervical and lumbar regions.

CIRCUMDUCTION
The end of the bone circumscribing a conical space; very limited.

ROTATION
Turning, revolving, the front of the vertebrae being turned to one side or the other; considerable rotation is possible in the thoracic region, less in the cervical region while it is very limited in the lumbar region.

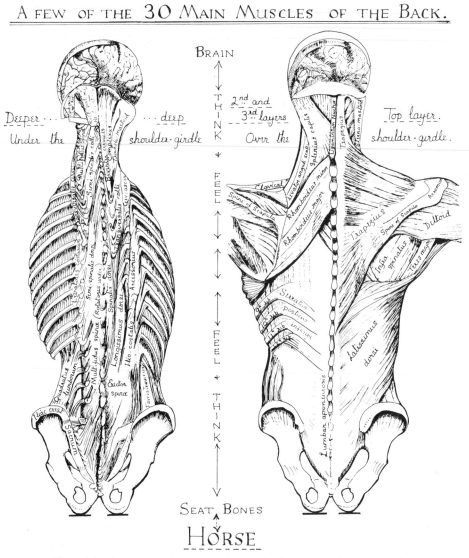

HORSE

By thoughtful play of his muscles with his skeletal frame the rider can use simple and complex leverages to influence the horses he rides.

A deep understanding of his own muscle-work is essential if the rider is to improve his horse's muscle-work, his form and his performance.

82

The movement of the horse's vertebral column is far more restricted than in its human counterpart, due to the extended size and shape of the horse's vertebrae and to his horizontal rather than vertical stance. Whereas movement in the cervical and coccygeal region is fairly free, the thoracic and lumbar regions allow only very slight flexion, extension and lateral flexion. This must be remembered by the rider in his schooling or dressage sessions; although lateral bending of the horse's spine is extremely limited, as the muscles develop his shoulders become more free and mobile; then the bending will appear more emphasised but this can only be achieved after many years of correct work.

The ligaments of the back

ANTERIOR LIGAMENT

A flat band extending from the front of the atlas to the front of the sacrum; it is firmly attached to each vertebra and disc.

POSTERIOR LIGAMENT

A flat band which runs up the back of the vertebral column from the sacrum to the atlas.

LIGAMENTAE FLAVAE

Consist of yellow elastic tissue; they unite the adjacent laminae. They maintain the four vertebral curves, support the spine when it is flexed, and assist in restoring it to the extended erect position.

SUPRA-SPINOUS, INTERSPINOUS AND INTERTRANSVERSE LIGAMENTS

Provide additional support.

THE LIGAMENTUM NUCHAE

The neck portion of the supra-spinous and interspinous ligaments.

The muscles of the back

"The muscles of the back" is a collective term for all the muscles situated at the back of the trunk, some of which extend around the sides. These muscles are largely responsible for man's erect posture and its stability, especially against a forward pulling force and for the stability and mobility of the upper and lower back. Those which control the upper limbs can be divided into two groups: those at the rear of the shoulder girdle which attach the shoulders and upper limbs to the trunk and those in the front which extend the head and the vertebral column. We shall look at this first group, noting that the most important back muscles for the rider to consider and learn to use correctly are:

TRAPEZIUS

A broad, flat muscle lying superficially on the back of the neck, shoulders and upper trunk. It originates at the occipital bone at the base of the skull, the spines of the seventh cervical and of all the thoracic vertebrae, together with the ligamentum nuchae, the corresponding portion of the supraspinous ligament. It inserts into the spine of the scapula, the acromion process at the shoulder joint and the back of the clavicle. Riders with nodding heads or round shoulders will appreciate its action. The trapezius draws the head back, extends the head and neck and keeps them steady on the top of the spinal column. It braces the shoulder blades, back, in and down towards the spinal column, and is used in expanding the chest; it assists in shrugging the shoulders, supporting the arms and in controlling their descent.

LATISSIMUS DORSI

A broad flat muscle stretching over the lower part of the chest and loins. The top part lies under the lower part of the trapezius. It originates at the lower thoracic vertebrae, the lumbar fascia and the crest of the ilium; it then converges to insert into the tendon attached at the bicipital groove of the humerus. Its *action* is a powerful extensor of humerus; adducts humerus and rotates arm inwards. When the arm is fixed it raises the body to the arms. (The last action is particularly relevant to the horse's carriage of his trunk – and of the rider).

LEVATOR SCAPULAE

Lies under the trapezius from the upper cervical vertebrae to the upper angle of the scapula.

THE RHOMBOIDEUS MINOR

Arises from the ligamentum nuchae and the spines of the seventh cervical and first thoracic vertebrae; it passes down and outward before being inserted into the spine of the scapula.

THE RHOMBOIDEUS MAJOR

Is situated below the minor described above. It arises from the spines of the upper five vertebrae, the lower part of the ligamentum nuchae and the supraspinous ligaments. Its *action* is for these three muscles to act together to elevate the scapula. (In the horse they help to free the scapula from the trunk, to enlarge its movement and that of the limbs beneath and behind it).

The second group of back muscles, those which extend the head and the vertebral column, lie below the muscles at the back of the shoulder girdle. The most significant of these are the splenius, serratus and erector spinae muscles. The splenius is situated at the back of the neck and of the upper part of the chest. Its action is to assist in supporting the head in an erect position. When both sides act together they draw the head backwards; acting separately they draw the head to that side or slightly turn the head towards the same side.

THE SERRATUS MUSCLES

Are situated in the upper and back part of the chest (superior) and at the junction of the thoracic and lumbar region (inferior). They originate from the ligamentum nuchae, the supraspinous ligament and the spinous pro-

Connections of the Latissimus Dorsi.

Balance, Posture and Influences

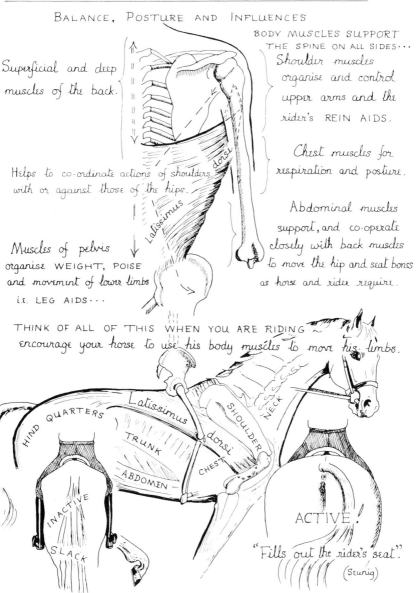

Superficial and deep muscles of the back.

Helps to co-ordinate actions of shoulders with or against those of the hips.

Muscles of pelvis organise WEIGHT, POISE and movement of lower limbs i.e. LEG AIDS···

BODY MUSCLES SUPPORT THE SPINE ON ALL SIDES···
Shoulder muscles organise and control upper arms and the rider's REIN AIDS.

Chest muscles for respiration and posture.

Abdominal muscles support, and co-operate closely with back muscles to move the hip and seat bones as horse and rider require.

THINK OF ALL OF THIS WHEN YOU ARE RIDING ~ encourage your horse to use his body muscles to move his limbs.

Latissimus dorsi

HIND QUARTERS
TRUNK
ABDOMEN
Latissimus dorsi
SHOULDER
NECK
CHEST
INACTIVE
SLACK
ACTIVE!
"Fills out the rider's seat"
(Stunig)

cesses of the last cervical, the thoracic and the first two or three lumbar vertebrae. They pass obliquely downward and outward (superior) and upward and outward (inferior), before inserting into the upper and lower borders respectively of the ribs. In *action* the serrati are vital respiratory muscles, they rotate the scapula, fix the lower ribs and tense the vertebral aponeurosis. Also known as the fencer's muscle for they are used when lungeing and when pushing. See also serratus magnus.

ERECTOR SPINAE

Three prolongations and associated muscles fill the grooves on either side of the vertebral column. Together they all form two tendonous and muscular masses of varying thickness which extend from the sacrum to the occipital bone. In *action*, when both sides act together they straighten the spine and bend it backwards; acting separately each muscle bends the trunk over to its own side.

The fifth and deepest layer contains a further twelve pairs of muscles, including the multifidius dorsi and the intertransversales. There are also the prevertebral muscles, running up and down the front of the spine. In the horse, all these muscles play a prominent part in lifting the trunk, to maintain a good form under the rider's weight.

This is but a sketchy view of the muscles of the back. To those few instructors who maintain that it is dangerous to talk about the rider's back in early lessons, I would ask them to glance again at these few paragraphs.

The back muscles are many, varied and strong and, like a group of unruly school children, if they are not trained correctly they will form bad habits. Just as undisciplined children may grow into vandals, so untrained back muscles can lead to poor posture and ill-health. In riders, bad riding faults may develop which will greatly impair their health and performance and also that of all the horses they ride.

The thorax (chest)

The skeleton of the thorax is both bony and cartilaginous. The rib-cage contains, supports and protects the thoracic cavity and the principal

Poor posture ~
Wrong muscles utilised.

Good posture ~
Rein aids connected by rider's back to the whole of his seat.

Restraining

Aggressive and/or worried stiff.

chest depressed
biceps active.

Forceful pulling.

Rib cage lifted clear of pelvis

(soft)

Smooth
'Happy talk.'

hard bumping.

Confident, calm + kind.

shoulder and tricep muscles active.

Spine supported by muscles at front, back and both sides.

Weight softly secure on two seat bones.

No excess tension.

86

THE THORAX (Chest).

BONE AND CARTILAGE.

The Rib-cage ~ 12 ribs.... all attached to and articulating with the 12 dorsal vertebræ at the rear.

Front view.

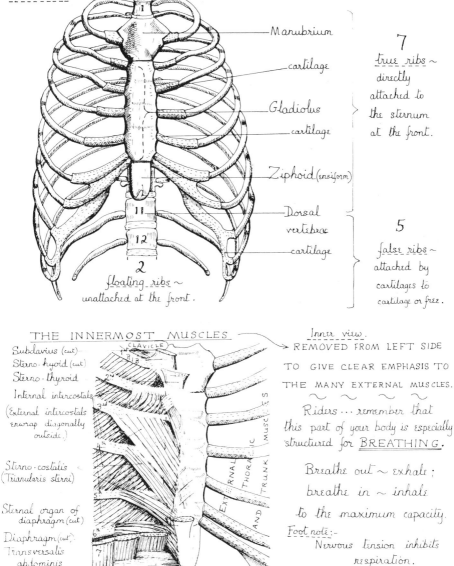

— Manubrium

— cartilage

— Gladiolus

— cartilage

— Ziphoid (ensiform)

— Dorsal vertebræ

— cartilage

7 true ribs ~ directly attached to the sternum at the front.

5 false ribs ~ attached by cartilages to cartilage or free.

2 floating ribs ~ unattached at the front.

THE INNERMOST MUSCLES

Inner view.
REMOVED FROM LEFT SIDE TO GIVE CLEAR EMPHASIS TO THE MANY EXTERNAL MUSCLES.

~ ~ ~ ~ ~

Subclavius (cut)
Sterno-hyoid (cut)
Sterno-thyroid
Internal intercostals
(External intercostals enwrap diagonally outside.)

Sterno-costalis
(Triangularis sterni)

Sternal organ of diaphragm (cut)

Diaphragm (cut).
Transversalis abdominis

CLAVICLE
1ˢᵗ RIB
2ⁿᵈ
3ʳᵈ

EXTERNAL THORACIC AND TRUNK MUSCLES

Riders ... remember that this part of your body is especially structured for BREATHING.

Breathe out ~ exhale;
breathe in ~ inhale
to the maximum capacity.

Foot note :-
Nervous tension inhibits respiration.

87

organs of respiration (lungs) and circulation (heart). Its walls are formed by the twelve true ribs, attached at the rear to the twelve thoracic or dorsal vertebrae, and at the front each rib is attached to the sternum by a short length of cartilage.

The sternum (breast bone) is composed of three parts, the manubrium, at the top; the gladiolus, the main body of the sternum originally formed from four sternebrae, the joins of which still show faintly on the bone, and the ziphoid or ensiform at the bottom. There are small indentations down each side of the sternum in which costal cartilages are accommodated. The intercostal spaces between the ribs provide attachments for three layers of muscles and their nerves – the external, internal and innermost intercostal muscles.

The dome-shaped diaphragm forms the floor of the thorax.

Movements of the thorax

There are so many joints in the thoracic region that although many of these joints are only capable of limited movement the sum total is considerable. There are several groups of joints. For example:

INTERVERTEBRAL
Between the vertebrae of the spinal column.

RIBS WITH VERTEBRAE
Double articulations, costo-vertebral and costo-transverse.

COSTAL CARTILAGES WITH STERNUM
Also related articulations of the ribs with their cartilages and between the cartilages themselves.

The rib-cage provides attachment to:
• The scalene muscles which help to fix the first ribs.
• Muscles which support the abdominal viscera.
• Extensor muscles of the back, which continue laterally as far as the angles of the ribs.
• Many of the major muscles which support the weight of the upper limb, some of these being trapezius, latissimus dorsi, serratus anterior and pectoralis major and minor.
• The diaphragm.
• The intercostal muscles.

Apart from the usual forms of movement the thorax carries out the inspiratory and expiratory phases of respiration, breathing in and breathing out; these are produced by an alternating increase and decrease in the volume of the thoracic cavity. These movements are so much a part of life that often they are overlooked.

However, if a rider is stressed with an unusual, exceptional or frightening experience he will often forget to breathe. As he holds his breath he

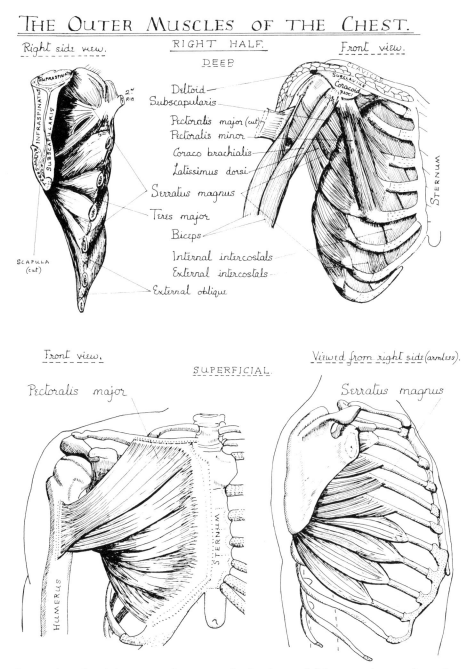

SUPRASPINATUS
2° RIB
INFRASPINATUS
TERES MAJOR
SUBSCAPULARIS

Deltoid
Subscapularis
Pectoralis major (cut)
Pectoralis minor
Coraco brachialis
Latissimus dorsi
Serratus magnus
Teres major
Biceps
Internal intercostals
External intercostals
External oblique

SCAPULA (cut)

CLAVICLE
SUBCLAVIUS
Coracoid
PROC:
STERNUM

Front view.   Viewed from right side (armless).

SUPERFICIAL

Pectoralis major   Serratus magnus

STERNUM

HUMERUS

loses the elasticity, suppleness and rhythm of his muscle work and
movement – and so does his poor horse! Riders must practise deep
breathing as a daily routine, it emphasises a correct habit, improves health
and stamina and improves voice production, an extra bonus if the rider is
also an instructor.

Muscles of the thorax

SCALENUS

Anterior, medius and posterior – these are attached to the second and seventh cervical vertebrae and insert into the first and second ribs. In *action* they raise and fix the first two ribs and are also weak flexors of the head and neck.

LEVATORES COSTARUM

There are twelve pairs on each side of the spine, at the top of the back of the chest. They arise from the ends of the transverse processes of the seventh cervical and the eleven upper thoracic vertebrae and pass obliquely downward and outward to insert into the upper border of the rib below them.

EXTERNAL INTERCOSTALS

Situated between the ribs, they run obliquely from behind forwards. They originate from the lower edge of the rib above to the upper edge of the rib below. In *action* they produce respiration and support the weight of the trunk.

INTERNAL INTERCOSTALS

Similar to the above except that the fibres run from front to rear forming a criss-cross pattern with the outer layer.

PECTORALIS MAJOR

This is situated at the front of the chest. It originates from the front of the sternum and ribs and inserts into the humerus. Its *action* is to adduct the arm and carry it across in front of the chest.

PECTORALIS MINOR

As its name suggests, this is a smaller edition of the above muscle, lying directly under it and supporting its action.

SERRATUS MAGNUS

Situated at the side of the chest, this muscle originates from the upper nine ribs and inserts into the front of the top edge of the scapula. In *action* it carries the scapula forwards and provides power for strong pushing movements. (In the horse, the serratus muscles help to lift the front of the trunk and then to move the freed shoulder blades.)

Many of the muscles of the chest are adductors and abductors of the upper limb. In the horse these chest muscles acting together with those in the hindquarters carry out the same movements. In *action*, when adducting, they pull the limb inwards, towards the trunk, or even across its central line; abducting they lift the limb out and away from the trunk. Both these actions are rarely used by the horse in his natural state; therefore these muscles have to be developed thoughtfully by easy lateral work such as leg-yielding before the horse can be expected to perform any of the more advanced dressage movements. The development of

The Diaphragm and its Attachments.

A sheet of muscle which can form a strong central support for his body if the rider uses it well ~ it is vital to good posture and respiration.

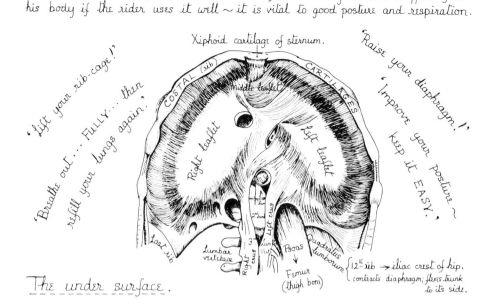

Xiphoid cartilage of sternum.

'Lift your rib-cage!'

'Breathe out... FULLY... then refill your lungs again.'

'Raise your diaphragm!'

'Improve your posture keep it EASY.'

COSTAL (rib)

CARTILAGES

Middle leaflet

Right leaflet

Left leaflet

Last rib

Lumbar vertebrae

Right crus

Left crus

Psoas

Quadratus lumborum

Femur (thigh bone)

12ᵗʰ rib → iliac crest of hip.
contracts diaphragm; flexes trunk to its side.

The under surface.

these muscles will do much to strengthen the whole of his musculature with a consequent improvement to his ability on the flat and over fences.

DIAPHRAGM

A dome-shaped muscle which forms a partition between the thoracic and the abdominal cavities. It originates from the lumbar vertebrae, from the back of the ziphoid process of the sternum, and from the inner surfaces of the lower six pairs of ribs. Its *action* produces respiration, being the chief muscle of inspiration; its cross-tie position in the upper body has just that effect on posture and the consequent freedom of movement of the hips.

The abdomen

The abdomen is the largest cavity in the body. It is of an oval shape, the top being bounded by the under surface of the diaphragm and the bottom by the lowest muscles in the pelvis. It can vary considerably in capacity and shape! If the latter is too rotund the rider's balance and his muscle work cannot have the necessary efficiency and ease required of horsemanship.

The external abdominal muscles

All the muscles in this group are of major importance to posture whether the person is standing or sitting. Combined with correct postural action of the back muscles, the external abdominal muscles keep the front of the pelvic bowl up so that the pelvis is in the required "neutral" position of vertical balance.

THE EXTERNAL ABDOMINAL MUSCLES.

DO use your tummy muscles to keep your pelvis upright.

DON'T "let your tummy muscles go" and "push your stomach forward" ~ the wrong way.

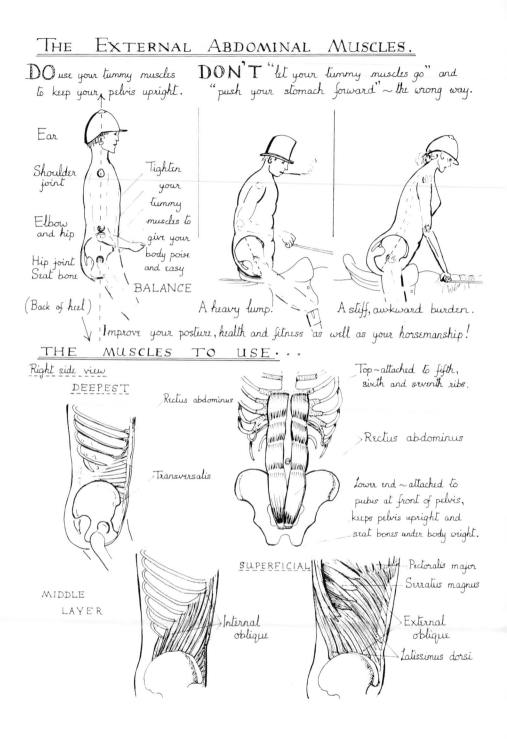

Ear

Shoulder joint

Elbow and hip

Hip joint Seat bone

(Back of heel)

Tighten your tummy muscles to give your body poise and easy BALANCE

A heavy lump.

A stiff, awkward burden.

Improve your posture, health and fitness as well as your horsemanship!

THE MUSCLES TO USE···

Right side view

DEEPEST

Rectus abdominus

Transversalis

MIDDLE LAYER

Top ~ attached to fifth, sixth and seventh ribs.

Rectus abdominus

Lower end ~ attached to pubis at front of pelvis, keeps pelvis upright and seat bones under body weight.

SUPERFICIAL

Internal oblique

Pectoralis major
Serratus magnus
External oblique
Latissimus dorsi

A long flat muscle down the front of the abdomen from the sternum to the pubis, at the front of the pelvis. In *action* it collaborates with the back muscles to keep the upper body erect, it flexes the spine forwards and supports the internal organs.

OBLIQUUS EXTERNUS ABDOMINUS
The fibres run obliquely from the lower ribs to the iliac crest. In *action* it flexes the trunk laterally, rotates the trunk and supports the internal organs.

OBLIQUUS INTERNUS ABDOMINUS
Similar to the above muscle in position and in action, except that the fibres run in the opposite direction.

TRANSVERSALIS ABDOMINUS
Runs transversely across the abdomen, lies beneath the two preceding muscles and assists their action.

QUADRATUS LUMBORUM
Runs each side of the four upper lumbar vertebrae and from the last rib to the iliac crest. In *action* it assists the abdominal muscles.

LINA ALBA
A line of tendon along the outside of the middle of the abdomen, from the ziphoid cartilage to the pubis.

(In the horse all these abdominal muscles play an important uplifting rôle – providing that the rider's lower legs at the girth ask them to do so!)

The Appendicular Skeleton

The appendicular skeleton controls the upper and lower limbs.

The upper limb

It is well for riders to recall that their upper limbs are specialised organs for grasping, that is, hanging on powerfully. Strong muscles, tendons and bones provide the limbs' power and this is intensified by man's subconscious ability to fix the joints of his upper limbs in positions which enable the muscles to work with maximum effect. Add to this knowledge the fact that by adopting a sitting posture man automatically increases his stability and thus his ability to hold or to pull is multiplied. It is small wonder that soft, smooth rein aids are not formed easily; they must be taught and learned, thought about and practised carefully in order that instinctive, prehensile reactions may be over-ridden.

Fortunately Nature is not entirely pitted against the rider achieving rein aids of "the right sort", for, due to a well-developed sensory nerve supply, and to the brain's strong connection with the upper limbs, they also have the ability to perform sensitive, finely controlled movements.

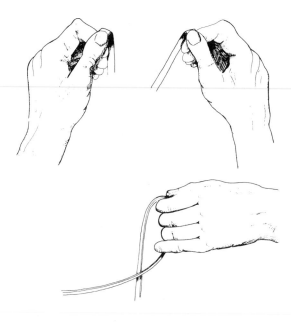

'Hookey', stretched out fingers with set wrists
and hard or sharp rein aids ~ usually
gloveless and often associated with
bootlace - thin reins.

However, a warning note must be attached here for riders. The fingers are the natural gauges of and for this sensitivity, particularly the tips of the fingers. Unless they are educated in their holding of the reins, the fingers will like to feel the reins with a too-del-i-cate touch between the tips of the fingers and the thumb. Whereas this is an ideal way to judge the quality of the rein, whether the leather is supple, thick or thin, it is too superficial to be even adequate as part of a rein aid which measures the work of the horse's body muscles and of his hindlegs. The instinctive, too-del-i-cate hold relates too closely with the prehensile clutch; it fixes the joints and employs the wrong muscles – the biceps instead of the triceps. Thinking rider, please read on!

Often it is presumed that the upper arm commences at the point of the shoulder. Of course, this is inaccurate, and if he is to acquire a correct feel for the posture and control of his upper limbs, the rider must understand that the shoulder girdle is their true beginning. Each limb has its own bony plate and strap which is firmly attached to the back of the trunk, not by bolts and screws, but by a strong and elastic web of muscles.

THE RIGHT SHOULDER BONES AND MUSCLES.

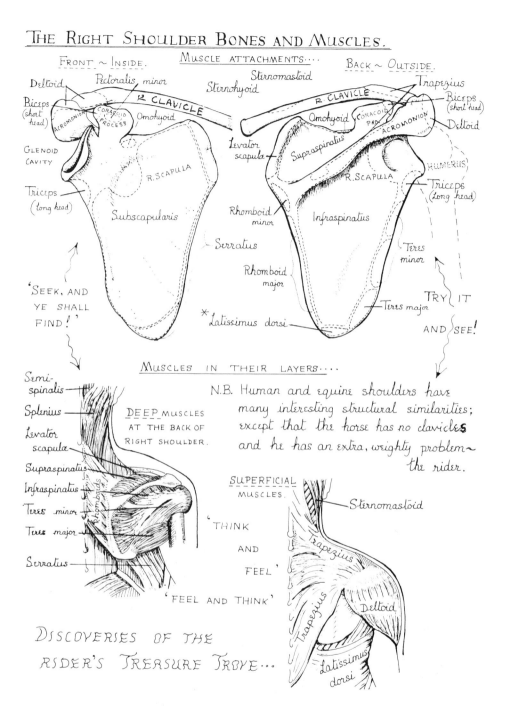

FRONT ~ INSIDE.

MUSCLE ATTACHMENTS····

BACK ~ OUTSIDE.

Deltoid
Pectoralis, minor
Sternomastoid
Sternohyoid
Trapezius

Biceps (short head)
R. CLAVICLE
Omohyoid
CORACOID PROCESS
ACROMION
R. CLAVICLE
Omohyoid
CORACOID PRO
ACROMION
Biceps (short head)
Deltoid

GLENOID CAVITY
Levator scapulæ
Supraspinatus
HUMERUS

R. SCAPULA
R. SCAPULA
Triceps (long head)

Triceps (long head)
Subscapularis
Rhomboid minor
Infraspinatus

Teres minor

'SEEK, AND YE SHALL FIND!'
Serratus
Rhomboid major
Teres major
TRY IT AND SEE!

* Latissimus dorsi

MUSCLES IN THEIR LAYERS····

Semi-spinalis
Splenius
Levator scapulæ
Supraspinatus
Infraspinatus
Teres minor
Teres major
Serratus
Rhomboids
DEEP MUSCLES AT THE BACK OF RIGHT SHOULDER.

N.B. Human and equine shoulders have many interesting structural similarities; except that the horse has no clavicles and he has an extra, weighty problem~ the rider.

SUPERFICIAL MUSCLES.
Sternomastoid
'THINK AND FEEL'
Trapezius
'FEEL AND THINK'
Trapezius
Deltoid
Latissimus dorsi

DISCOVERIES OF THE RIDER'S TREASURE TROVE···

FRONT VIEWS

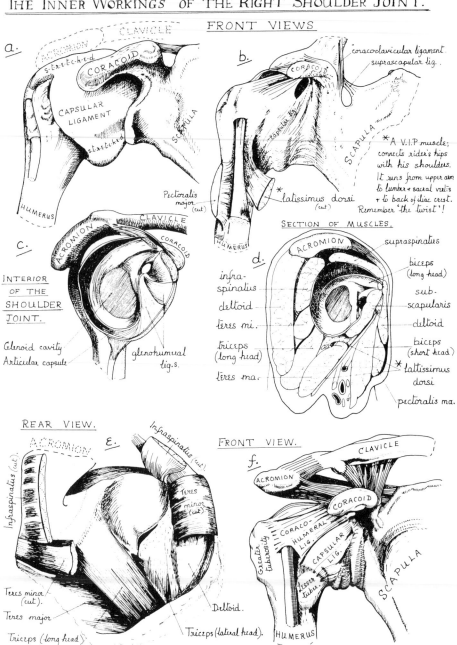

a.
ACROMION
CLAVICLE
s-t-r-e-t-ch-e-d
CORACOID
CAPSULAR LIGAMENT
stretched
SCAPULA
HUMERUS

b.
coracoclavicular ligament.
suprascapular lig.
CORACOID
SCAPULA
Pectoralis major (cut)
HUMERUS
* latissimus dorsi (cut)

* A V.I.P muscle; connects rider's hips with his shoulders. It runs from upper arm to lumbar + sacral vert's + to back of iliac crest. Remember 'the twist'!

c.
INTERIOR OF THE SHOULDER JOINT.
ACROMION
CLAVICLE
CORACOID
Glenoid cavity
Articular capsule
glenohumeral lig.s.

SECTION OF MUSCLES.

d.
ACROMION
supraspinatus
biceps (long head)
sub-scapularis
deltoid
biceps (short head)
* latissimus dorsi
pectoralis ma.

infra-spinatus
deltoid
teres mi.
triceps (long head)
teres ma.

REAR VIEW.

e.
ACROMION
Infraspinatus (cut)
Infraspinatus (cut)
Teres minor (cut)
Teres minor (cut).
Teres major
Triceps (long head).
Deltoid.
Triceps (lateral head).

FRONT VIEW.

f.
CLAVICLE
ACROMION
CORACOID
CORACO-HUMERAL LIG.
Greater tuberosity
CAPSULAR LIG.
Lesser tuber
SCAPULA
HUMERUS

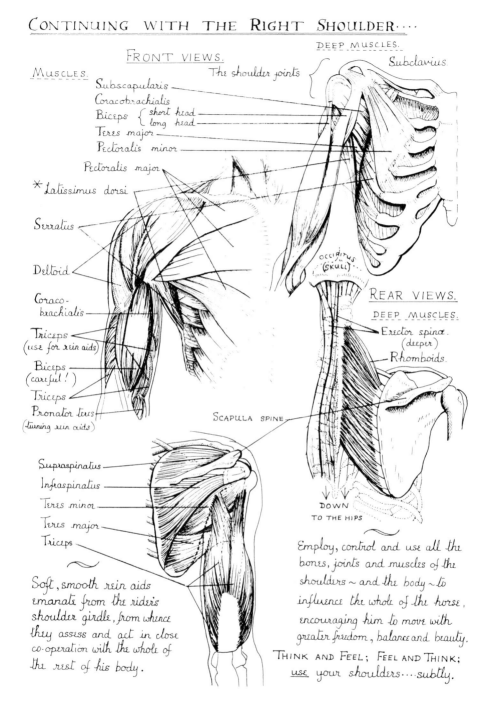

FRONT VIEWS.

DEEP MUSCLES.

Subclavius

MUSCLES.

The shoulder joints

Subscapularis
Coracobrachialis
Biceps { short head
long head
Teres major
Pectoralis minor

Pectoralis major

* Latissimus dorsi

Serratus

Deltoid

Coraco-
brachialis

Triceps
(use for rein aids)

Biceps
(careful!)

Triceps

Pronator teres
(turning rein aids)

OCCIPITUS
(SKULL)

REAR VIEWS.

DEEP MUSCLES.

Erector spinæ.
(deeper)

Rhomboids.

SCAPULA SPINE

Supraspinatus
Infraspinatus
Teres minor
Teres major
Triceps

DOWN
TO THE HIPS

Soft, smooth rein aids
emanate from the rider's
shoulder girdle, from whence
they assess and act in close
co-operation with the whole of
the rest of his body.

Employ, control and use all the
bones, joints and muscles of the
shoulders ~ and the body ~ to
influence the whole of the horse,
encouraging him to move with
greater freedom, balance and beauty.
THINK AND FEEL; FEEL AND THINK;
use your shoulders····subtly.

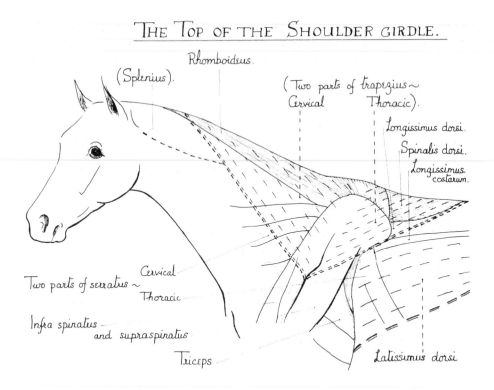

Rhomboideus.

(Splenius).

(Two parts of trapezius ~
Cervical   Thoracic).

Longissimus dorsi.

Spinalis dorsi.

Longissimus costarum.

Cervical

Two parts of serratus ~
Thoracic

Infra spinatus
and supraspinatus

Triceps

Latissimus dorsi

The shoulder girdle consists of four bones, a left and right clavicle or collar bone and a left and right scapula or shoulder blade. Those riders who have broken their collar bones, sometimes more than one apiece, may wish they were like horses who have no collar bones, but then horses do not stand up on their two hindlegs – at least, well-trained horses don't!

The clavicles of man allow his upper limbs to swing clear of his upright body and transmit part of their weight to be borne by the trunk, also they provide attachments for a number of major muscles. The medial end of each clavicle articulates with the manubrium, or top of the breast-plate, and with the cartilage of the first rib, while the lateral end articulates with the acromion process of the scapula.

The scapula is a flat, triangular spade-shaped bone which forms the back part of the shoulder girdle. It is supported by, controls and provides attachments for no fewer than seventeen muscles.

The muscles of the upper limb

To compile a list of the muscles of the upper limb would seem simple enough, but, in fact, so many muscles are involved that such a chore would defeat its object. A list of every muscle together with its situation and action would daunt even the most enthusiastic reader. For instance, to move one shoulder in one direction requires the co-ordination of a remarkably wide range of muscles. Those of the neck, the chest, the back and the abdomen are all employed in varying degrees for any movement the rider may make with one of his shoulders. If it is realised that there are over fifty muscles in each arm (excluding the shoulder region) perhaps the reader will think me wise rather than lazy if I select only a few muscles which have special uses and interest for the rider.

The muscles of the shoulder region have three main purposes, those of respiration, posture (including the carriage of the upper limb) and leverage. They control all the movements of the upper limb and as such are the mainstay of the rein aids; some of these muscles also protect the vulnerable shoulder joint.

Movements of the shoulder girdle (scapula and clavicle)

Although the scapula is the main motivator, its movements are always accompanied by movements at each end of the clavicle and usually at the shoulder joint as well, as the humerus is worked from and by the scapula. The scapula is very mobile; it may be moved upward, downward, forward or backward on the wall of the chest or rotated medially or laterally. The muscles involved are:

UPWARD
Levator scapulae, upper fibres of the trapezius and the two rhomboids.

DOWNWARD
Serratus anterior, pectoralis minor, subclavius and the lower fibres of the trapezius – all aided by gravity.

FORWARD
Serratus magnus and pectoralis minor. When the arm is fixed, they are assisted by the pectoralis major.

MEDIAL ROTATION
Levator scapulae and the rhomboids.

LATERAL ROTATION
Serratus anterior and trapezius.

These movements of the scapula are of great importance to all the arm movements. By its mobility the scapula plays the muscles through the shoulder joint, almost as if it were a pulley. This clever arrangement saves the shoulder joint from the stress and strain which it would suffer if the arm movements and the carriage of its full weight were to originate there. The balance and control of the human upper limb is a wonderful example of perfection to any engineering expert or professor of mechanics. However, such perfection is too easily put to naught if the rider does not use it with a matching degree of trained skill.

Muscles of the shoulder girdle

As well as being employed for respiration, the widely ranging shoulder girdle muscles govern the posture and movement of the rider's upper body and of his upper limbs. Every movement or non-movement (stiffness) emanating from this region will have a repercussion throughout the whole of the rider's seat.

Whenever he rides, the rider must use his brain well to attune the muscle work of his shoulders to the rest of his musculature as well as to that of his horse. Many riders hold their shoulders in a set position as if they are carved from a single piece of wood. They round them or raise them, they stoop them forward or do their best to shrug them up to their ears. Riders' shoulders must be held with a good and easy posture; they must be free – and relatively loose upon the trunk so that they may be used in concert with all the other bones, joints and muscles of the seat.

The same principles apply to the horse. By means of his skilled horsemanship the rider must encourage the horse to carry them both in balance and with the maximum freedom of his shoulders. Unless the horse's shoulders are loose and free he has to be "a leg mover". His powerful hindlegs cannot engage forward under his body, as virtually there is no room for them to do so. Although his head may be raised, there can be no true lightness of the forehand nor can the movement flow through the great muscles of his body.

Muscles connecting the shoulder girdle to the trunk

THE POSTERIOR, DORSAL OR REAR DIVISION

- Levatores costarum
- Trapezius
- Rhomboideus
- Latissimus dorsi

from a "supple poll" but not a nodding head at the top to the deep back muscles below

THE ANTERIOR, VENTRAL OR FRONT DIVISION

- Scalenus
- Pectorals
- Serratus anterior
- Subclavicus

respiration, carriage of rib-cage to improve poise of upper body and to "free" back and pelvic area.

THE SHOULDER JOINT

It is common knowledge that the shoulder joint is a ball-and-socket joint, the large globular head of the humerus (upper arm bone) being the "ball" and the shallow cavity near the top outer edge of the scapula (shoulder blade) being the socket. However, many riders are not aware of the intricacy and value of the secondary joint, that of the outer end of the clavicle (collar bone) with the scapula's acromion process, the large, oblong bony projection which overhangs the cavity or socket of the true shoulder joint.

Muscles of the arm

As we have seen, there are over fifty main muscles in each arm and it is not practical here to describe them all. It is probably best to reserve the students' energies and thoughts for the larger muscles of the upper arm. If the reader will pay close attention to their respective attachments and actions, as described below, his interest must be caught by the fascination of which muscle goes from where to where and by what it does. Thus he

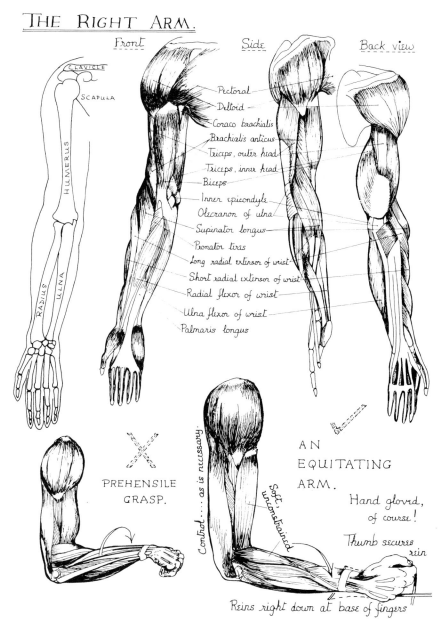

THE RIGHT ARM.

Front Side Back view

CLAVICLE
SCAPULA
HUMERUS
RADIUS
ULNA

Pectoral
Deltoid
Coraco brachialis
Brachialis anticus
Triceps, outer head
Triceps, inner head
Biceps
Inner epicondyle
Olecranon of ulna
Supinator longus
Pronator teres
Long radial extensor of wrist
Short radial extensor of wrist
Radial flexor of wrist
Ulna flexor of wrist
Palmaris longus

PREHENSILE GRASP.

Control ..... as is necessary.

AN EQUITATING ARM.

Soft, unconstrained

Hand gloved, of course!

Thumb secures rein

Reins right down at base of fingers

will see that it is important that riders should think of their upper limbs as extensions of their upper bodies, rather than as arms and hands stuck on to the body independently, like the limbs of a doll. It will help him to understand, for example, how the arms can make the teres muscles connect and work with other shoulder, neck and back muscles. He will then get a true feeling for rein aids which form a smooth connection with the whole of the horse's body, through to his two hind feet. By soft feeling through his arms and the reins from his back and his shoulder blades to the horse's mouth the rider can assist the horse to balance himself and to move and work his body freely in answer to the rider's forward-driving aids. The rider's hands should never grasp or pull – rather, they should analyse, measure and prescribe. If he understands more about the where and how of the muscles of his arms, the rider will have "hands" which are well-carried, steady, light and unobtrusive in their action and an asset to his horsemanship.

These bones, joints and muscles are also of the greatest interest when related to the horse's physiology. The humerus or upper arm bone connects the point of the shoulder joint to that of the elbow. It is a vital part of the area commonly referred to as the horse's shoulder. In the horse the humerus is a short, stout bone which provides attachments for many of the large muscles which connect the neck, shoulders, trunk and foreleg; this, and the joints at either end of it, play an important role in the carriage of the horse's forehand and in his overall balance and agility.

Movement of the shoulder joint is considerable. It is governed by the scapulohumerus muscles which join the arm to the shoulder blade.

Muscles on the outside of the shoulder

DELTOID

A powerful multipennate muscle which lies on the point of the shoulder, as an 'epaulet'. Its *action* is to raise the arm at a right angle with the body; it rotates the arm inwards and flexes it; it rotates the arm outwards and extends it.

SUPRASPINATUS

It assists the deltoid muscle in adducting the humerus and in rotating it inwards.

INFRASPINATUS

Has a wide attachment on the outer surface of the scapula from which it is inserted into the middle of the greater tuberosity of the humerus. Its *action* is to rotate the arm outwards, as is required to give an open or leading rein aid.

TERES MINOR

Is attached to the outer edge of the scapula and inserts into the lower facet of the greater tuberosity of the humerus. Its *action* is to rotate the arm outwards. The rider can feel and use its close connection with the triceps, the large muscles at the back of the upper arm.

Muscles on the inside of the shoulder

SUBSCAPULARIS
Passes from subscapularis fossa on the inner surface of the scapula to the lesser tuberosity of the humerus. Its *action* is to rotate the arm inwards.

TERES MAJOR
A thick muscle which runs from the lower outer edge of the scapula to the upper end of the shaft of the humerus on its inner side. It is united with the latissimus dorsi for short distance. Its *action* is the adduction and inward rotation of the arm.

The brachii muscles of the arm

CORACO-BRACHIALIS
A thin muscle which passes between the tip of the coracoid process of the scapula to insert halfway down the inner side of the humerus. Its *action* is to adduct and flex the arm.

BICEPS
As its name indicates, it has two heads both of which are attached to the scapula, the short head to the tip of the coracoid process and the long head to the shoulder joint. It lies along the bicipital groove of the humerus and inserts into the tubercle of the radius, and the deep fascia of the forearm. In *action* it is a powerful flexor and supinator of the forearm. The rider should make full use of the latter action and as little as possible of the former. He must guard against pulling with his biceps.

BRACHIALIS
A broad muscle in front of the elbow joint. Its *action* is to flex the elbow.

TRICEPS
A powerful muscle at the back of the arm; it arises by three heads – the long head from the scapula, where it works closely with the teres muscle and the latissimus dorsi. The lateral and medial heads arise from the top half of the humerus. It inserts into the back of the elbow joint at the olecranon process of the ulna. Its *action* is to extend the elbow joint and forearm and, most important from the rider's point of view, is the triceps' action of drawing back the humerus and adducting it to the thorax. Here is a vital factor for softly restraining rein aids.

There are of course many more arm muscles, those of the forearm, wrist and fingers, but for riders, of particular if not arresting interest, are the two sub-headings under which these muscles are grouped:

- Extensors and supinators
- Flexors and pronators

For some readers, two of these words, *supinator* and *pronator*, may be new, and indeed dictionaries are not anxious to disclose their meaning, whilst anatomical text-books ensure that the lay reader is utterly confused by the technical jargon! To paint a practical picture – if a person is lying on his back with the palms of his hands uppermost, on the beach, in the sun, his forearms are in the supine position; if he sits up, bends his elbows and turns the palms of his hands downwards to face the sand, this turning movement is called pronation.

The four actions are usually grouped in the two pairs: extensor and supinator, and flexor and pronator.

Although those are the actions which are naturally paired, the turning of the forearm to and from supination and pronation is more effective when the elbow is flexed softly. The rider's elbows should never be flexed and fixed; he must guard against this natural muscular double action as this will make his rein aids very harsh. He must also be careful to keep his upper arms close to his body so that he can make full use of them to make a subtle play with the bones, joints and muscles of his shoulders and trunk and to ensure that there is a smooth follow-through from his shoulders to the reins without interruption from elbows which are stuck out. It is hoped that the reader will remember a note of warning which was given in Book 1: flexion, pronation and pulling tend to go together and in the rider this combination results in the "English" hand position so condemned by Müseler and many other past and present masters.

Reminders

The rider's rein aids have their origin at the shoulder blades, then ... elbows softly flexed; forearms supinated to keep the bones parallel and the tissues between them free; reins down at the base of the fingers, the ends of which are flattened to allow free movement in the base joints, resulting in "happy talk" within the rein aids.

As has been mentioned earlier, the rider's shoulders work in close collaboration with his pelvis. By thoughtful, subtle movements of his shoulder's bones and joints the rider can organise his muscles and his body weight through his pelvis right down to his seat bones. The shoulders and their muscles can have a considerable effect on many other bones, joints and muscles with which they are associated. Even distant muscles can be hampered or assisted; a tense rounding of the shoulders can immobilise the rider's lower legs; on the other hand, a smooth backward movement of the rider's inner shoulder will enable the inner hip to be moved forward simultaneously, inviting the horse to move freely in his body. In this way the rider and horse can perform as one as they negotiate a circle or turn.

This brings me, rather naturally, to the pelvis and the lower limbs.

THE RIDER'S MIDDLE PART.

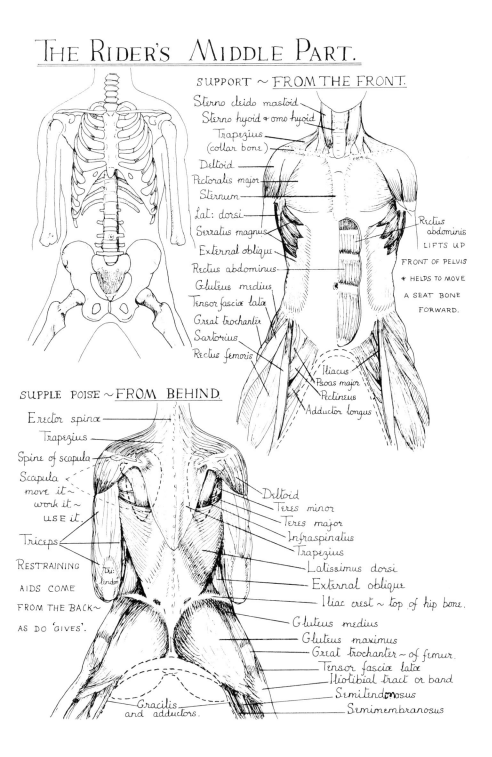

SUPPORT ~ FROM THE FRONT.

Sterno cleido mastoid
Sterno hyoid & omo hyoid
Trapezius (collar bone)
Deltoid
Pectoralis major
Sternum
Lat: dorsi
Serratus magnus
External oblique
Rectus abdominus
Gluteus medius
Tensor fasciæ latæ
Great trochanter
Sartorius
Rectus femoris
Iliacus
Psoas major
Pectineus
Adductor longus

Rectus abdominis LIFTS UP FRONT OF PELVIS & HELPS TO MOVE A SEAT BONE FORWARD.

SUPPLE POISE ~ FROM BEHIND.

Erector spinæ
Trapezius
Spine of scapula
Scapula < move it ~ work it ~ USE it.
Triceps
RESTRAINING AIDS COME FROM THE BACK~ AS DO 'GIVES'.
tri: tendon

Deltoid
Teres minor
Teres major
Infraspinatus
Trapezius
Latissimus dorsi
External oblique
Iliac crest ~ top of hip bone.
Gluteus medius
Gluteus maximus
Great trochanter ~ of femur.
Tensor fasciæ latæ
Iliotibial tract or band
Semitendinosus
Semimembranosus

Gracilis and adductors.

The lower limb

As there are over fifty muscles in each leg, these will not be tabulated or described in too fine a detail. As with the earlier description of the arm, I will try to confine the theory to aspects, movements and muscles which are of special interest to the rider.

Firstly, an essentially practical point. The legs are both heavy and strong, factors which are most helpful to the rider for they aid his balance and stability when he sits astride his horse. Although a certain length of leg is an advantage, legs which are too long can be a disadvantage in that they make communication more remote by being far removed from the rider's brain and ... from the horse's sides.

"A good leg for a boot"; "He uses his legs very well"; "His legs are always in the correct position". These are compliments which surely make the horseman happy. The first denotes that visually the form is good; the second may imply either that the rider's legs are seen to move with vigorous biffs and bangs or that, although little movement is seen, the horse is full of impulsion and is going in a good form. The third comment may mean the observer has noticed that the rider's heels are well down, drawn back and immobile or that the lower legs are constantly feeling the horse's sides close to the girth, with only occasional, individual, moves to the area on the horse's ribcage known as "behind the girth".

It is so important that riders should think what they are doing with their legs, how they are doing it and for what purpose. Still legs which are still purely for the sake of being still, "maintaining a good position" are possibly the worst of all, for the stillness on a moving animal's back causes him discomfort and stifles his natural movement.

The rider must use his legs for the horse more than for himself. The rider's legs create the impulsion, they help the horse with his balance, with his gait programmes, to guide him, to animate him and to give him confidence. Every second that a good horseman sits on his horse he employs both legs to assess the horse's form and to encourage him to improve it.

At the top of the lower limbs is:

The pelvis

The pelvis is a strong, basin-shaped arrangement of bones through which the weight of the head, trunk and upper limbs is transmitted to the lower limbs when man stands or moves about.

The pelvis comprises four bones, the two innominate or hip bones, the sacrum and the coccyx. These four bones are separate yet joined. Extremely little movement occurs either at the three joints between the four bones or at the fifth lumbar vertebra where the pelvis joins and becomes the bottom part of the spinal column.

The angle at which the pelvis is tilted, or not tilted in the perfect horseman's seat, is sometimes a subject for debate. Those who assert that it should tilt forward at the top have no logical argument to support their theory. On the other hand, there are substantial reasons for the axis of the rider's hip bones to be poised vertically above his seat bones. These reasons are:

HEALTH

It is an established fact that poor posture – standing with head poked, rounded shoulders and a hollow back – causes unnecessary strain to a person's physique in general and to his joints and internal organs in particular. It is interesting to note that Mr. Tucker, the consultant and surgeon quoted earlier, puts great emphasis on the importance of good posture for health and fitness, "The pelvis tilted so that it is at right angles to the ground."

However, it is the sitting rather than the standing posture that is of real interest to the rider.

ANATOMY

To quote *Gray's Anatomy*: "In the sitting posture the body rests on the medial and lower parts of the ischial tuberosities and a coronal plane drawn through the anterior superior iliac spines passes through the acetabule. The lumbosacral angle is considerably reduced and the projection of the sacral promontory is correspondingly diminished." If this sounds incomprehensible to the lay reader it can be translated in more simple terms. When a rider sits on his horse, automatically his two hip

MR W.E.TUCKER'S POSTURAL TRAINING   ADAPTED FOR THE RIDER.

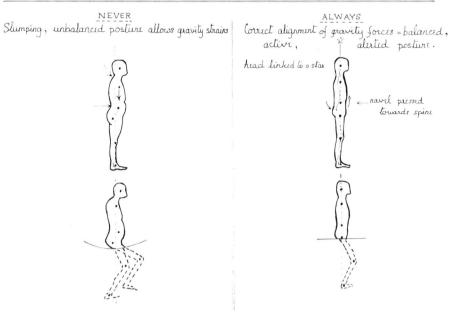

NEVER
Slumping, unbalanced posture allows gravity strains

ALWAYS
Correct alignment of gravity forces = balanced, active, alerted posture.

head linked to a star

navel pressed towards spine

bones assume a more upright posture and the hollow in the small of his back virtually disappears; the spine is straightened. That simple anatomical fact is the basis of the rider's upright, balanced seat.

The above two facts link together to provide a very tangible reason why riding promotes good health. It is a sport which is taken sitting down and as such a considerable amount of strain is removed from the body, which in turn is given the most advantageous posture by the simple act of sitting.

At no time do medical or equestrian experts advocate tipping the top of the pelvis forward and hollowing the small of the back. Clearly such a move would be detrimental to the health and the performance of both horse and rider.

BALANCE

As in the upright, dressage or everyday seat, the weight of the rider's body rests on the lower edges of the two hip bones instead of on the two feet at the bottom of the legs. The angle of the pelvis and the curves of the vertebral column are altered as they adapt to the sitting posture. The centre of gravity of the rider's head is poised immediately over the centre of the hip joints in the pelvic girdle which now supports the whole of the weight of the rider's trunk. When the rider adopts a more forward or light seat he will use the structure of his pelvis to balance and carry his weight down to his knees, heels and shortened stirrups.

ADAPTATION

The rider's pelvis is given much additional work to do. It is responsible for balancing and carrying the rider's upper body and for giving it

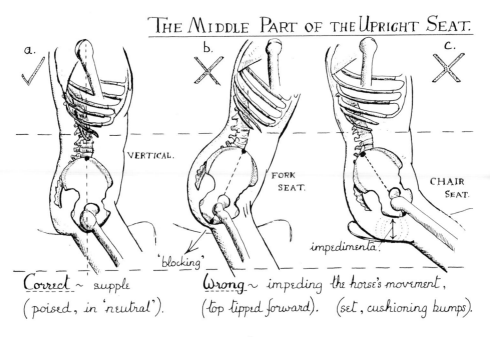

THE MIDDLE PART OF THE UPRIGHT SEAT.

a.   b.   c.

VERTICAL.

FORK SEAT.

CHAIR SEAT.

'blocking'

impedimenta.

Correct ~ supple   Wrong ~ impeding the horse's movement,
(poised, in 'neutral').   (top tipped forward).   (set, cushioning bumps).

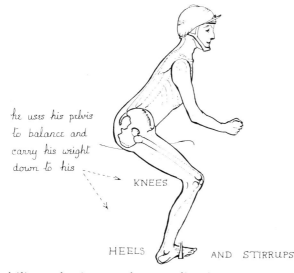

he uses his pelvis
to balance and
carry his weight
down to his

KNEES

HEELS   AND STIRRUPS

stability. Also its muscle co-ordination programmes have to be reorgan-
ised and considerably rearranged whenever the rider wishes to move his
trunk as well as his lower and upper limbs efficiently while he is seated.

Q.E.D.

On no account must the rider be led to imagine that he should tip
forward the tops of his hip bones when practising the upright balanced
seat. Of all rider postural faults this "fork seat" is the worst, not only for
his health and performance but also for those of his horse. If the rider's
pelvis is tipped forward the lower back is hollowed and the weight of the
body is pressed on to two backward shoving seat bones which "dig" into
the horse's back with a deadening press. This blocks the movement of the
horse's back muscles which then cannot bring his powerful hindlegs
forward, under his body. Inevitably a fork seat rider will turn his horse
into a shambling, pottery leg-mover – they cannot help themselves.

In order to sort out the "what, where and how?" of the rider's lower
limbs it is necessary first to become acquainted with the bones of the
pelvic region.

THE HIP, OR INNOMINATE BONES

So called as they "bear no resemblance to any known object"!

Two innominate bones, one on each side, form the pelvic girdle of the
lower limbs. They support the rider's balance and stabilise and carry the
weight of his body when he is riding with an upright seat.

Each innominate or hip bone consists of three parts: the ilium, the
ischium and the pubis all of which meet to form the cup-like cavity on the
outer surface, the acetabulum which articulates with the head of the
femur.

The Left Innominate (hip) Bone.

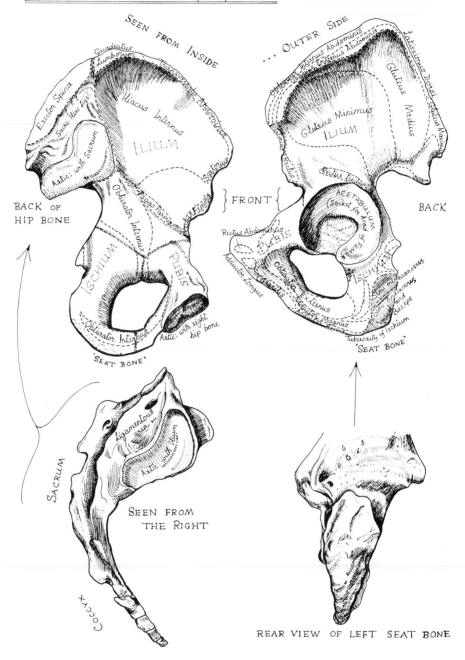

SEEN FROM INSIDE

... OUTER SIDE

Quadratus Lumborum
Erector Spinæ
Sacro Iliac Lig.
Transversus Abdominis
Iliacus Internus
ILIUM
Artic: with Sacrum
Psoas Parvus
Obturator Internus
Psoas Magnus
Ileo Femoris
ISCHIUM
PUBIS
Obturator Internus
Artic: with right hip bone
'SEAT BONE'

BACK of HIP BONE

} FRONT {

Obturator Internus Abdominis
Obliquus Internus Abdominis
Latissimus Dorsi
Gluteus Maximus
Gluteus Medius
Gluteus Minimus
ILIUM
Obturator Rectus
Rectus Tendon
ACETABULUM (Socket for head of FEMUR)
Rectus Abdominis
PUBIS
Adductor Longus
Gracilis
Obturator Externus
Adductor Magnus
Adductor Brevis
ISCHIUM
Semimembranosus Semitendinosus and Biceps
Tuberosity of Ischium
'SEAT BONE'

BACK

Ligamentous area
Artic: with Ilium

SACRUM

COCCYX

SEEN FROM THE RIGHT

REAR VIEW OF LEFT SEAT BONE

110

The penultimate section of the spine is formed of five fused vertebrae; it is triangular in shape.

THE COCCYX

The "tail end" of the spinal column is formed of four fused coccygeal vertebrae. The first of these may be separate, it articulates with the sacrum above. The coccyx gives attachment to the gluteus maximus muscles which are so important for the correct use of the rider's hips and lower legs and which cannot be employed by the rider if he sits with a hollow back and his "tail" out behind him, or with a chair seat and his "tail" tucked under him too much.

The pelvis is an area with which the rider must be fully cognisant. He must learn how to move his hips, which muscles to employ, and for what purpose to organise, re-arrange or alter the effects of balance or leverage as required by himself for the better riding of his horse. He must learn how to shift his weight unobtrusively and to move with his horse; how to improve the posture of his seat and the clarity of his riding influences by using simple forms of leverage coupled with muscular action and counter action.

THE HIP JOINT

A synovial ball-and-socket joint, the large, globular head of the femur or thigh bone being the "ball" and the acetabulum of the hip bone being the "socket".

The cup of the acetabulum is much deeper than the socket of the shoulder joint. This depth gives strength and security to the hip joint which has such a major postural duty to perform; also it puts a safeguard on the amount of movement possible within the joint itself.

Movement of the hip joint

The movements of the hip are surprisingly extensive; it is capable of flexion, extension, abduction, adduction, circumduction and rotation.

However, in spite of its great mobility it is a very stable joint. This is due to the depth of the acetabulum with its surrounding cartilaginous ring shaped like an upside-down horseshoe, and to strong binding ligaments and short articular muscles which secure the ball-and-socket joint – the thigh into the hip bone.

FLEXION

The iliacus and psoas muscles, assisted by rectus femoris, sartorius and pectineus.

EXTENSION

Gluteus maximus, assisted by the hamstrings, the iliotibial tract, the weight of the lower limb and gravity. Gluteus maximus also stabilises the knee.

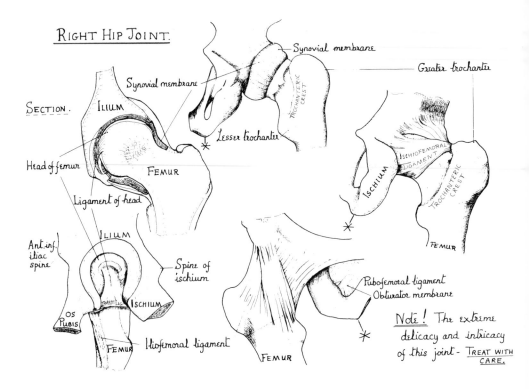

RIGHT HIP JOINT.

SECTION.

Synovial membrane

Synovial membrane

ILIUM

Head of femur

FEMUR

Ligament of head

Ant.inf. iliac spine

ILIUM

OS PUBIS

ISCHIUM

FEMUR

Iliofemoral ligament

Spine of ischium

Lesser trochanter

TROCHANTERIC CREST

Greater trochanter

ISCHIUM

ISCHIOFEMORAL LIGAMENT

TROCHANTERIC CREST

FEMUR

Pubofemoral ligament
Obturator membrane

Note! The extreme delicacy and intricacy of this joint - TREAT WITH CARE.

FEMUR

ABDUCTION

Tensor fasciae latae, gluteus medius amd min. All abduct the femur and rotate it in.

ADDUCTION

The three adductor muscles of the thigh and pectineus (known as the horse-gripping muscles!), the gracilis muscles and gravity.

ROTATION

Medial or inwards – the iliacus and psoas muscles assisted by the anterior or front fibres of the gluteus medius and minimus; lateral or outwards – the gluteus maximus assisted by the short muscles at the back of the hip joint.

As the large adductor and flexor muscles are situated and co-operate closely together in the thigh area, the action of "gripping up" is a very natural one albeit not conducive to good riding. Thus aspiring horsemen have to oppose such inborn actions, they have to learn to grip downwards – a difficult technique to perfect.

One of the most important hip movement mixtures for riders is a combination of *extension*, *abduction* and *medial rotation* as this brings the seat bone forward and softens its action on the horse's back.

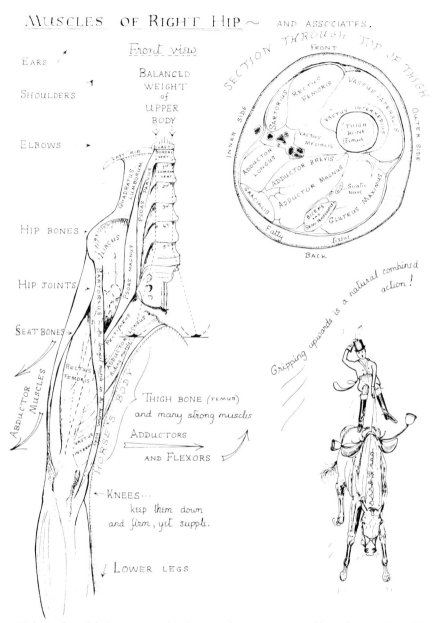

MUSCLES OF RIGHT HIP ~ AND ASSOCIATES.

Front view

BALANCED WEIGHT of UPPER BODY

EARS

SHOULDERS

ELBOWS

HIP BONES

HIP JOINTS

SEAT BONES

ABDUCTOR MUSCLES

RECTUS FEMORIS

THIGH BONE (FEMUR) and many strong muscles

ADDUCTORS

AND FLEXORS

KNEES··· keep them down and firm, yet supple.

LOWER LEGS

SECTION THROUGH TOP OF THIGH

FRONT

INNER SIDE — OUTER SIDE

SARTORIUS — RECTUS FEMORIS — VASTUS LATERALIS — VASTUS INTERMEDIUS — THIGH BONE (Femur) — VASTUS MEDIALIS — ADDUCTOR LONGUS — ADDUCTOR BREVIS — GRACILIS — ADDUCTOR MAGNUS — Sciatic Nerve — GLUTEUS MAXIMUS — BICEPS AND SEMI TENDINOSUS — Fatty — Tissue

BACK

Gripping upwards is a natural combined action!

Riders should discover which muscles to use to effect the various hip movements when they are dismounted, in front of a mirror. Exercises to improve the range and control of these movements should be practised daily. When they ride, the instructor should help the riders to feel and get the timing right for their horses. Tiny seat bone moving programmes which synchronise perfectly with each and every horse's gaits are a sure sign that correct riding techniques have been learned and have become correct riding habits.

The thigh

The femur or thigh bone is the largest, longest bone in the body. There is a head at its top end, which articulates with the acetabulum, a neck and two trochanters, a great and a lesser trochanter. These provide leverage to muscles which rotate the long thigh bones. The lower end of the shaft of the femur is larger than the top; it divides into two condyles, an inner and an outer, which are cartilage covered, articulate with the patella or knee-cap and with the tibia or shin bone, and form the top part of the knee joint.

The femur provides attachment for twenty-three muscles, some of the most important of which have been mentioned in connection with the movement of the hip joint while others are involved in the movements of the knee joint.

The length and strength of the femur should be used to the rider's advantage to stabilise his seat. If the lower end of the femur is fixed low on the saddle it will steady the hip bone at the top of the femur against even strong forces – centrifugal or speed. Such a use of the thigh will help the rider to retain perfect balance, to shift his weight unobtrusively, to invite the horse into a new direction and to encourage lateral suppleness by giving the horse a knee and leg around which to bend.

The knee joint

Anatomically speaking the true leg starts here. In equestrian language, from the knee down is referred to as the lower leg – as opposed to the thigh, being the upper leg.

The knee joint is synovial and is of a modified hinge type between the lower end of the femur, the patella and the upper end of the tibia.

The patella

A triangular shaped sesamoid bone situated in front of the knee joint which it protects; it forms the point of the knee. The four muscles which comprise the quadriceps extensors are attached to the patella's upper border and the ligamentum patellae to the lower apex. When the knee is fully extended, protective ligaments prevent the joint from hypertension (over-tension) and the knee is thus locked and stable. The popliteus muscle unlocks the joint by rotating the femur while simultaneously pulling the lateral meniscus back to prevent it from being crushed in the joint.

Two semilunar fibrocartilages sub-divide the joint, between the femur and the tibia. Skeletally the knee joint is not strong; its stability is dependent on strong ligaments and powerful muscles.

Movements of the knee joint

The knee joint is capable of flexion, extension and slight rotation. The respective muscles are:

Biceps femoris, semitendonosus and semimembranosus. The hamstring muscles, assisted by the gracilis and sartorius muscles, also indirectly by the gastrocnemius of the calf, popliteus and plantaris muscles. Where the lower legs are held firm or "fixed" against the horse's side, the hamstring muscles support the pelvis upon the head of the femur and draw the trunk backwards, "behind the vertical".

THE RIGHT LEG.

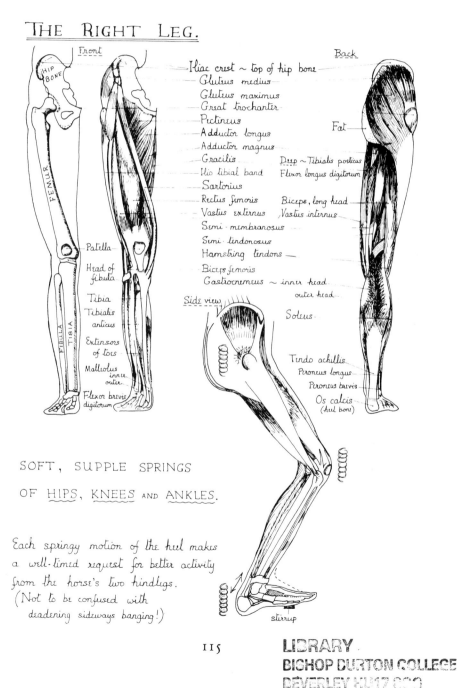

Front

Back

HIP BONE

FEMUR

FIBULA   TIBIA

Patella

Head of fibula

Tibia

Tibialis anticus

Extensors of toes

Malleolus
inner
outer

Flexor brevis digitorum

Iliac crest ~ top of hip bone
Gluteus medius
Gluteus maximus
Great trochanter
Pectineus
Adductor longus
Adductor magnus
Gracilis
Ilio tibial band
Sartorius
Rectus femoris
Vastus externus
Semi-membranosus
Semi-tendonosus
Hamstring tendons
Biceps femoris
Gastrocnemius ~ inner head

Fat

Deep ~ Tibialis posticus
Flexor longus digitorum

Biceps, long head
Vastus internus

outer head
Soleus

Side view

Tendo achillis
Peroneus longus
Peroneus brevis
Os calcis
(heel bone)

stirrup

SOFT, SUPPLE SPRINGS

OF HIPS, KNEES AND ANKLES.

Each springy motion of the heel makes a well-timed request for better activity from the horse's two hindlegs. (Not to be confused with deadening sideways banging!)

The quadriceps extensor extends the leg upon the thigh.

ROTATION OUTWARD
The biceps femoris.

ROTATION INWARD
The popliteus and semitendonosus muscles assisted by the semimembranosus, the sartorius and gracilis.

The lower leg

There are two bones in this region:

THE TIBIA
The largest and second longest bone in the human body. The upper end is expanded to form two condyles which articulate with the femoral condyles. The shaft of the tibia is triangular in cross-section; the front ridge, the crest of the tibia, is prominent down the front of the leg – the shin. The expanded lower end is longer on its inner side to form the medial or internal malleolus or the "inside ankle bone". The lower end articulates with the astragalus or talus which connects the leg to the foot.

THE FIBULA
Situated on the outside of the tibia to which it is connected at both extremities; it is the most slender of all the long bones. The lower end projects below the end of the tibia and forms the outside ankle bone.

There are sixteen main muscles attached to the bones. The work of these muscles is to fix the bones of the leg in a perpendicular position, to co-ordinate for progression, to move the limb at one end when the opposite end is fixed, to flex or extend the foot and to strengthen the ankle joint for stability or movement.

The ankle joint

The hinge joint where the leg joins the foot is the ankle joint. It is formed by three bones, the two lower ends of the tibia and fibula which meet with and rest on the astragalus (or talus). The connecting surfaces of these bones are covered with cartilage, bound together by a capsule which is extended to form four thick, strong ligaments. These are the anterior, posterior, internal lateral and external lateral.

The ankle joint and the foot below it are far from being large and stout; quite the contrary, they are small and frail in stature when compared with the weight and bulk of the body they have to support and carry.

Movements of the ankle joint

FLEXION OR DORSIFLEXION
When the dorsum, or top, of the foot is raised up towards the shin. In addition to the work of the strong ligaments, the main muscles which flex

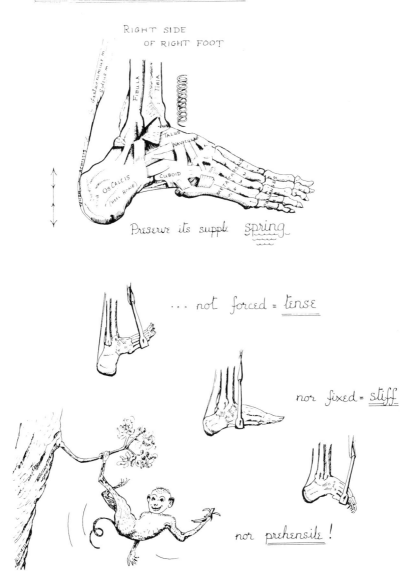

RIGHT SIDE
OF RIGHT FOOT

FIBULA

TIBIA

TALUS

NAVICULUM

OS CALCIS
(HEEL BONE)

CUBOID

Preserve its supple *spring*

... not forced = *tense*

nor fixed = *stiff*

nor *prehensile* !

the ankle joint are the tibialis anticus, peroneus tertius, extensor longus and digitorum and the extensor proprius hallucis.

EXTENSION OR PLANTARFLEXION

(Plantar being the under surface of the foot.) When the heel is raised and the toes are pointed downward. The muscles involved are the gastrocnemius, soleus, plantaris, tibialis posticus, peroneus longus and brevis, flexor longus digitorum and flexor longus hallucis.

When the sole of the foot is turned to face inward. The muscles employed are the tibialis anticus and posticus.

EVERSION
When the sole of the foot is turned to face outward, the muscle employed is the peroneus.

The foot

As far as the rider is concerned, "a foot is a foot"! – and there the matter could rest. However, there are a few more pertinent facts to be considered. We stand on our feet, and so does the horse sometimes, but that is never his fault, of course.

The foot is arched to support our weight and it provides an effective lever to work the muscles of the leg as required for locomotion or for applying the leg aids. There are two other natural functions of the foot which, although of little consequence to modern man in general, should be understood by the horseman. Amongst native tribes far removed from civilisation, feet are used to obtain proprioceptive information – where and how to tread or move – and also may be used for grasping, mainly with the toes. Both of these natural instincts may be revived by the feel underfoot of the stirrups' tread, just behind the toes.

Constructively there are two factors for the rider to consider. Firstly, the arched nature of the feet provides them with the resilience necessary to support the weight of the rider's body, especially when he is riding with shortened stirrups and a light seat, galloping or riding over fences. Secondly, the construction of the foot gives the rider a very powerful lever with which to influence the bones, joints and muscles of the whole of his lower limbs. By a strong lowering of the heel – one or both – he can effect a quick and powerful action in the hip joint above; the os calcis or heel bone seems to have been specially constructed for the horseman.

Conclusions

Under normal conditions, when man sits he rests – or even sleeps. Those who work while sitting use their upper limbs with which to write, type or sew, while their trunks and lower limbs remain almost stationary; their brains may work hard but physical exertion is cut to a minimum. There are some who use their feet as well as their hands whilst they are sitting, such as an oarsman, a cyclist, a pianist or the drummer in a dance band. The rider's task is far more complicated even than the last group.

The rider has to exert his brain and mental powers, as well as learn physical techniques, in order to consider, analyse, help and work his willing but large and ungainly equine partner. The rider must possess knowledge and understanding; he must be trained to think quickly, kindly and calmly; he must act with skilled dexterity and care, to feel, anticipate, adjust and organise all the parts of his body with the finest selection of reactions exactly to suit his horse.

All equestrian experts agree that the middle part of the rider is of the utmost importance. Physically, the rider's hips, his pelvic area, is the crux of the whole of the rider's seat for his horse – it is the "seat of his seat"!

In the sitting posture, the pelvis bears all the weight of the rider's upper body and stabilises its balance and poise. Of equal value is the rôle of the pelvis as the "team captain and manager" to the rider's physical aids, those body movements which signal a running commentary of messages to the horse whenever he is worked by and with his rider.

The pelvic girdle is a comparatively large bony structure within the human skeletal frame. The rider's pelvis can be quite cumbersome if its owner does not appreciate its unwieldiness and has not learned how to place, control and use it. Even to make a slight shift of the pelvis to the right with the weight of the upper body above it, when the horse is walking, requires a considerable physical effort on the beginner rider's part and his first attempts will probably be rather clumsy. However, learn this shifting he must in order to invite his horse to the right, and to enable him to carry his rider there in perfect balance. (This has already been discussed in connection with the weight aids.) In fact, these clumsy, early shiftings usually feel far more clumsy to the rider than they appear to the instructor or other observers – a comforting fact for the pupil.

Due to its comparative solidity, breadth and strength, the pelvis can exert considerable leverage power on the different muscles attached or related to it. The rider must learn to use the moving, tilting and shifting of his pelvis with dexterity. Tiny but thoughtful movements here can have an incredible effect on the ploy and play of the muscles in the whole of the rider's body and thus on those of his horses. As the brain thinks through the thought aids so the pelvis is the hub of the rider's physical influences on the horse he rides. To use a musical simile, we could liken the rider's brain to the conductor and the body to the orchestra, with the two seat bones as ... the double bass!

Riders must be taught which muscles are attached to the pelvis and what are their actions so that they can use them with minimum effort and maximum effect. By an improved knowledge, understanding and practised feel of the importance of his seat, the rider can become a horseman of real value. He will learn to stabilise his pelvis with one group of muscles to provide a support whilst tensing another group against it, or he can utilise the strength of the pelvis directly to oppose two or more groups of muscles actively against each other. Best of all – he will learn how to allow and then to encourage the horse to move with greater freedom and activity in all his gaits.

The following description of one of the effective body movements will provide an opportunity for the rider to think about it, even to try it out as he sits in the chair before putting it into practice with his live partner – the horse.

If the rider thinks of riding his horse through a turn or circle to the right, he will prepare with half-halts as necessary and shift his weight to

"**FEEL** how your pony's hind legs are moving underneath you...."

I said 'FEEL', Emily....not 'look'!

LATER...

"In rising trot, see how I rise (slightly and lightly) as my horse brings his inside stifle forwards".

THEN... try to get the same feel with your inside seat bone, in sitting trot ~ invisibly."

the right, supporting this positioning of his seat with a firm, lowered right knee and heel. If then he uses the muscles under and behind his right shoulder and upper arm, to turn it back against the right hip which is moved forward, this particular movement of the rider's body has an amazingly powerful effect on the horse's body when he is moving through a turn, a circle or a lateral movement which requires a right bend.

Of course, the rider must remember to regulate the horse's balance, rhythm and activity and the bending of his body by thoughtful use of his outside aids – the left (outside) shoulder is brought forward while the left hip stabilises the rider's left lower leg just behind the girth to keep the horse's hindlegs under his body. Both lower legs maintain impulsion as and when necessary.

The rider must be very supple throughout his body. He must ensure that neither his inner shoulder nor his inner hip become "stuck" backward or forward, they must move freely with the horse's muscle movement. The strength of the subtle "twisting" can be increased or diminished within each stride as the rider feels it is needed. The effect of this double action on the rider's part will be to encourage further forward engagement of the horse's inner hindleg and of a bending in his body so that his central line conforms easily and exactly with the line of the circle or with the requirements of the movement being performed. This activity and bending on his inner side can only be managed by the horse if he is perfectly balanced and his rider's seat invites and allows him to use all his muscles, particularly those on the inner side of his body, to the fullest extent, comparable with his present standard of training.

Besides reading about it, every rider must prove for himself that his horse will turn and bend entirely as a reaction to the rider's weight and to this turning of his shoulders and hips – there is no need for the rider to apply one iota of extra pressure on the inner rein. The rider will soon learn to feel the large muscles on the inner side of the horse's body rise and swell under his forward moving inner seat bone as they bend the joints of the massive hindleg on that side and bring it forwards under the horse's huge body. If the rider thinks and feels . . . and feels and thinks . . . extra well, he may discover an additional quality to improve his riding of sitting trot. He should try to discern and pick up the faintest murmur of a rising trot with his inner seat bone; an imperceptible but clearly felt rising, timed with the outside diagonal and working in rhythm with the horse's inside hindleg. If, after all this, the reader is still able to get out of his chair he should go and put it to the test immediately, together with his horse.

The instinctive reactions of the talented rider must be preserved; they must be enhanced by additional knowledge and understanding – talent can only shine when it is nurtured by the brain.

7 Applying Physiology

This chapter contains an outline of the main points of the two prime subjects to which instructors and riders should give constant consideration. They are *the rider's seat* – his position; and *the rider's aids* – his influence on the horse. Although both subjects are covered in Book 1, in some detail, I hope that the following paragraphs will form a short "continuation and refresher course", applying the knowledge of physiology gained from the previous chapter.

The Rider's Position – The Balanced Seat

That the rider must be well balanced when he rides is an obvious and logical fact. The actual position he adopts must be flexible and adaptable to suit a wide variety of conditions. At either end of the scale are the straight or upright seat and the light or forward seat with a full range of variations in between.

Although the variety of position must be pre-selected to a degree by the rider before he adjusts his stirrups, all riders should use and return to a straight, upright (or dressage) seat as often as possible. In the upright seat the rider is in the best position for the horse to carry his weight at all but the fastest paces, because the rider is then near to the centre of gravity of the horse and is sitting on the strongest part of the horse's structure rather than on the weak loins. Also, when riding in an upright position the rider can best feel and influence his horse through his seat, from his seat bones and throughout the whole of his body.

For these reasons the straight or upright seat will be accorded the most attention in this chapter. We shall begin with the seat bones and work down and thence upwards.

The rider should sit easily in the centre of the saddle when the horse is halted and when he is being ridden on straight lines. This should be checked from the side and from the rear. However, the rider must be ready and able to adjust his hips as and when necessary.

The rider should shift his weight to the appropriate side before riding a change of direction, and whenever he is riding on a curving track he should shift, and must keep, his weight to the inside with his inner seat bone slightly forward so that it allows free action of the horse's back muscles underneath it.

When viewed from the side, the rider should be seated in the centre of the saddle; however when riding a curved or circle track and when viewed from behind, his seat should be seen to be slightly to the left or the right of the saddle and the horse's central line, according to the direction being taken.

EFFECTS OF THE RIDER'S SEAT.

The Balanced Seat.

Upright~
 for dressage.

Forward~
 for jumping.

TREAT WITH CARE

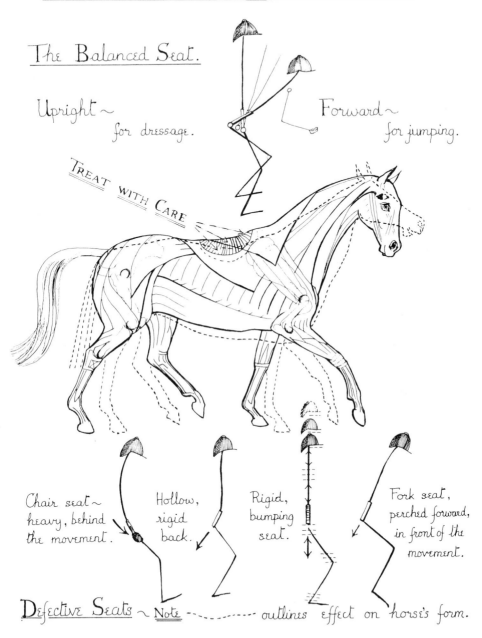

Chair seat~
heavy, behind
the movement.

Hollow,
rigid
back.

Rigid,
bumping
seat.

Fork seat,
perched forward,
in front of the
movement.

Defective Seats ~ Note ----------- outlines effect on horse's form.

Bird's Eye Views....

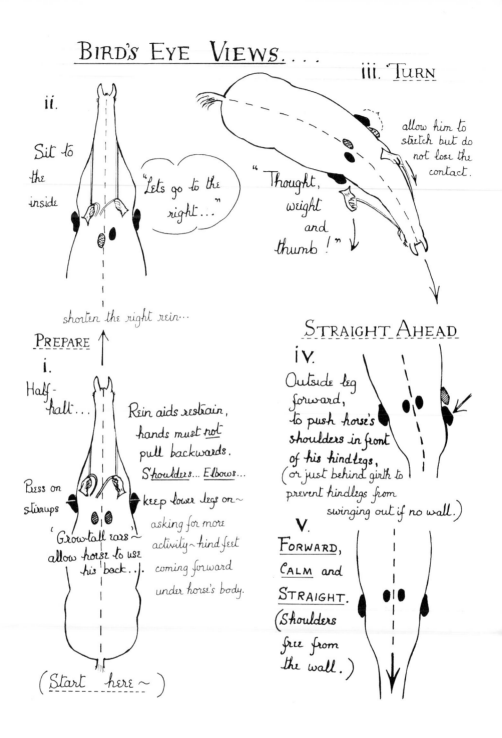

iii. Turn

ii.

Sit to the inside

"Let's go to the right..."

"Thought, weight and thumb!"

allow him to stretch but do not lose the contact.

shorten the right rein...

Prepare
i.

Half-halt...

Press on stirrups

'Grow tall ears' allow horse to use his back...

Rein aids restrain, hands must **not** pull backwards. Shoulders... Elbows...

keep lower legs on ~ asking for more activity ~ hind feet coming forward under horse's body.

(Start here ~)

Straight Ahead
iv.

Outside leg forward, to push horse's shoulders in front of his hindlegs, (or just behind girth to prevent hindlegs from swinging out if no wall.)

v.

Forward, Calm and **Straight.** (Shoulders free from the wall.)

This shifting of the rider's pelvis puts the weight of his body in perfect balance for the turning and his upper body can then remain vertical and poised, inviting and moving with his horse's changes of direction. Only by so shifting his seat can the rider use his weight aids correctly and co-ordinate all his other aids to maximum effect and yet with minimum effort and outward sign. Only thus can he avoid being a cumbersome burden for his horse to carry.

The rider should sit as far forward on the saddle as he can with comfort so that he is as near to the horse's centre of gravity as possible. The rider must not allow his seat to slide to the back of the saddle as that part of the horse's back is weaker. Also, it will be difficult for the rider to remain with the horse's movement without an effort or a certain clumsiness. If the rider's seat bones are allowed to slide backwards under an upright position, there is a danger that in an endeavour to improve his balance he may tilt the top of the hip bones forward. Automatically this will stiffen his hips and hollow his back which will result in an impulsion-blocking influence on the horse beneath him.

The solution to the backward slide is simple: the rider must think, he must find out the cause, cure it and ask his instructor or another friend to check that the correction is complete. The most probable causes are a careless and bad riding habit, too-short stirrup leathers, or a faulty saddle which needs additional stuffing at the rear.

The rider should sit with a natural ease and poise, on his two seat bones. The positioning of the rider's middle part is of the utmost importance – it can truly be said to be the foundation on which his horsemanship rests!

The pelvis should be in a "neutral" position – this is imperative for good riding, for only then can the rider balance and poise his upper body "with nonchalant ease" above his two seat bones and thus feel and communicate with his horse through the whole of his body.

In addition to the advantages for balance and poise, the neutral position of the pelvis ensures economy of effort with only a few of the muscles and tendons of that area in action. It also facilitates immediate effectiveness, for from a neutral position the rider can call upon additional muscles for increased support and strength as and when he wishes; he can move or put more weight on to one seat bone or change to increase his influences as may be required – there are no unnecessarily tense muscles prohibiting these subtle changes.

Few riders know the skeletal shape of the human pelvis, some do not even know that "the rider's hips" is a loose term for the hip joints. This is a dangerous omission in their riding education, for to misinterpret the advice that "the rider's hips should be well forward" into "the top of his hip bones should be well forward" could end in near disaster for their future riding – although, of course, the forward tilt of the pelvis is a required factor in the light or forward seat.

The two most common faults in the positioning of the pelvis, both of which are grave riding faults for they have a seriously adverse effect on the whole of the rider's position and his influence on his horse, are:

(i) When the tops of the hip bones are tilted forwards, the spine above is often over-hollowed with a marked stiffness in the rider's loins. This results in a *fork* or *"hanging"* seat – the rider's general attitude looks and is doubtful, timid and precarious.

(ii) When the tops of the hip bones are tilted back – this is usually combined with too high knees and thighs below, and a rounded spine above. This results in a *chair seat* with a general impression of slovenly and thoughtless heaviness.

Many riders are astonished at the small size of the seat bone area at the bottom of the rider's hip bones. That is the moment when their minds are most receptive to the principle of the concentration of weight upon a small area. They will understand this with utmost clarity if the instructor reminds them of the damage stiletto heels can do to the lovely woodwork of a parquet floor – or how "short" the wearer can become, suddenly, at a cocktail party held on a well cared for lawn! The principle is the same: the force of the concentrated weight is multiplied a hundred-fold! Often a rider will confirm that "the penny has dropped" by exclaiming, "Oh yes! my saddle has two well-marked dimples in its seat." If this is taken one stage further and the "dimples" are inspected often it will be found that they are neither symmetrical nor central, which is of course both revealing and damning. The rider in this instance does not sit straight and does not use his weight aids correctly. He stays stuck to the same two little

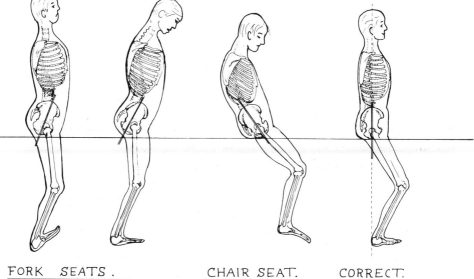

FORK   SEATS .
Stiff. Falsely posed. Diffident.

CHAIR SEAT.
Careless. Uninterested.

CORRECT.
Positive thoughts; balanced, easy.

126

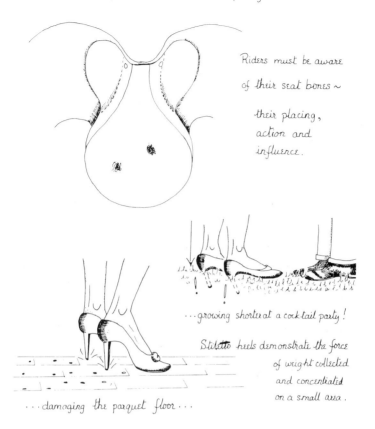

Riders must be aware
of their seat bones ~

their placing,
action and
influence.

...growing shorter at a cocktail party!

Stiletto heels demonstrate the force
of weight collected
and concentrated
on a small area.

...damaging the parquet floor...

spots and leans his upper body to left or right – pulling hard on the inner rein of course! His left hip is permanently blocking the forward movement of his horse's left hindleg because the horse's back muscles are not allowed to function freely under that "stiletto" seat bone.

The instructor can help riders to further understand the severity of the common fault of setting or putting added weight on to the seat bones for downward transitions, by means of a simple but effective demonstration for which he enlists the aid of a dismounted pupil.

The instructor asks him to lean forward, putting his hands on a table or similar firm support, approximately 70 centimetres from the ground. The pupil must now imagine that he is a horse! If the instructor then stands behind the pupil, puts his two thumbs on the pupil's back at either side of his spine, just behind the shoulder blade and says, "Can you feel my thumbs? Imagine that they are the rider's seat bones. Now, we're going to halt." He then presses hard with the nail end of both thumbs whereupon a sensitive pupil will hollow his back away from the uncomfortable pressure – as will a sensitive horse.

127

"Now we'll do it again with the imaginary rider, growing tall ears and pressing lightly on the stirrups, to allow the seat bones to move freely and lightly. This allows the horse to use (fill out) his back muscles in order to bring his hindlegs further under the mass of his body to make a smooth and perfect halt."

The relief and understanding felt by the second method will usually convey a very clear message to those who watch and make a life-long impression upon the pupil who helped with the demonstration.

Another very useful practice demonstration may be given during a line-up discussion period, when riders and horses are settled and in need of a rest. The instructor tells the class to knot their reins evenly, on their horses' withers and to put their whips under their thighs, drop their hands down on either side of their hips, lean forward just far enough to slip the fingers (palm side uppermost) underneath the seat bones and then to sit upright again. "Now feel the weight you put on your seat bones!"

The instructor should then tell the class to feel how the seat bones move and change in weight as the riders look "up to the left; up to the distant trees ahead; down to the right", and so on. If the horses are quiet and steady, the instructor can suggest that his pupils repeat this exercise, in their own time, with their eyes shut, quietly to appraise the feeling with greater clarity and emphasis. This is a particularly valuable exercise for riders who have ridden for many years without giving any real thought to the influence of their weight aids, especially if they are sitting on a hard saddle. It is guaranteed to make them believe in the truth of the statement that "the rider's weight aids commence as soon as he sits on his horse's back"!

The instructor can develop the analysis and discussion value of this little exercise by inviting his pupils to feel how a seat bone will slide in, towards the centre of the saddle, when extra weight is applied to it in a leaning-over posture (collapsed inner hip). They can then compare this faulty slide in the *wrong* direction with a slight shift in the *right* direction, while the hip bone in question is kept vertical with its seat bone forward, as if it were pulled by a puppet string from its top, the iliac crest. This imaginary puppet string can be of inestimable value in the imagination of instructors and riders as a guide to level hips, to the moving forward of an inner hip bone, and to correcting crooked hips or an over-weighted seat bone.

Riders are constantly being told to sit on their two seat bones, and that of course is quite correct – as far as it goes. However, if the instructor goes on to ask, "What does a seat bone look like? Does it look like the lower edge of a dish standing on its end, a polo ball, a navicular bone, or what?", most riders will plump for the navicular bone. Few realise that the seat bone is a slang term for the ischial tuberosity at the lower edge of the large hip bone. Although this simplest version of its full title may make pupils hesitate, a sketch or diagram will always arouse interest. Similarly if a pupil who is very stiff and seems quite incapable of sitting down in the saddle especially at sitting trot, is told that he must relax, the pupils will nod his head, try harder and bump more. However, if the instructor halts the class and asks the rider how many muscles, tendons and ligaments he has in the middle part of his body in and around his pelvis, he will usually shrug his shoulders, but if pressed might offer a number between two and four.

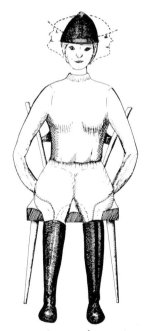

Rider analysing her seat bones.

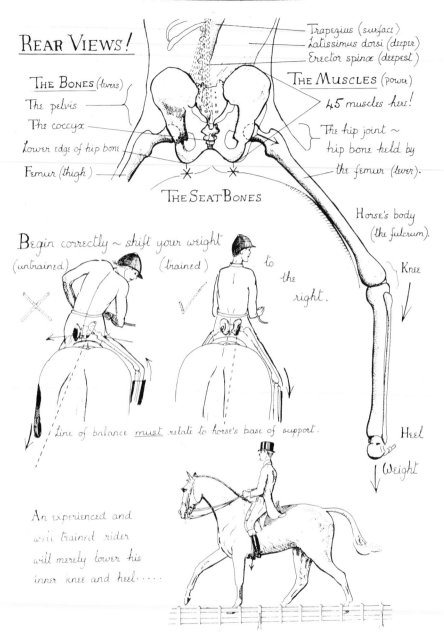

REAR VIEWS!

THE BONES (levers)

The pelvis

The coccyx

Lower edge of hip bone

Femur (thigh)

THE SEAT BONES

Trapezius (surface)
Latissimus dorsi (deeper)
Erector spinae (deepest)

THE MUSCLES (power)

45 muscles here!

The hip joint ~ hip bone held by the femur (lever).

Horse's body (the fulcrum).

Knee

Heel

Weight

Begin correctly ~ shift your weight

(untrained)   (trained)   to the right.

Line of balance *must* relate to horse's base of support.

An experienced and well trained rider will merely lower his inner knee and heel·····

I remember enacting this very scene during a Pony Club course for instructors at Talland. A rather small mum had been having a very uncomfortable time on a newly-acquired big, young horse who was a lovely mover – but was also awkward and stiff. In her own answer to my query she was more enterprising than most and suggested she might have six muscles, tendons and ligaments. When I told her that the correct answer was around seventeen she looked astounded but believing and I could see her releasing excess tension left, right and centre! The exercise which followed contained some sitting trot and there was marked improvement. At the next line-up she looked positively radiant and asked the spectator sitting just behind me, in the gallery, "Why didn't you tell me that, Peter?"

I gulped . . . "Who was Peter?" Her husband.

"What was Peter?" A doctor of medicine . . . Oh help!

"Was I right?" I asked.

"Pretty good," said Peter.

"Could I have raised it to twenty?"

"No, that would have been too many". . . .

As with many good tales this one has a postscript which serves well to emphasise its point. Several months later I was asked to speak on "the use of the rider's back" at the British Horse Society's study day when doctrine and provocative or controversial subjects are debated and discussed. I was honoured by the invitation and collected my facts and drew several supporting diagrams, but all the while those seventeen muscles kept niggling at the back of my mind. I was well aware of my responsibility (then and now!) and determined that every fact must not only be absolutely correct but also have been checked to be so. I was not sure that seventeen was the right number. None of the text-books were in the least interested in supplying me with the confirmation I required. I thumbed my way back and forth through several more technical tomes like a hound casting over a foiled line. At last, in the early hours of the morning my searching was rewarded: my third "draw" through the heaviest book revealed the staggering information that there are in fact no less than forty-five muscles attached to the pelvis!

MIND AND LEGS COMMUNICATE ~

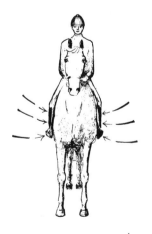

Messages inside his boots !

The rider's legs should hang down against the saddle and the horse's sides beneath. The legs themselves, together with the hip joints and the pelvis above, must contain no excess tension, for constraint leads to, and is synonymous with, stiffness. On the other hand, the legs must not hang down on either side inanimate like a boxer's punch-bag, they must contain and be capable of considerable strength and control and be applied with tact and precision. The more of the horse's trunk muscles that the rider's legs can touch, feel and call into action, the better will that rider's influences be on the whole of the horse's skeletal and muscular systems and the better and more easily will he be able to make a marked improvement on the form and performance of every horse he rides. Impulsion is the energy created in the horse by the rider's forward-driving aids, mainly his lower legs which should massage the muscles for movement. Finally, three reminders:

(i) "From the hips, stretch down."

(ii) "Remember the magic spot." (As described in Book 1.)

(iii) M. de la Guérinière's directive that "the rider's spur should touch that portion of the horse's belly which is just four fingers behind the girth" (and M. de la Guérinière rode with long-necked spurs!).

The angles of the rider's hip and knee joints should be as open as suppleness and comfort will allow for all normal riding on the flat. However, when riding at speed or over fences of more than 60 centimetres, these angles and those of the ankles should be closed by shortening the stirrup leathers to a length which suits the rider's balance and the relative demands of the task in hand, to make him more balanced, supple and secure.

A cautionary note should be added here concerning the rider's hips: the instructor should warn his pupils not to be over-energetic (or over-zealous) when practising exercises intended to open the hip joint to improve their upright seats for dressage. All such exercises must be done with a thoughtful stretching, at a contemplative speed rather than as "physical jerks". The hip joint is a very delicate one, carefully held by many small and larger ligaments, none of which must be torn or damaged. The original pair of hip joints should be encouraged to last a lifetime!

The rider's feet should be in a natural position – with the toes not forced up, in or out. A lowered heel hardens the calf muscles and is desirable when applying leg aids and when riding over fences with shortened stirrup leathers, but this tension must not override suppleness for feel especially when riding on the flat.

Toes which face the front or turn in and cause an unnatural outward "break" at the ankle joints are indicative of faulty instruction; this riding fault detracts from the leg's effectiveness and the rider's style, possibly leading eventually to arthritic troubles if not corrected soon enough.

If toes turn out too much this can indicate unwanted tension in the hips

Imagine a narrow gate!

or pelvis above. To correct this fault the instructor has a chicken and egg situation! With some pupils, "Relax your hips and all the muscles in your pelvis", will do the trick, while with others, "Keep your stirrups a little closer to your horse's sides – as if you are riding through a narrow gate", will cause an automatic easing of the hips above.

When riding with stirrups, the balls of the feet should rest on the stirrups and the toes should be a little higher than the heels. However, when riding without stirrups, the legs and feet should hang naturally so that the feet are horizontal or the toes slightly lower. Instructors should never tell their novice pupils to force up their toes when they are riding without stirrups for such action causes strong tension in the pectineus and three adductor muscles which in turn causes the pelvis to tip forward and a partial locking of the hip joint – just where the rider needs to be most supple. Unfortunately some untrained "instructors" do not consider this obvious fact, they are conscious only of the smart appearance of their class, "Boots look best when toes are raised, so raised they must be!", a grievously faulty instruction, revealing considerable lack of thought and training.

There are two exceptions to the last rule! These being:

(i)   The instructor may tell his more experienced pupils to raise their toes when riding school movements, practising rising trot or when jumping fences without stirrups for then he wishes them to increase the firmness of their legs and to develop their riding muscles.

(ii)   Some young riders raise their toes because they are afraid that their boots will fall off if they don't! Usually an additional pair of socks removes the worry and tension.

The rider's upper body should have a good posture – it should have a natural poise, being a combination of straightness and controlled suppleness. "From the waist grow tall!"

Too few riders realise the importance of a correct posture of the upper body: so often backs are slouched, shoulders are rounded, elbows fly out, hands turn over, and necks and heads are poked forward with eyes cast down – and mouths seem to follow a similar pattern!

Unless the rider sits with a correct and easy poise vertically above his seat bones, his loins and hips will be cramped and rigid. A good posture of the rider's upper body will allow his hips and loins to be supple and to absorb and direct the horse's movement.

The spine

Of all parts of the human anatomy, it is about the rider's spine that even acknowledged experts let their imaginations run riot rather than running on a line which is following the true facts. Spines are thought to be able to "wiggle like a rope", to contain bends which even a highly trained contortionist would find impossible and are accorded a force and strength quite beyond the bounds of possibility.

Let us take a careful and clinical look at the construction and articulation of the human spine. A genuine skeleton's spine wobbles and clanks, because all the live tissues which support the spine, keeping it fairly erect, and preventing it from clanking, have long since shrivelled up and departed! Whereas the skeleton will provide a picture of the intricacies of the vertebrae, it is the substance of the less permanent, attached tissues which are of greater importance to an understanding of the rider's back.

THE CENTRAL COLUMN OF THE RIDER'S BODY

The spine and its countless ligaments act as a mainstay which provides many attachments for all the main muscles, not only of the body's trunk, but also of its head and of its upper and lower limbs. It may be kept rigid by these muscles and ligaments, or they may allow it to be fairly flexible and pliant.

It is what lies between the vertebrae that gives the spine its peculiar but scientifically very clever shape, that restricts the "wobble" and prevents the clanking. Through the very centre of the spine runs the spinal cord, a most vital component of the whole of the human nervous system. This is common knowledge, but the "discs" which lie between each and every vertebra are rarely understood. These discs are composed of fibrous and fibrocartilaginous tissue with a "soft centre" which is filled with a yellowish, pulpy and highly elastic substance. If the spine is strained, contorted or bruised the cushioning discs between the vertebrae may be damaged. A slipped disc is in fact a split disc – the central substance pushes out like toothpaste from a tube with a split in it. The paste hardens as it emerges and it is the hardened lump which causes pain as it presses on nerves where it should not! A further and extremely sobering thought must be added here: such a split and the consequent loss of elastic filling are irreparable.

This simple explanation of the case history of a "slipped disc" is included here so that instructors and riders may understand not only the shape and movements of the human spine but also its frailty and the danger of asking too much of it.

The rider should not try to change the natural basic shape of his spine: its arrangement has evolved so that it may support the head vertically above the pelvis or feet. Its shape and arrangement must not be meddled with nor must the spine itself be abused. The muscles, tendons and ligaments are what the rider can and should organise and rearrange, stabilise or ease whenever he rides his horse, as a truly leading partner.

THE LOINS

The loins, or the small of the back should be straight but unconstrained. They should not be humped, hollowed or too loose. They, together with the rider's pelvis, absorb the horse's movement below and transcribe it into a composure above.

The Latissimus Dorsi.

FIND AND USE IT, RIDERS !

By the scope of its dimensions and attachments it can assist you to balance and control your posture and movement and thereby refine your influences on your horse.

'Keep your shoulder blades flat and level.'

Feel it co-ordinate bones and muscles which lie under its wrapping.

'Keep your elbows close to your sides, for efficiency and tidiness.'

FEEL the latent strength of a subtle turning of the right shoulder against the right hip.

'Keep your pelvis upright, usually in a 'neutral' position.'

THINK of your weight aids at all times ~ allowing, inviting and controlling.

FEEL AND THINK ~ AND ~ THINK AND FEEL
how is your horse moving ?
Is he using his latissimus dorsi too ?

THE FRONT OF THE CHEST

This should be uplifted and the lungs kept well and regularly filled. The shoulders should be back, down, comfortable and exactly level. Riders must remind themselves frequently that the muscles across the back of their shoulders must be employed to control and carry the head and the upper limbs and to cause a further strengthening to the deep back and pelvic muscles lying beneath them if and when this is required. However, they should also remember the dangers of an inhibiting stiffness caused by overtensing these or any muscles.

These should be well carried, above and out of the shoulders "as if the top of your head were linked to a star" to quote Mr. Tucker again. The head should appear to be a firm and thought-filled continuation of the spine. It should never tilt to one side or forwards nor should it "wobble" – this latter fault is a sure sign of stiffness in the hips and/or lower back, the shock-absorbers have not absorbed! Riders must remember how comparatively heavy are their heads and that if they are not poised correctly above their spines then their balance and their aids to their horses will all be put out of order.

Many riders stiffen unwittingly in their necks, for this reason a head-turning exercise should be practised frequently during every week's work routines. Head rolling, head turning, or "the nose making the sign of infinity" are all excellent for this purpose. These exercises are described in Book 1.

The rider's arms should hang freely but close to his sides. "The upper arms belong to the body". "The elbows should never stick out nor come behind the central line of the body". Both of these faults result in heavy, hanging hands which have an adverse effect on the whole of the horse's movement – and who can blame him? He must have free, or well directed, use of his head and neck which are his balancing pole, as well as containing many vital component parts of the mechanics of his movement.

The rider must keep his elbows down as if weighted and must preserve a soft suppleness within the joints. The positioning of the elbows (in and down) is a most important factor as unless this guideline is remembered the rider cannot (physically impossible, cannot) employ the muscles over and under his shoulder blades to give light or firm rein aids or to employ the deeper muscles of his back.

The hands should be well-carried, independent, gentle and sympathetic. The positioning of the rider's forearms, wrists and hands has already been fully described in Book 1. To pick out and condense a few facts is not easy, for all the points every rider should remember. However, if the refresher points were rationed to eight facts then this would be the list:

• The forearms "untwisted", that is with their inner surface turning upwards, never downwards.

• The wrist having a continuation of the forearm's turning and being slightly rounded, never stiff, hollowed or over-rounded.

• The hands turned with the thumb-part uppermost, the reins tucked well down at the base of the fingers, the fingers themselves bending to move smoothly, mostly at their base joints, the middle joints having a similar, harmonising bend and movement, while the last joints, before the fingernails, stay softly straightened, so that the tips of the fingers have free play over the thumb cushion, towards the elbow. The thumbs should be bent with their tips helping to hold the reins.

• The reins should be untwisted and thought of as a continuing part of the rider's hands and arms to the horse's mouth – hence "rein aids".

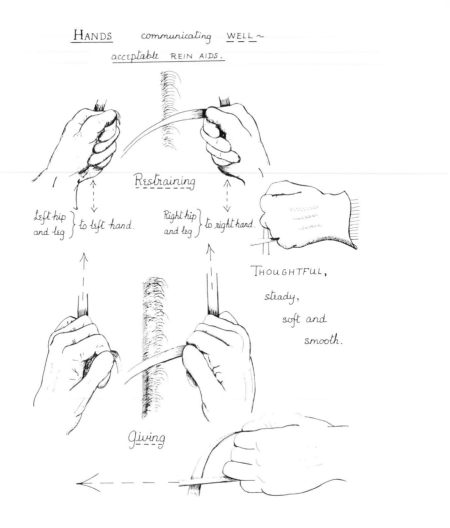

<u>*Restraining*</u>

Left hip } to left hand.
and leg }

Right hip } to right hand.
and leg }

THOUGHTFUL,

steady,

soft and

smooth.

Giving

- The rein aids start, receive their control and have a fluent continuity of movement from the back of the rider's shoulder girdle; this is supported by the spine which gains its support from the middle part, the pelvic area of the rider's seat.
- The rider should try to uphold the rule of the two elbow-to-bit lines: *below* the elbow, forearm, hand, rein to the horse's mouth and *inside* them all to the mouth. The latter is frequently "broken" by the rider's inner hand at or just in front of the withers. "Watch it – and don't do it!" The inner hand should never be brought in too near to the withers.
- The rider's hands should be unobtrusive – even in white gloves! They should be capable of conveying a vast range of messages, directives and assurances with smooth precision, tact and a trained but delicate touch.
- Although the hands' restraints may have to be strong occasionally, they should be still in their holding.

Faulty Hands.

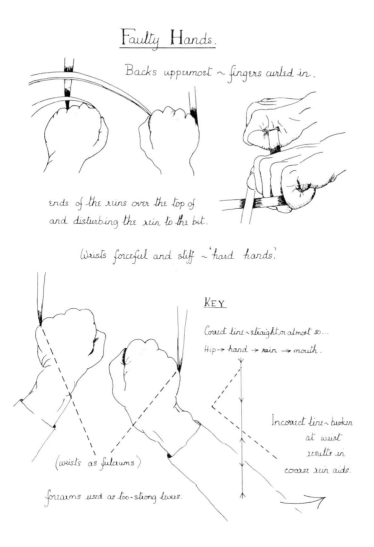

Backs uppermost ~ fingers curled in.

ends of the reins over the top of and disturbing the rein to the bit.

Wrists forceful and stiff ~ 'hard hands.'

(wrists as fulcrums)

forearms used as too-strong levers.

KEY

Correct line ~ straight, or almost so...
Hip → hand → rein → mouth.

Incorrect line ~ broken at wrist results in coarse rein aids.

The vertical line of the upright position of the balanced seat. The imaginary "line" taken from the rider's ear, through his shoulder and hip joints to the back of his heel, has been left until last in this refresher course, not to test the reader – "Ha! she has forgotten it!" – but because this line is only meant to be a guide; over-emphasis can lead to disastrous false positioning.

Riders are rarely built to a similar pattern – although it is true to say that many patterns meet with success. Every individual has conformation problems; it is up to the instructor to make the best of every pupil he has to teach. Although he may suggest a medically approved slimming diet if the rider is unstable and clumsy due to being overweight, there is nothing more that he can do to change his pupil's shape. The instructor must never force a false position upon any rider: an effective yet sympathetic natural horseman who has poise and a certain stylishness must be the overall aim.

Finally, *good posture* is something which riders cannot practise too often – not just while riding but when standing, sitting and walking – being aware of the human skeletal framework and of holding and balancing it correctly by feeling, stretching, positioning and easing the various muscles and tissues which control that framework. Only by being aware of these tiny actions which contribute to good deportment will the rider be able to improve the horses he rides by utilising the actions of his own skeletal and muscular systems to develop those of his horse.

The Aids

As with the rider's position, these notes on the rider's aids are all set out in Book 1. They are there for study, deeper consideration and digestion. What follows is a form of "light refreshments" to be served as an aperitif before riders or their instructors get down to the plat du jour – of the schoolwork!

The main aids with which the rider may influence his horse are:

The thought aids

These commence as the rider approaches his horse. They are used in three main directions:

(i) Early preparation. Choosing the best place, footing and ground-plan.

(ii) Togetherness. Two-way mental communication with the horse or horses with whom the rider, trainer or instructor is working – telepathy.

(iii) Awareness. Of the environment, other riders and of his horse's form and work.

The weight aids

These include the following factors:

POSITIONING

How the rider places his pelvis and his upper body above it has a major effect on the horse carrying him. A rider who sits softly with an easy poise is much less tiring to carry and easier to follow and obey than is a rider who is heavily slouched, stiffly bumping or whose legs clamp on to the horse's body with a vice-like grip.

BALANCING

The rider using his body to help the horse's balance or as a counter-balance when he is overriding evasion or resistance.

SHIFTING

By actually shifting his weight, albeit almost imperceptibly, the rider can greatly influence the horse carrying him. If the rider sits centrally

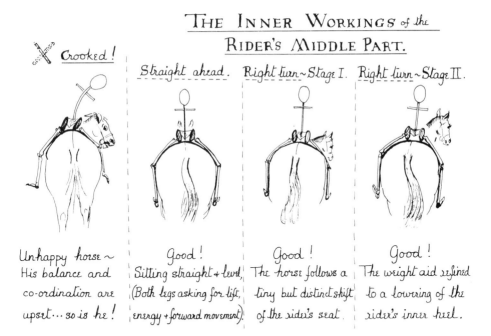

Crooked!

Straight ahead. Right turn ~ Stage I. Right turn ~ Stage II.

Unhappy horse ~
His balance and
co-ordination are
upset... so is he!

Good!
Sitting straight + level,
(Both legs asking for lift,
energy + forward movement).

Good!
The horse follows a
tiny but distinct shift
of the rider's seat.

Good!
The weight aid refined
to a lowering of the
rider's inner heel.

while the horse moves along straight lines on level footing then horse and rider are in the same equilibrium – they are perfectly balanced together. However, if the horse inadvertently moves away to the right, if the movement is strong, fast and abrupt, the inexperienced rider will fall off – his weight has shifted the wrong way and he has lost his balance! On the other hand, a trained rider can use his ability to shift his weight exactly as he wishes in order to produce a definite, unseen influence.

INVITING

By shifting his weight in advance, towards the direction in which he wishes his horse to go, the rider warns, invites and tells his horse of his intended change of course, track or movement. The shifting must be a light, subtle movement – it should never be clumsy, abrupt or stiff. This is one of the most fundamental of all the rider's physical influences – the harmony and effectiveness of all his other natural aids depend upon it. For this reason riders and their instructors must not be nervous about learning or teaching this technique from the earliest lessons – the sooner it is learned the earlier it will be assimilated and become an easy, natural, subconscious habit. Remember, the rider's weight aids commence as soon as he sits on the horse's back.

DRIVING

By pushing his seat bones forward and keeping the top of his hip bones back the rider can strengthen his back muscles, rather as a lowered heel strengthens the calf muscles. This is an extra aid which is taught at a later

GOOD TEACHING ～ SURE FOUNDATIONS.

stage in the horseman's career, when he rides well enough to school his own horses and to retrain problem horses. This bracing of the back gives the rider's seat extra strength, for example, for horses who baulk or are nappy. This extra driving should never be overdone in amount or in frequency: the rider's upper body should remain vertical, he should not lean backwards.

RESTRAINING

This may be carried out with a strong seat as has just been described – but better by far is a "tall" restraining seat. Here the rider presses lightly on his stirrups while "growing tall ears". This allows the horse's back muscles to fill out with an arched rather than a hollowed appearance. The horse's back muscles must be allowed this free play in order that he may bring his hindlegs forward and to balance the mass of his body weight on all four legs as he makes a smooth downward transition or halt.

ANALYSING

Through his seat bones and the surrounding tissues the rider feels how his horse's skeletal and muscular systems are working. He can feel nervous or physical constraint, or excess tension, and he can feel when the horse is freewheeling – "a leg-mover", "going like a sewing machine" are terms used to describe a horse who is not working genuinely, through the whole of his body.

By sitting softly and with an easy poise the rider's pelvis and the lower part of his spine move with the movement of the horse's back – his seat in no way impedes the movement, rather it encourages the horse to work the whole of his body, particularly through his strong back muscles.

Thus, the influences given by the rider's weight aids may be:
- Forward-driving.
- Sideways-inviting – to change direction.
- Sideways-moving – as in lateral movements.
- Restraining.

The weight aids are the foundations of all the physical aids: unless they are used correctly, with forethought, timing and tact, there can be no "harmony of the aids" nor real horsemanship.

Every rider should be taught to be acutely aware of the effect and influence which the weight of his entire body has on the horse he rides – from ears to toes, of man and horse. He must remember the four main directives for his weight aids:

(i)   The rider's body must be correctly poised and balanced so that he can place and use it, accurately and pliantly, exactly where, when and how he wishes, with a subconscious ease, in order to create the best "tune" or movement within and from his horse. *He must never upset his horse's balance.*

(ii)   Whenever the rider wishes his horse to proceed along a straight line he must poise and balance his body softly on his two seat bones which are placed exactly centrally above the horse's central line. The respective axes of the rider's ears, shoulders, elbows, hips, knees and ankles should be level as they all co-operate together to urge the horse forward along an absolutely straight course.

(iii) Before asking for a change of direction the rider should make a light, accurately measured shift of his weight to invite the horse into the new direction and to help him to take it by giving him a perfectly balanced load to carry – again, all the rider's axes must be level; he must never lean to one side or the other.

(iv) Whenever he is riding on a curved line, the rider must be extremely careful to keep his weight shifted sufficiently to the inside, with his axes level and his inner hip (hip joint and seat bone) well forward, in order that he will remain in balance and will allow his horse to use his back muscles freely. The rider must open the angle at the front of his hip joint as far as is possible without force or constraint, with a lowered knee and heel so that his inner seat bone cannot slide out and is able to move forward with the horse's movement.

Riders and instructors, please note that it is essential to remember the golden rules of *thought, weight* and *feel*. Riders must discipline themselves and instructors must keep on their toes, seeking every opportunity to explain and teach these "grass roots" whilst tactfully but firmly removing the weeds of bad, rough riding habits.

The leg aids

As the aids or signals given by the rider's legs are readily understood by the horse and are therefore one of the most effective of his forward-driving influences, the rider's leg aids must be ever-present – and never absent. The rider's boots should contain a constant supply of encouraging messages.

These messages may be further emphasised, extended or refined by trained and thoughtful use of whips and spurs. For details of these aids and their application, see Book 1.

There are four groups of four leg aid refresher points which riders and instructors may find useful:

(i) Desired qualities
- Position.
- Placing.
- Effectiveness.
- Tact.

(ii) Place for reaction
- By the girth – impulsion, softening, bending.
- Just behind the girth – sideways-moving, in a supportive role for bending and impulsion.
- Occasionally – a little further back, moving over or otherwise controlling the hindquarters when asking for more bend with the inner leg.
- Occasionally – in front of the girth – urging a sluggish horse, softening a spoiled, stiff horse, straightening a crooked horse.

(iii) Main influences
- Forward-driving.
- Sideways-moving.
- Regulating – or containing.
- Bending.

(iv) Undesirable qualities
- Weak position – heels rising or toes turned unnaturally in or out.
- Wrongly placed – stuck forward, or used too far back.
- Absence.
- Overuse – stiffness, gripping or thoughtless banging, numbing the horse's mind as well as his sides.

The rein aids

The term preferred to that of "hands", the latter being only a portion of the whole – often far too busy a portion at that!

As was said earlier the rider's rein aids must be based on and used in conjunction with the whole of his seat; they must be totally independent and yet work in close co-operation and fullest harmony with all his other aids.

"Position" is possibly the most important and helpful reminder. Not only must the rider discipline himself into a general posture which is habitually correct in order to support his trunk, shoulders, arms and hands so that the latter may have precisely the desired influence through the reins, he must also carry and move his hands correctly.

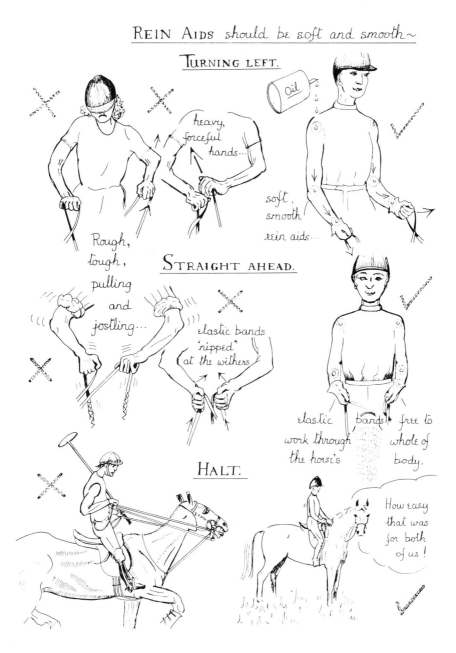

REIN AIDS should be soft and smooth~

TURNING LEFT.

heavy, forceful hands...

Oil

soft, smooth rein aids...

Rough, tough, pulling and jostling...

STRAIGHT AHEAD.

elastic bands 'nipped' at the withers

elastic bands free to work through whole of the horse's body.

HALT.

How easy that was for both of us!

The rider's hands should always be carried with the thumb part uppermost. They should act with a smooth turning which brings the fingernails into view or even uppermost; they should yield or give by moving the little finger part of the hand towards the horse's mouth. Their feeling on the reins should be soft, smooth and consistent – never hard, jostling or rough, nor should they ever pull backward.

Remember – there's a horse's mouth at the end of the reins and further, remember the fragile construction of the horse's mouth.

The voice aids and tongue clicking

The rider's influences with his voice and tongue can be extremely beneficial to both the horse – and the rider. However, the three words, "Quiet, short and meaningful", are perhaps the most helpful reminders concerning these aids.

The value of the simple corrective exercises of conversing, saying, humming or singing for riders who are too tense or who have too little rhythm in their make-up must be remembered by instructors and by the riders themselves.

Feel

Although feel and talent are two invisible qualities which are bound together and interdependent, feel can be developed by correct training, combined with plenty of practical experience for which the rider must be fit. If he is tired he will make posture evasions and gain wrong feels.

The rider can only improve the vital quality of feel if:
- He is well instructed from the first lessons he receives.
- The ponies and horses he rides give him the correct feel.
- He learns all he can concerning how the horse "ticks" and moves, and . . .
- . . . how to analyse this movement through his seat and with his brain.

Through understanding and practice he develops his own natural qualities of belief and confidence, sensitivity and sympathy, patience and generosity, all combined with mental and physical suppleness – and *thought*.

Conclusion

A couple of quotes and a summing up.

The rider must sit naturally "with his loins and hips supple, thighs and legs steady and well stretched down." (F.E.I.)

"Only the rider who knows how to contract and relax his loin muscles at the right moment is able to influence his horse correctly." (F.E.I.).

This sounds such a simple directive, but if it is realised that there are approximately forty-five muscles, tendons and ligaments in the hip area (pelvis) alone for the rider to organise, and that these pass downwards to the legs and upwards to and through the loin area, to and through the shoulders to the head, to be joined by many other muscles as they go, the true complexity of the rider's problem can be appreciated.

Mental and physical unconstrained self-control and discipline are, as we have seen, essential qualities for athletes, skiers, swimmers, gymnasts, dancers and riders alike. However, the rider has the greatest task of all, for he does not have the firmness of the ground on which to stabilise his poise and movement. He sits upon his horse, a live creature who is also his partner with independent thoughts, moods, urges and actions, all of which have to be led by the rider.

The horse should carry himself and his rider easily, willingly and with pride, answering invisible aids. The rider should find his horse comfortable to sit on in all his gaits. Together they should appear balanced in all ways, calmly confident yet with undaunted courage, giving a heart-warming gaiety to their performance and an overall harmony to their partnership. There is a heart, a spirit and many feelings to be considered as well as a position when pupils are taught to ride horses!

A "Tail-piece"

Often the doctrine on the rider's seat and the use of his back and weight as aids is inadequate, muddled, evasive or misleading. Put the two last failings together and the so-called "doctrine" then becomes destructive to the rider's position, his ability, to his vulnerable embryonic vestiges of feel, as well as to his physique and general well-being. Incorrect teaching on these subjects can implant bad habits, thoughts and actions, creating major riding faults which are among the most difficult to correct.

It is because these subjects are so important, and yet at the same time they are misunderstood and badly taught or quite often avoided altogether, that they are grouped together here as a tail-piece. Thus they should be easy to find for reference purposes, both initially and repeatedly thereafter!

The rider's seat

This term can mean the whole of the rider's position or it is sometimes used, less correctly, to refer only to the pelvic or hip area – his bottom. This latter area is agreed by all experts to be the most important, and yet also the most difficult part of the whole of the rider's seat to "get right" and it is the part which provides the vital link between all three subjects under present discussion. As he rides the horse forward and straight with a calm but resolute purpose the rider's seat is governed by trained thought and feel as it combines with the horse's movement.

The use of the rider's back

Some people exclaim vehemently that it is dangerous to teach the use of the rider's back until the rider is advanced in age and experience. With my tongue well in my cheek I exclaim, nearly as vehemently, "I am convinced that all pupils should be taught the use of the rider's back from their very first lessons; in fact, I believe that it is dangerous not to do so." This usually has the desired effect of waking up every person present – then comes the qualifying explanation which justifies my counterstatement.

The novice rider must be taught *the use of his back for himself*, long before he can be taught how to use his back for his horse's benefit. Unless he learns the skeletal shapes and landmarks and the relevant muscles and their effects he rides with a great disadvantage. Without such knowledge it is far more difficult for him to acquire a correct position or "seat for his horse" which combines good posture with balance and a natural ease and grace – and which is effective with minimum effort.

Yes, certainly it is irresponsible not to educate beginners about the correct use and carriage of their backs. They should receive interesting short lectures on basic human anatomy with special regard to the effects from and for riding. If they understand the delicate structure of the human spine with its four natural counter-balancing curves, they will be less likely to abuse it. Current illogical directives such as "wobble your spine like a rope", "make your back loose" or "like springs" are worthless, even harmful instructions.

A pupil should be taught how to use his back in three stages:

(i)   As a beginner, to understand the mechanics and to feel a correctly poised and balanced seat, the spine being the "tree trunk" of his whole position or seat for the horse.

(ii)   To establish this position – practising and perfecting the ploy and play of his muscles, positioning and using his bones with supple ease, until he can retain a correct, balanced seat on a variety of horses, in all circumstances – well, nearly all circumstances! (We are human, after all!)

(iii)   The pupil may then be taught how to give his aids subtle or more definite emphasis by correct use of the muscles of his back – when he is sufficiently educated and experienced.

The weight aids

These have been mentioned in detail already. At this stage, let it suffice to say again, "The rider applies his weight aids as soon as he lowers his weight on to his horse's back, by means of his seat bones, his knees, and/or stirrups depending on the form of the balanced seat being used at the time." This undeniable fact being accepted, equally acceptable should be the fact that pupils be made aware of their weight as an aid and taught how to use it correctly from their earliest riding lessons – to be fair to their horses and to achieve maximum effect, enjoyment and success themselves as riders.

Before enlarging on the weight aids, it is imperative to return to the link which connects these three subjects – for they are all interrelated and must be regarded as such. The rider must know and understand the basic facts of his own anatomical structure. The middle part of the rider is of the utmost importance to the standard of his horsemanship, from his waist to his thighs, but particularly the pelvic or hip area.

True, bottoms may be large, small or indifferent – each is a personal problem. However, the position can be improved considerably if, during early and subsequent lessons, the following facts are taught:

- The whole area – skeletal and muscular – must be supple and without constraint. It must receive the messages from the horse's musculature, particularly from his back muscles, and it must provide a sure foundation for the correct poise and posture of the whole of the rider's body including his head and limbs; it must allow the horse to move his many back muscles freely under it.
- The positioning of the hip bones should ensure that when viewed from the front or back they are equally upright and their front edges face forward. When viewed from the side the line of balance should be vertically upright – "in neutral gear" so to speak, so that the whole pelvis may move well with the horse's movements. If the top of the hip bones are pushed forward, the result is a faulty "fork-seat". The rider's weight is no longer taken on the two seat bones, the small sitting areas at the bottom of the hip bones; the lumbar ligaments hold the rider's spine rigid at the loins, or in the small of his back, and his weight is pitched down and backwards, in a manner which is hardly conducive to the horse moving with free forward movement. A fork seat all too effectively "blocks" the ease of movement of the horse's large back muscles and of all the other muscles connected with them. On the other hand, the opposite fault of a slouched or "chair seat" can have an equally retrograde effect on the horse's movement for the rider's gluteal or buttock muscles, being tucked too much underneath the pelvis, render it insensitive to the horse's movements, and even cushion his bumpings from the rider himself so that he remains blissfully unaware of the detrimental effect he is having on the movement of the horse beneath him.
- Beginners should be taught to make a small, invisible shift of their bottoms to prepare the horse for an intended change of direction. It is no good shilly-shallying or being even half-hearted about this point. They must learn the correct method so that they do not slide (literally) into the two connected bad habits, those of bottoms slipping out, away from the direction of the curve or turn, and a collapsing of the inner hip – together with the whole of the inner side, above that hip. This fault causes most of the rider's weight to be moved on to the horse's outer side. Then, following his natural inclination, the horse would like to turn away towards the outside under the unbalancing rider burden – but no! Strong pulls on the reins and his mouth dictate that he must, positively *must* keep going in what to him feels a most awkward way, in the "wrong" direction. Invariably he will comply for the horse is a wonderfully generous creature.

• Later, when riders become more experienced and their seats (position) become established, they will easily manage to attain the desired weight shifting, subtly and invisibly, by lowering the inner heel to indicate direction and to keep in perfect balance through a short turn, small circle or, later still, a canter pirouette.

This lowering of the inner heel and knee has an important mechanical effect on the hip bone. The femur is used as a lever with the horse's body as the fulcrum. Lowering the knee end of the femur means that the top, hip end, shifts the pelvis towards the same side. That is, if the right heel is lowered this brings the hips over to the right. The lowering also opens the hip joint at the top of the leg which allows the hip bone on the same side to move forward, and it keeps the whole of the pelvis level and stable. All these actions are so slight that they are imperceptible to any but the most trained of eyes. They are of vital importance to the horse's balance and movement and thus to the whole of his training. These actions can only be triggered off by the lowering of the inner heel if the rider has been taught to shift his weight thoughtfully from his earliest riding lessons.

The value and method of using the weight aids

The use of the weight aids, the theory and the practice, should be taught in two stages, the first for beginners and the second, later, for riders of some education and experience. As a quick guide, children should be moving on to the second stage by the time they are taking their Pony Club B Test, and adults by Stage III.

As I have said earlier, as soon as the rider sits on the horse, his weight is applied as an aid, for better or for worse. If one watches a number of classes – in a riding school, at a horse show, ponies, hacks, hunters, jumping and dressage, or at hunter and horse trials – one will see a variety of good and bad styles and results, some sick-making performances and some which are a joy to watch. Usually the main keys of balance and harmony are either obviously missing or they are present. Definitely there is a technique to keeping in balance and, even better, to being able to lead the horse with invisible weight aids. How is this basic technique learned?

Many young people grow up with ponies and horses as a part of their lives. They play cowboys and Indians, they ride as often on a blanket or bareback as they ride on a saddle and, as a duckling takes to water, so these children learn in the best, most natural way to stay in perfect balance during all their ponies' gyrations – or, at least for most of them! During the inevitable chase, or competitive element which always enters children's fun-time with ponies, the rider finds he can guide his pony with his weight. He learns to make lightning-quick adjustments to his seat, moving a little to the right or to the left on his pony's back just as and when the need arises. Daily his prowess grows – the pony teaches the technique – the child soon learns that if his seat slides out he loses his balance and falls off. This is the natural training – quick thinking, quick

STYLES ··· BAD ··· AND ··· GOOD ···

··· sick-making ·····   ····· a joy to watch ·····

INDIANS !

going ·······   going ·····   ·· gone !

A live creature's reaction ···   ···is delayed···

a machine's reaction is instant, and its base of support is very narrow.

reactions and quick adjustments for balance which can be seen each year amongst the finalists of the Prince Philip Games at the Horse of the Year Show or in top-class dressage or jumping events.

These young riders are the lucky ones, they have learned the first stage of the technique of the rider's weight aids by natural methods – the best ones, of course.

However, nowadays, there are many new riders who did not have the opportunity to learn to ride as children. These riders have to learn the technique and feel of actually shifting their weight slightly to the inside a few strides before they wish their horse to take a new direction. It is most important that instructors understand the necessity for teaching this technique, and for reminding and correcting their pupils frequently during every lesson until, quite quickly, it becomes ingrained in their way of riding as a subconscious habit. Unless this technique is taught in early lessons the riders will have endless problems of "crookedness", "collapsed inner hips", "seat sliding to the outside" and other heinous riding faults, which will crop up continually on examiners' and judges' sheets and will produce other related riding faults which will impede their careers and their horses' performances.

Some experienced instructors, who learned the first, the natural way, themselves, may question whether it is correct to teach pupils actually to shift their weight. Whereas it is easy to prove the value of the teaching by means of a demonstration with a group of inexperienced riders – in fact, this never fails! – that method is not possible here and now. Explanations will have to suffice.

If a cyclist is riding on a large, flat and level area, such as a deserted municipal car-park, and if that cyclist keeps pedalling at a steady rate but removes his hands from the handlebars, he can cause his bicycle to take a right-handed curve by putting a little more weight on to his right seat bone which he keeps where it is, on the right side of the saddle. Providing his confidence, balance and skill are good he will find such turning very easy to accomplish and very "instant".

Why then, will not this simple press on the inner seat bone work for a rider when he wishes his horse to turn or to circle to the right?

Of course it will work for an educated horseman, especially if he is riding his horse at a faster pace, because he will have learned how to make his weight adjustment correctly – probably by riding without a saddle, as a child – the best, most feeling way.

If the differences between the bicycle and the horse are considered this will help instructors to gain a fuller understanding of the pupil's problem with regard to his thought aids, his balance and his weight aids.

(a) The bicycle is a machine, it has no brain, no feelings and its reactions are instant, being mechanical.

(b) The cyclist's saddle is narrow and is so shaped, with a pronounced central line, that the cyclist's seat is stabilised with the seat bones clearly on either side of the bicycle's line of balance.

(c) The bicycle's base of support is narrow, being only a few centimetres wide; the bike rider's base of support is wider (often considerably so!), thus it is easy for him to influence the direction his bicycle takes by means of a more weighted seat bone – and pedal. There is almost no risk that he will tilt the line of balance beyond the area of the base of support.

When the beginner sits on a slow-moving novice horse the picture and the mechanics are very different.

(a) The horse is not a machine and should never be considered as one. Because he has a brain, a complex collection of systems and a cumbersome body to organise together with a rider-burden on top of it, his reactions to his rider's signals are far from "instant": they are often surprisingly slow.

(b) The horse's saddle has a seat which is comparatively broad, like a slippery chair seat – or board – depending on the particular saddle or the state of the human bottom concerned!

(c) The horse's base of support is comparatively wide – certainly wider than the rider's base of support as he sits upon the saddle.

If the beginner rider does not make a little shift of his weight to the right but leaves his seat bones as if for "straight ahead" and then presses on his right seat bone hoping to turn right – immediately several things will go awry . . .

Even a little uneducated press, without keeping the hip bone upright, will cause his right seat bone to slide away to the left. (Please try this for yourself when sitting on a chair with a firm seat – for example, a dining or lecture room chair, and again when riding at walk, while sitting on your fingers, nails down.)

This movement, and the sliding it can cause to a seat which is not yet controlled, knocks the line of balance for six; the horse's equilibrium has to be upset, he cannot follow his rider's aids because, applied in this way they are contradictory and confusing. The horse does not turn to the right – the rider resorts to pulling on the right rein; the horse then turns to the right because he is a living and generous creature – whereas no bicycle would turn right if the cyclist's weight was out to the left. The beginner rider starts to believe that if he wishes to turn to the right, he must, positively *must*, pull the right rein. He will probably have to pull quite hard too, due to his weight having been displaced way out to the left, with the inevitable accompanying collapse of the right hip, and the upset of his and his horse's balance.

"Don't slide out to the left!", is not nearly such a helpful or easy correction to follow as is, "Sit a little more to the right." The looks of amazement, pleasure and excitement that always accompany the latter correction can be among the most rewarding moments of teaching a group of novice riders – or when helping young instructors how to teach a group of beginners. Then the riders' reactions and comments, "It works!", are doubly rewarding.

I do hope that if any experienced instructors still doubt the truth and value of teaching this technique, simply, clearly and determinedly in very early lessons, they will be open-minded enough to give it a try themselves – and I know they too will reap the rewards as their pupils assimilate correct methods, understanding and feeling in less time than ever they have done before. Also, in due course, they will realise that only those riders who have been taught this correct basic technique will be able to retain a position which is straight, supple and balanced even when the demands increase through more difficult movements or courses.

Crookedness is not only a major riding fault, it is also very common and is very difficult to erase. Often it becomes a habit which is positively ingrained into the rider's seat, and is the most hotly denied of all faulty habits. Some riders slide out equally badly whether their horse is turning left or right; some slide out in one direction only, for example, to the left when they are riding a right circle or turn.

Pupils must have been taught how to sit in perfect balance for their horses before the demands are raised. They can learn through natural practice on ponies or in a riding school – a combination of both is the best. Learned the lesson must be, in order to be fair to the pupils and the horses.

Many exercises can be composed to provide riders with opportunities to learn how to use the weight as an aid with subtlety and tact, and in complete harmony with every horse they ride. These educational exercises give the instructor a marvellous means of working a number of riders and horses together and giving them all "the best of both worlds", the natural and the educational, spiced with *fun*.

As the novice rider becomes more educated, experienced and proficient, his seat (his whole position) will be established. It will be correct in posture and placing, it will be balanced and supple – a seat which is truly *for the horse*. The shifting which the rider makes before he wishes his horse to take a new direction will soon soften into a minute, subconscious and entirely invisible shift: only the horse will feel it and be guided and helped by it.

The timing of the shifting is extremely important, this is where the thought aid combines with the weight aid. Correct timing is the element which produces the much sought-after harmony, a quality possessed only by a true horseman – a very rare bird, these days. Only by a complete understanding, and by an interplay of feel, thought and correct shifting, poise and use of his whole body can the rider lead the horse to follow his aids and intentions.

As was mentioned in Book 1, hands which always follow the horse are sometimes ineffective and are often too late. The rider's hands should frequently "give" a split second earlier so that they offer the horse an invitation to stretch forward to the bit, for example, over a fence. Similarly, the good horseman can use his weight as an invitation to his horse, to go forward, to slow down or to change direction, providing that his brain triggers off the timing of the aid so that it is given early enough for the horse to follow it smoothly and easily.

The rider must be with his horse literally – laterally and longitudinally. A rider can be left behind, laterally, riding a small circle just as badly as he can be left behind, longitudinally, over a fence.

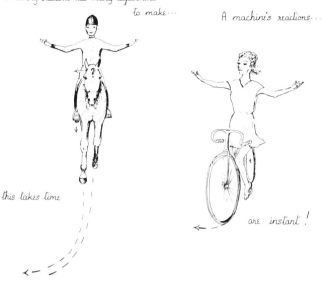

A living creature has many adjustments to make...

A machine's reactions...

this takes time

are instant!

So we come to the "when" of the timing. This is where the logistical, mechanical theorist will come unstuck, for the horse is a complex, cumbersome, living creature; he is not a machine capable merely of simple actions which can be scientifically programmed. His brain has to receive the messages – both physical and mental signals – which are then sorted out and transmitted through the horse's vast body until, eventually they come out at his toes!

It is through his sympathetic understanding of this – the living creature as opposed to the machine – that the naturally trained rider will often have the edge over the town-bred theorist.

If a comparison is made between a cyclist and a rider as each rides the same ground-plan this should help the reader to understand why the rider's weight aids have to be programmed so much earlier than a mechanical expert would comprehend or even tolerate.

If the two riders are asked to ride a change of rein within a 20 metre circle on their bicycle and horse respectively, to get the best result their methods will be similar but different! To ride a well-shaped 20 metre circle, they will both have to sit in perfect balance to suit exactly the speed and the curve as well as the force of gravity; also they will have to produce enough impulsion – from the pedalling of one and the forward-driving aids of the other. So far so similar – the method differs as soon as there is a change of direction in the middle. The cyclist makes his slight shiftings during the moment when he changes his course on the centre line; the horseman, to be worthy of that title, should make much earlier shiftings. Of course it is absolutely understandable that it may be difficult for a non-horseman to comprehend and accept this fact which is largely based on feel.

Why is there this difference in the timing? Because the bicycle is inanimate and the horse is a living creature with all the mental and physical complications that that implies; he must be warned and he must be prepared for the impending change of direction and he must be invited to make it, smoothly and easily, in perfect balance. This excellent state of affairs can only be accomplished if the rider shifts his weight early enough. Critics who may find this teaching offends their theories of physics and locomotion, should try riding a young or a trained horse at walk, on long reins, through the simple figure of changing the rein within the circle. They will see for themselves how well it works. Then, maybe, they will make better dancing partners in the ballroom as well as in the arena!

Most pupils are amazed when their instructor demonstrates the length of time it takes even a well-trained horse to change course, following the instructor's thought and weight aids. This is always an enlightening and convincing demonstration: it should be carried out at walk on loose reins, the instructor exaggerating the lateral shifting of his seat bones at first so that his pupils can see for themselves how many strides the horse will take before he follows his leading partner in the new direction.

Instructors must never tire of explaining that the rider must always be ahead of time with his thoughts and the shifting of his weight, so that he leads his horse to follow the softest and smoothest of aids. The timing of his leadership should be akin to that of a good conductor in front of his orchestra as suggested earlier.

The horse's balance is also very dependent upon his rider's knowledge, feel and judgement of rhythm, speed and impulsion.

An under-ridden horse will idle along, he will neither develop muscularly nor will his performance improve. An overridden horse will often hold his breath as well as hold his body rigid, flattening or even hollowing his back as he is hurried along beyond his own personal point of balance. The animation of his muscle work as a whole will be stunted as he strives to keep his balance while moving his legs hastily as directed by his rider.

The rider must be aware constantly of his responsibility to select a rhythm and speed and to create just the right amount of impulsion which are finely judged to be exactly suitable for his individual horse partner.

These balancing factors are of prime importance to the riding horse's well-being as well as to his performance, whether the rider is executing turns on the spot, novice or advanced exercises on the flat, show jumping or riding for a medal on a cross-country course.

To finish on a positive note we will return to the good horseman, for the final stage: weight aids with finesse.

When the trained rider wishes to tell his horse that together they will turn to the right, he will already be sitting absolutely in balance as he makes a preliminary half-halt. Then he lowers his right heel and knee which moves his seat slightly to the right, opens the angle of his hip joint and keeps his pelvis level and under control. Thus the right seat bone is

THOUGHTS WHEN RIDING A SERPENTINE LOOP.

Rider (the leader).
'I have shifted my weight in advance, to prepare and to invite my partner to take a new direction . . .'
(Already I have shortened – not tightened – my right rein)
CENTRE LINE
Horse (the follower).
'He no longer wishes us to go on that curve to the left . . .'
'Ah! now together we can go in balance and harmony to the right . . .'
Rider (the leader).
I must :– ride FORWARD on the new loop I have planned ~ THINK and connect with his brain waves (at his poll), look well ahead. keep my weight to the right ~ use both legs for a good form, balance and impulsion, using them as and where required to keep his body muscles active and his central line matching the curves of the track ~ my rein aids must be soft, the right hand free from the withers as he work towards the outside rein.

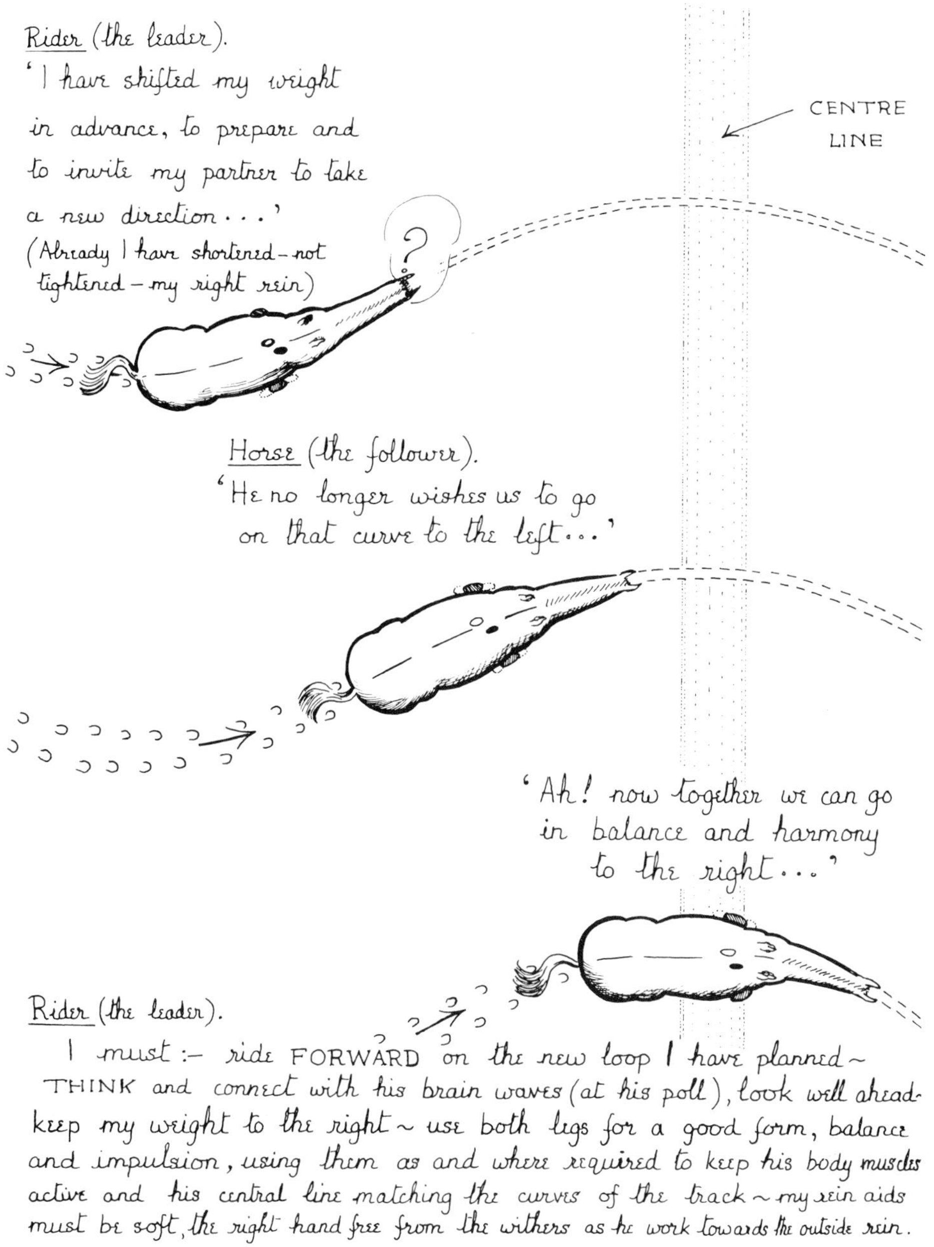

kept forward and to the right of the horse's central line by the rest of the rider's leg and the muscles of his middle and upper body. The right seat bone does not slide away to the left when the rider gives it more weight to carry because, firstly, it has never formed that bad habit and, secondly,

Pat to encourage, to reward ~ give it often, whenever it is needed or deserved.

WELL DONE! ——— THOUGHTS

Rider's

MEANINGFUL FEEL

Not too hard ~
not too soft ~
just firm enough to
make a small vibration
through to the horse's
systems and to his
heart . . .

Horse's → AND

his spinal cord ~ brain, nerves.

his spinal column ~ bones.

his muscles ~ 44 here ~ related to a further 666!

due to the trained posture and control of the whole of his body, the rider is able to keep his hip bone relatively straight – remember the puppet string! At the same time his thigh bone (femur) keeps his seat bone in a correct position through its connection at the hip joint. The horse's body forms a middle area fulcrum while the lowered knee guards the situation at the lower end of the femur.

The two seat bones are the foundations of the rider's seat. Once the rider learns how to place his seat bones correctly, just where and as they will be required and to balance his whole seat from them with a supple poise, then, and only then, will he be able to join his horse's movement and to give aids which are soft, subtle, and easy for his horse to understand and to follow.

I hope that this chapter will have helped riders to understand the real challenge of horsemanship, that its field is far wider and deeper than most beginners envisage: it is a great test of prowess – of the rider's ability to channel and then direct the horse's mental and physical resources which cannot be learned in a mere year or two.

8 The Rider's Partner

Equilibrium; centre of gravity; balance; free forward movement; regularity; straightness; suppleness; impulsion; submission; lightness; the stiff side; mouthing; bridling; flexion; positioning and bending.

All these names and phrases are used by horsemen in their discussions and by instructors in their lectures with an assumption that the listener knows their meaning. It is entirely possible that the listener does not know enough, if anything, about these words, in which case the whole lecture will remain only partly, if at all, understood. However, such is human nature that it is unlikely that the listener will confess that most of the discussion or lecture has flown off at a tangent and that as far as he is concerned it has gone way above his head. It is important that these terms should be explained and understood.

Desirable Qualities of the Riding Horse

EQUILIBRIUM

A word which is used sometimes as an alternative for balance, either to avoid repetition or to give the text an added impact or sophistication, or as a kind of one-up-manship for the lecturer who may use it to "blind them with science". However, equilibrium is included here because it means much more than balance. Equilibrium signifies a balanced state of mind as well as of body; the equal balancing of the mind between conflicting ideas, reasons or motives – composure; a state of rest or balance due to the action of forces which counteract each other. Equilibrium is the name applied to a body when it is in a state of equal balance or equipoise; when the several forces acting upon a mind or body balance each other; due proportion between parts. These are facts which can be gleaned from any dictionary. The part upon which the body rests is termed its *base of support*.

The maintenance of equilibrium is dependent on two factors:

(i)   The joints which unite the main segments of the body must be held firm by the ligaments and muscles surrounding them.

(ii) The vertical line of gravity must pass through the base of support – however narrow the base of support may be, if the line of gravity falls or even wavers outside it, the body's equilibrium is lost, and its mental state will be upset too!

A subject's equilibrium may be stable or unstable. Any object remains stable only if its vertical line of gravity falls within the area of its base of support. These are the essential facts. Man's equilibrium is more unstable than stable, because his base of support is so small in comparison with his

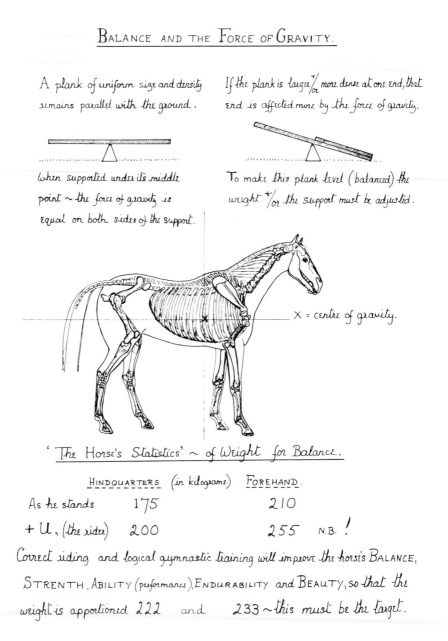

A plank of uniform size and density remains parallel with the ground.

If the plank is larger $^t/_{or}$ more dense at one end, that end is affected more by the force of gravity.

When supported under its middle point ~ the force of gravity is equal on both sides of the support.

To make this plank level (balanced) the weight $^t/_{or}$ the support must be adjusted.

X = centre of gravity.

' The Horse's Statistics' ~ of Weight for Balance.

	HINDQUARTERS (in kilograms)	FOREHAND.
As he stands	175	210
+ U, (the rider)	200	255 N.B. !

Correct riding and logical gymnastic training will improve the horse's BALANCE, STRENTH, ABILITY (performance), ENDURABILITY and BEAUTY, so that the weight is apportioned 222 and 233 ~ this must be the target.

height. He is more stable when he stands still in an alert, active posture or as a soldier stands at ease. He is least stable when he stands on one toe and he is not particularly stable when he sits on his two seat bones – especially if they have managed to slide off course when he was not thinking.

The horse is similar in these respects. When his base of support is reduced to the size of one hoof he is extremely unstable and vulnerable to the smallest overbalancing influence. Also, under normal circumstances, the faster the horse moves, the further forward will his centre of gravity shift and it will become more difficult for him to retain his equilibrium.

CENTRE OF GRAVITY

That gravity is the force which draws bodies towards the earth is an accepted fact. Any object which can produce a seesaw motion will provide a practical illustration, such as a strip of wood balanced on a cotton reel or similar support. As long as the piece of wood is symmetrical, the pull of gravity will be equal all along it: it will remain horizontal if the cotton reel is situated under its central point – it will be "pulled" down equally on either side of the cotton reel. If however, the wood is thicker at one end or a small, additional object is attached to one end, then the plank will only be level if the cotton reel is moved nearer to the more bulky end in order to find its centre of gravity with the weight distributed evenly at either end.

Man's centre of gravity is situated on a level with his second sacral vertebra when he is standing and slightly higher when he is seated. Whenever he is in an upright position, standing or seated, his head, neck, shoulders and arms should be aligned and kept in perfect balance above the centre of gravity.

The horse is considerably heavier at his front end, even when his proportions and symmetry are near to the ideal. The heavy, bulky front part of the horse's trunk has no bony support or "props": it is suspended between the shoulder blades and kept in place by a veritable sling of muscles – that is all. Then man decides to climb "on board" and those muscles have to support him as well. It is hardly surprising that novice horses ridden by inexperienced riders never get off their forehands.

The horse's centre of gravity is situated approximately at a point where a vertical line passes upwards behind the ziphoid cartilage at the back of the sternum (breast bone) and crosses a horizontal line drawn along the top of the lower third of the horse's trunk.

In their natural state, man and horse have comparatively few problems in retaining their equilibrium even under pressure, as can be seen when children are playing or being coached at ballet school, on the ice rink or in the gymnasium, or when young horses are playing at liberty. The problems really commence when man decides to ride the horse.

Of course it is true to say that anyone can learn to ride – they can be taught the skill of the craft, the sport or the art. However, in order to learn these skills the would-be rider must understand the fundamental difficulties which are likely to beset both him and his steed. Only by understanding these difficulties may they be overcome.

Put a man on a horse and we have two unstable bodies together, one on top of the other which maximises their instability – and then we expect them to move together and to perform incredible and unnatural feats. To do so the rider must achieve the four following:

(i)   The horse's base of support is considerably larger from front to rear than it is from one side to the other. This is why the rider must be extremely careful to place his body and use his weight aids exactly to suit his horse. *He must never upset his horse's balance.*

(ii) Proceeding along a straight line, the rider must be poised and balanced softly on his two seat bones which are placed exactly centrally above the horse's central line.

(iii) Before turning right, the rider makes a light, accurately measured shift of his weight to the right to invite the horse into the new direction. This aid must be given well in advance because unless both horse and rider are highly trained, a signal to turn cannot be answered by a quick reaction from the horse. He is a big, awkward creature with hundreds of bones and muscles to be organised; his brain is a long way from his muscles and even further from his feet, so he needs this preparatory signal to prepare himself to make the turn which lies ahead.

(iv) When riding on a curved line, the rider must stay in balance; that is, with his weight shifted sufficiently to the inside, so that he presents his horse with a perfectly balanced load to carry.

Throughout all these thoughtful adjustments and shiftings the rider must keep the axes of his ears, shoulders, elbows, hips, knees and ankles level. He must consider how best he can use the whole of his body to help the horse to use the whole of his body – both in perfect balance, together.

BALANCE

The *British Cavalry Manual* definition of a balanced horse was concise and easy to learn. My memory has retained it with ease from my pre-Pony Club B Test days to the present time, although scientific formulae and historical dates have long since been forgotten! The two short paragraphs run as follows:

> Balanced. A horse is said to be "balanced" when his own weight and that of his rider is distributed over each leg in such proportion as to allow him to use himself with the maximum ease and efficiency at all paces.
> The head and neck form the governing factors (the balancing pole) in weight distribution and it is by their position that the horse carries his centre of gravity forward or backward as his paces are extended or collected.

This definition was revised for the civilian *B.H.S. and Pony Club Manual* with the addition of "the balancing pole" and other explanatory sentences. The object in including the definition was to help new and young riders to understand that whenever ridden horses are moving, their centre of gravity is being displaced constantly in one direction or another, and to emphasise that only by correct riding and logical schooling methods and exercises can they build up the muscles of their horses' backs and hindquarters so that they are able to carry their riders with ease and efficiency.

Whereas heavy, cold-blooded horses can provide excellent means of transportation, better quality, warm or hot-blooded horses will provide the best "ride". It must be appreciated fully that the horse must learn to make incredible adjustments both to his way of thinking as well as to his way of moving when he is encumbered by a rider-burden. Thus, clearly, it is the rider's responsibility to understand the problems he has created for his horse and to learn how to ride him as well as possible. It is a grave injustice to blame the horse for man's inability to train and ride him.

FREE FORWARD MOVEMENT

A term used to describe a highly desirable quality in a ridden horse. It is one of the essential ingredients of "impulsion" and both are contained in "good form". Free forward movement implies that the horse moves forward over the ground, carrying his rider willingly, calmly and ably.

Free Forward Movement first—
the young horse gaining strength,
a new balance and trust...

His mature, trained counterparts...
perform with efficiency, grace and pride,
using their weight with
a new-found balance
to produce thrust,
spring
and
power.

A STRAIGHT HORSE.

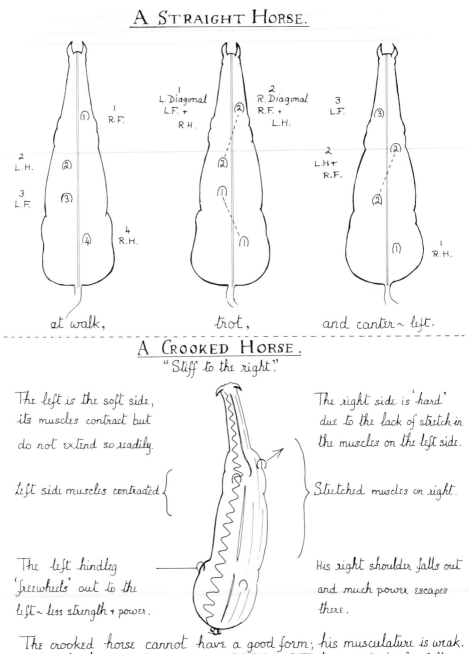

at walk,   trot,   and canter ~ left.

A CROOKED HORSE.
"Stiff to the right."

The left is the soft side, its muscles contract but do not extend so readily.

The right side is 'hard' due to the lack of stretch in the muscles on the left side.

Left side muscles contracted {

} Stretched muscles on right.

The left hindleg 'freewheels' out to the left ~ less strength + power.

His right shoulder falls out and much power escapes there.

The crooked horse cannot have a good form; his musculature is weak. Until the horse is trained to be STRAIGHT he cannot develop fully.

STRAIGHT AND SUPPLE.

The horse must be straight on straight lines...
at walk, trot and canter...

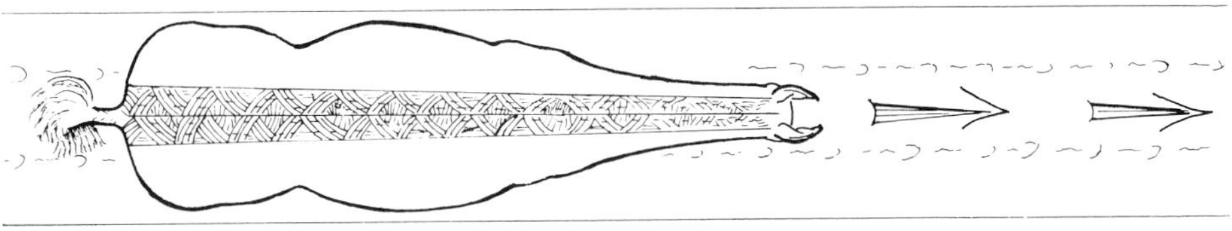

... and relatively 'straight' on curved lines.

The curve of
the horse's central line
must match that of
the track on which
he is working

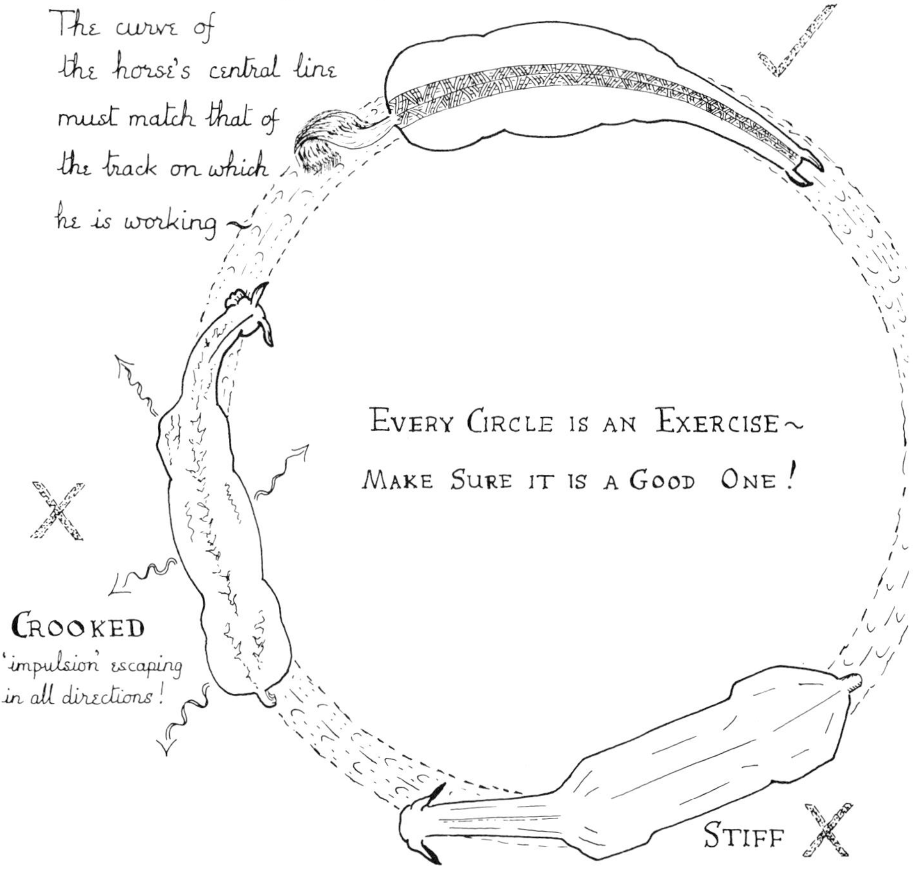

EVERY CIRCLE IS AN EXERCISE ~
MAKE SURE IT IS A GOOD ONE !

CROOKED
'impulsion' escaping
in all directions !

STIFF

He accepts and obeys his rider's aids and, as a result of correct training, he is able to move with good, ground-covering strides in a confident if not proud manner. His musculature has been developed so that his appearance and his movement look even more beautiful than they do when he is not being ridden.

REGULARITY

The freedom and regularity of the horse's gaits, his straightness, suppleness, impulsion and submission – lightness: all these are highly desirable qualities for the well-trained riding horse; all are important parts of the whole and they must go hand in hand together.

The true meaning of these qualities is seldom defined and taught by instructors. Sometimes they may be reeled off glibly as an imposing list in a manner more reminiscent of a parrot than that of a teacher, but too often the mere mention of them causes immediate worry and depression amongst riders and instructors alike, who tend to become overwrought about the whole subject especially if they do not understand enough about it.

Statements such as, "All horses are crooked", or, "Never use leg-yielding because it teaches the horse to fall out with his shoulders", and questions like, "Which is his stiff side?", are common, accompanied by a steely-eyed stare which is enough to paralyse any pupil's or candidate's mind.

This negative and accusative approach is wrong for it puts all the blame on the horse, which is unjust. It is better to make a positive approach. Rather than making a quagmire out of what might only be a bit of soft going, the instructor should feed small pieces of information in a carefully selected, relevant and constructive manner and sequence.

The gaits were described fully in Book 1 which can be used for reference and revision. In all the gaits, the sequence of footfall and rhythm must be true, the horse must move with an assurance, ease and balance, with good rider-carrying and ground-covering strides. His form must be consistently good throughout all his work and he should be obedient and responsive to his rider's wishes. The horse should have a light-hearted happy spirit and a bounce in his steps which enables him to use the ground as a springboard rather than a toneless, dead running track – thus is cadence born.

STRAIGHTNESS

The word does not imply merely that the horse's spine is straight, it means that both the longitudinal halves of his body are supple and working equally efficiently while all four of his legs are carrying fair proportions of the rider's and the horse's weight.

The horse must be straight on straight lines at walk, trot and canter and he must also be relatively "straight" on curved lines – the curve of his central line being identical to that of the track on which he is moving. A few school movements are accepted exceptions to this rule. For example,

Some Exceptions to the Straight Rule ~

Suppleness Continues to Improve.

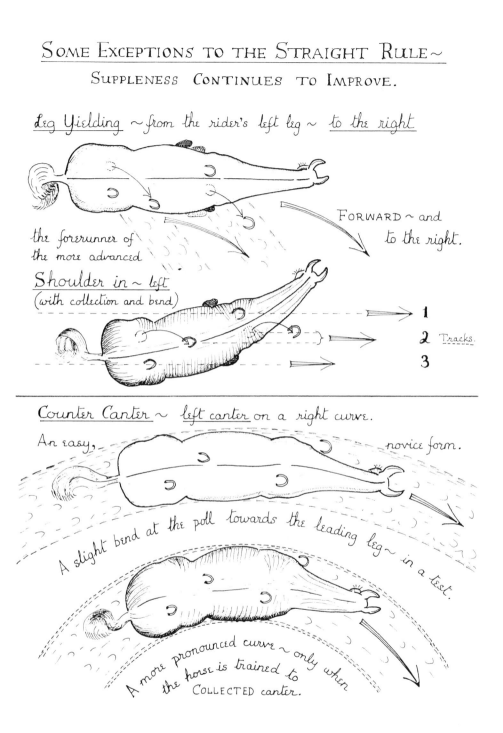

<u>Leg Yielding</u> ~ from the rider's left leg ~ <u>to the right</u>

the forerunner of
the more advanced

FORWARD ~ and
to the right.

<u>Shoulder in</u> ~ left
(with collection and bend)

1

2 <u>Tracks.</u>

3

<u>Counter Canter</u> ~ <u>left canter</u> on a right curve.

An easy, novice form.

A slight bend at the poll towards the leading leg ~ in a test.

A more pronounced curve ~ only when
the horse is trained to
COLLECTED canter.

lateral movements such as leg-yielding, shoulder-in and counter-canter. These exercises are used during the horse's training to improve his straightness and suppleness.

The rider's first aim in the early stages of his riding and/or of his horse's training is to feel that his horse is working equally well in both sides of his body.

All riders, from beginners upwards, must be taught to think and to feel for the whereabouts and the workings of the horse's body as a whole; and of his four quarters in particular, that his shoulders and forelimbs are straight in front of his powerful, propelling hindquarters. Riders must learn to think about "the two elastic bands" mentioned in Book 1. They

STRAIGHTNESS ∼ or the lack of it ···

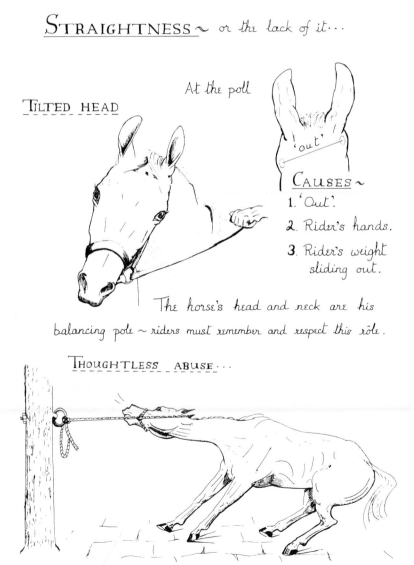

TILTED HEAD

At the poll

'out'

CAUSES ∼
1. 'Out'.
2. Rider's hands.
3. Rider's weight sliding out.

The horse's head and neck are his balancing pole ∼ riders must remember and respect this rôle.

THOUGHTLESS ABUSE ···

should try to develop a feel for these as well as for the regular timing of their horse's hind feet as they are set down and lifted off the ground, so that later they may be able to influence the horse to move his hindlegs with a better activity which passes through his back and is felt through the rider's rein aids and the whole of his seat.

Horses may fail to be straight in different parts of their bodies – they may have been born that way or have suffered an injury during training or while out at grass or even in the stable. Any crookedness, even if only of a very slight degree, will affect the whole of the horse's form.

A true horseman develops an eye which picks up the slightest trace of crookedness as well as those reflecting the horse's well-being or ill-health. Students must be encouraged to look more closely at horses and to become more aware of what they are seeing – nearly every horse displays his own little case history if only we know how to look.

The following provide a few examples of the clues and detection that the horseman's eye can make.

• The horse may be dead in his mouth, a puller, or one who crosses his jaw. Most probably he will be found to have a wolf tooth or two, and the cure will lie in its removal, not in strapping his jaws together with a grakle noseband. There is a possibility that the hands or any part or the whole of the rider's seat, at the other end of the reins may be at fault.

• The horse may not be straight in his poll, he may tilt his head when he is ridden due to soreness in that area. Closer investigation may reveal that the skull, atlas and axis bones are not truly aligned. A common cause of this misalignment is the practice of tying up a horse to an immovable object with a stout rope attached to one side of the headcollar or halter. This condition will require skilled treatment.

• The horse's spine is particularly vulnerable to injury as even minor disturbances can cause misalignments in the vertebral column which may affect the *shoulders* and the *hips*, or these may be put out independently. Even the simple and natural feat of rolling can cause these displacements any of which can become chronic if they are allowed to remain out of alignment.

SUPPLENESS

This term is not always correctly understood. Often it is referred to hopefully as something which will "happen later", or it is confused with a looseness which is altogether too loose or with a bend which is altogether too bent! The suppleness which is a required quality in every sort of riding horse, must be elastic, pliant, strong and resilient resulting from correctly developed muscles. To be supple a horse needs to be fit and in good condition; a thin horse lacks the muscle tone and strength to move his skeletal frame under his rider with good strides at all gaits – he will have to tense himself and conjure up forced, false energy and then he cannot be supple. Conversely the movement of a horse who is fat but not fit will be impeded by the stodgy rolls of fat on his ribs and his hind-

SUPPLENESS ~ longitudinal (lengthways).

In the early days...

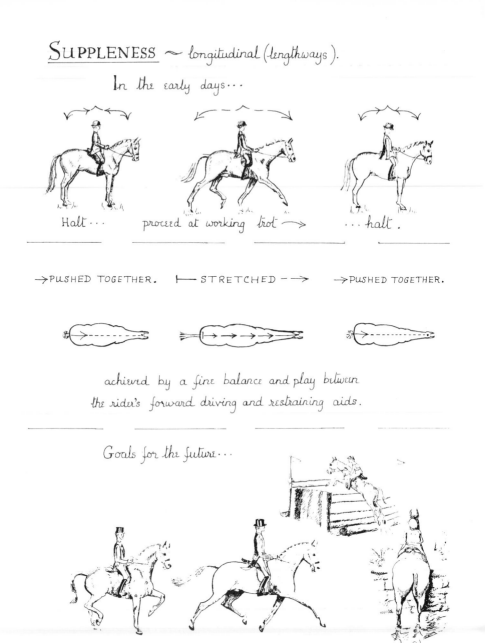

Halt...   proceed at working trot →   ...halt.

→PUSHED TOGETHER.   ├── STRETCHED ─→   →PUSHED TOGETHER.

achieved by a fine balance and play between
the rider's forward driving and restraining aids.

Goals for the future...

quarters. Fit condition, straightness, balance, impulsion and suppleness must all be present in full measure to ensure a good performance and a long, useful, healthy life. The horse's joints and muscles, his mind and his footwork must all co-ordinate with balance, elasticity and a confidence which precludes constraint. If ever excess tension is present the horse cannot be truly supple. Unwanted constraint will show in his eyes, his ears and probably his tail, as well as in his general demeanour and movement.

SUPPLENESS ~ lateral (sideways).

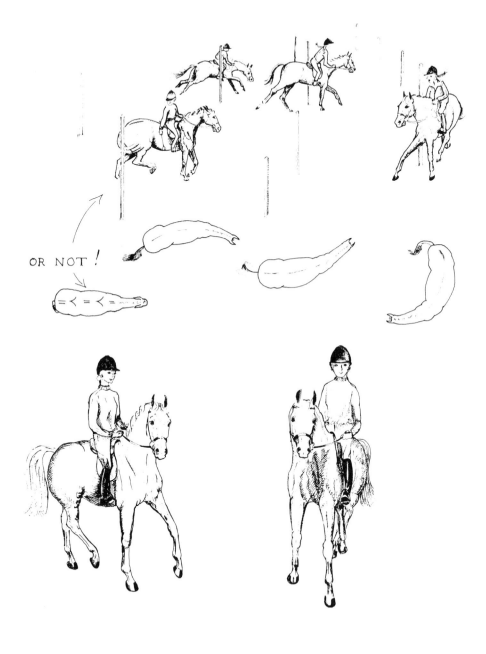

OR NOT !

As the demands become greater, so the horse should become more supple as a direct result of correct, logical and patient training.

The whole of the horse's musculature will be developed by correct training, his strength must be combined with suppleness if he is to become a top-class riding horse, so that he may make the fullest use of his whole body. His musculature must be full of a vibrant elasticity which extends to all his joints and enables him to co-ordinate his body and limbs to perfection and thus to move over the ground with powerful, free and light-footed, yet secure, strides.

To a large extent, suppleness of the horse's body depends upon the calm and contentment in his mind. The more tense he is, the more flat-footed and heavy his steps will be. General Viebig pointed this out to me during one of his courses for British dressage riders held at Talland for the British Horse Society. Before re-entering the indoor school after the lunch break he said, "Wait a minute and listen."

Then I heard it: "Thud, thud, thud; bang, bang, bang . . ." the heavy, trotting feet were accompanied by equally heavy equine breathing.

"And that, you will see", said General Viebig, "is the smallest, most lightly-built horse on the course."

We opened the door to find that his guess had been absolutely correct: the animal in question was an elegant show hack! That listening lesson has remained in my mental instructor's notebook as an example of the detrimental effect of overdriving, using unnecessarily forceful aids, so typical of an ambitious rider trying too hard.

The human athlete who is capable of working out his own training programme with a sensible increase of effort-demand can and often does cause himself to suffer serious injuries. One tiny error in the timing mechanism of his co-ordination can cause damage to muscles, tendons, ligaments or cartilages – such mistiming may even shatter a bone. The horse has the same problems, only greater. He is a much larger animal, usually his scale of intelligence is not so high. If the rider is over-forceful, using strong forward-driving aids which are, at the same time, opposed by hard restraining aids (pulling hands), then he creates too much impulsion or energy within the horse. As he is filled with this excess tension the horse's joints lose much of their elasticity, co-ordination is impeded requiring more mental effort, while his steps become heavier and heavier all due to the lack of suppleness. The purity of his horse's gaits, his straightness and his suppleness must be nurtured, encouraged and developed by the rider. Force by means of gadgetry or hard riding will annihilate good form and will never develop it.

The horse should be supple longitudinally, that is through correct schooling he will be able to lengthen and shorten his frame and his steps. He should also be supple laterally, that is be able to bend his whole body to match exactly the curved track he is following. This lateral bend should be equally easy for him to the left or the right, and later, he should show a more marked suppleness when it is joined with collection in the more advanced lateral movements.

Impulsion is the extra energy required by the horse in order to carry his rider efficiently, with ease, pride and grace. This extra energy may be created in the horse by the trained use of the rider's mental and physical forward-driving aids combined with tactful restraints.

To create impulsion the rider uses his thought aids as well as his posture and weight, carefully and exactly co-ordinating with every bone, muscle and sinew in his body to stimulate the horse's mind, body and movement with a powerful yet calm forward urge. The power is produced by muscular action which uses the weight of the mass of the horse's body, combined with a highly efficient leverage system of bones and joints to give carrying and propelling strength particularly to the horse's hind-quarters.

A young horse cannot be expected to exhibit the same amount or degree of impulsion as can his more mature, well-trained counterpart. At first the young horse will have to learn to move forward over the ground freely while he develops a new balance and a stronger musculature. True, his rider will use his forward-driving aids to achieve this desirable state of affairs, but he must keep his influences very simple, as for a child at nursery school. He will ask the young horse to go forward, to change direction in large and easy curves and to halt, mainly with his thought and seat aids (his whole "position"), but with very little use of his rein aids. Impulsion cannot yet be created for it cannot be contained – restraining aids have not been taught in the curriculum other than as an occasional use for basic control!

When, after many months of patient and systematic training, the horse has developed sufficiently mentally and physically and the three basic gaits have been established into a good working form, then the rider may add a more positive impulsion to his horse's work.

Impulsion will add power, spring, agility and lightness to the horse's movement and carriage, and his gaits will become more expressive, active and cadenced. Due to the impulsion emanating from his hindquarters, the whole of the horse's body will appear balanced, athletic, full of life, spirit and confident strength. Without impulsion there can be no true collection.

Two common misconceptions

(i)   Excess tension must never be confused with impulsion. Although there must be a certain tension in the horse – for without any tension or muscle tone the horse would fall flat on his face having been overcome by his own weight and the force of gravity – there should never be one iota of excess tension. A tense horse will be subject to nervous and muscular contractions and the consequent stiffness will stifle the flow of impulsion through the horse. Excess tension is the root cause of many faults in the horse's form; for example, the horse may be in a bad shape – he may not be well, his carriage and musculature may be developing incorrectly. He

Impulsive Misconceptions!

"the horse must be totally relaxed..."

Without any tension the horse would fall flat on his face.

"activity..." ①

Rider 'stoking up' an excess amount of tension ~
constraint eliminates impulsion.

may appear to be stiff in the lower jaw, poll, back, ribs or in his hindlegs, stiff-legged from the croup down to his feet. His action, under the rider, will be impaired, he will take short, awkward and irregular steps. He may show one or several of the many resistances to, or evasions of, his rider's wishes. All these problems may be caused by an over-zealous or inconsiderate rider who has "stoked up" too much nervous energy in his horse instead of seeking for the logical growth of an appropriate and reasonable degree of impulsion.

Rider substituting speed for impulsion.

However, impulsion
will develop with
correct training...
it will grow...

as the horse gains confidence and strength and can readjust his balance.

(ii) Speed must not be substituted for impulsion in the rider's understanding. If the tempo or speed of the rhythm of the gait in which the horse is working is set too fast, it will upset that horse's balance and co-ordination.

Every horse has his own gait programmes which are "set" in his head. Each gait has a limited range within which the rate of footfall is convenient and comfortable for that horse. If he is hustled out of his natural rhythm the horse can no longer remain unconstrained and supple. Speed

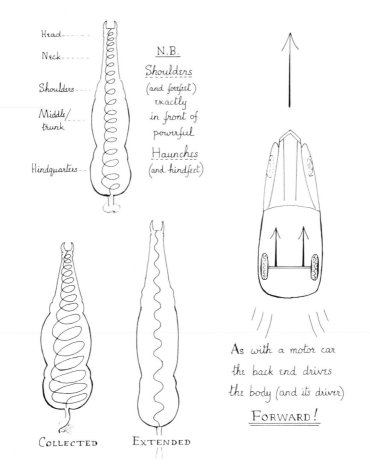

Head ------
Neck ------
Shoulders ----
Middle/ trunk ------
Hindquarters --

N.B.
Shoulders
(and forefeet)
exactly
in front of
powerful
Haunches
(and hindfeet)

COLLECTED   EXTENDED

As with a motor car
the back end drives
the body (and its driver)
FORWARD!

obliterates the desired impulsion by unnecessary and wasteful effort; the horse who is forced to hurry will run along, fast becoming a "leg-mover", for his rider does not allow him the time to work through his whole body and to move confidently and freely forward with good, regular, ground-covering strides.

Students must be encouraged to think of and for impulsion and good form as a natural course of events as well as a basic requirement during all their hours of riding whether they are in a lesson, out hacking, hunting or competing and they must inspire the same quest within their pupils.

IMPULSION

This is the extra energy needed by the horse in order to achieve a good form whenever he carries a rider. This energy is created by the rider who transmits it to his horse by means of a thoughtfully measured interplay between his forward-driving and his restraining aids. The seat of impulsion is in the horse's hindquarters which are mechanically strong enough to push the combined weight of horse and rider forward – or forwards and upwards as the gaits develop cadence or extra expression and brilliance, or when the horse jumps a fence.

As the motor car's energy is measured in horse-power it can provide a useful simile when explaining impulsion. A horse who is crooked or stiff can be compared with a car which has a flat tyre, damp plugs, a worn gasket and several faults in its electrical system – it will not start or if it does it won't go forward very well! A straight, supple horse will compare with a well-tuned Bentley, Metro or Rolls Royce – depending on its make and shape!

Only if the horse works *straight* forward through the whole of his supple body will he be able to use his energy or power to the maximum effect – and with the minimum of effort on his (and his rider's) part. Then his mental state will become calm, confident and happy and the strain to his physique will never exceed that which is logical, fair and humane.

SUBMISSION

"To yield one's person to the power of another; to acquiesce to the authority of another." In equestrian terms, submission does not imply that the horse is forced into a cowed, servile state – far from it. He retains his dignity and his confidence grows as he becomes more obedient. Riders have a responsibility to enlarge their horses' trust – they must never abuse it. Horses will only produce their best performance if they love their rider as well as the work he gives them to do.

Submission means that whenever he is working the horse responds obediently to his rider's wishes; he allows his mind and his body to be guided by his rider, submitting his will as well as his muscular resources. He shows an obvious enjoyment in working for his rider and a pride in carrying him well. His obedience is due neither to fear, pain nor forcefulness: he is proud not cowed.

LIGHTNESS

Some riders who prefer the sport to the art of riding, that is, hunting and polo rather than dressage to an advanced standard, look a little confused when a dressage rider talks of lightness as a desired quality in a well-trained horse.

"I thought a horse should have a steady contact – almost leaning on the bit, to get good marks in a dressage test – surely that is what is meant by the horse being *on the bit*", is a typical comment from a sporting type!

I remember being invited to give a commentary to the Riding Clubs at an open day at one of our leading showing establishments. After giving a most polished performance on two beautiful horses of championship standard the lady rider who owned the yard, halted, dropped the reins, looked me straight in the eye and said, "One thing I would *never* do with my horses is – dressage!"

177

"But", I spluttered, "that is just what you *have* been doing, quite superbly for three-quarters of an hour ... and I've been telling the members just that!"

It was then her turn to look puzzled. "But my horses are not on their forehands, leaning on my hands – I like them to be light and to have presence."

"Exactly so", I said, after which we had a lively and enlightening discussion and remain great friends to this day.

The goals for a well-trained horse of any discipline or sport are very similar, and for best, long-term results, classical methods which combine science and feel are the best for all horses. Of all the criteria by which a horse's training may be judged perhaps "lightness" is the one which most lifts riding to an art form.

General L'Hotte, of the French school, defined lightness as:

The bringing into action by the rider and the use by the horse of those muscles alone which are necessary for the intended movement. The action of any other muscle creates a resistance and thus detracts from the lightness. The better schooled the horse and the more skilful the rider, the more perfect is the lightness.

This little definition should be committed to memory and passed on to pupils as they become sufficiently educated and experienced to understand its meaning and to put it into practice.

Lightness should affect the whole of the horse. It is in no way connected with inconsistency or superficiality. The rider uses his skill and tact, his physical and mental weight and power to ask his horse to move his body in perfect balance, strength and poise so that all his movements are secure but light – so that he uses the ground more as a springboard and less as a landing platform along which to plod or run with heavy or quick insecure steps.

The degree and quality of a horse's lightness can be judged not only by his footsteps but also by his mouth, for that is at the bottom end of his lower jaw. It is the suppleness at the top end of the lower jaw which reveals the horse's lightness to his rider's aids.

The German manual says that, "the horse should chew the bit," the F.E.I. dressage rules ask that he should "quietly chew the bit". The French require, "a murmuring" or, to quote L'Hotte again, "the horse must be neither silent nor over-talkative."

If the submission of the lower jaw is a measure of the horse's lightness, a well-trained horse should not require a drop or crossed noseband. All gadgets are a sure sign of the rider's endeavours to conceal or to overcome resistances by false means. Tight nosebands have many more disastrous effects than their users realise – or they would not have to be endured by so many of today's horses, especially at competitive events. If the horse's mouth is clamped shut, it is true that the judge cannot see the horse open his mouth or roll up his tongue. His resistance may be concealed to novice eyes, but an experienced judge will see and be considerably more worried by the greater effect of such repressed resistances which are then evident in the horse's form (the horse may be constrained and lack activity in his hindquarters). The horse should be able to move his lower jaw, calmly and softly as he responds lightly to his rider's influences, showing that he is using his whole body, willingly, exactly as his rider wishes. The rider's aids should be matchingly light, so slight as to be virtually invisible.

THE STIFF SIDE

This problem, a major one, is common and is rarely appreciated or understood. Many so-called "problem horses" will display resistances or evasions which are in reality subsidiaries of the root cause, their one-sidedness. "The most difficult goal to achieve in equitation is that of keeping the horse straight."

Most horses are somewhat one-sided, just as human beings are left or right-handed. It is a natural phenomenon. There are many different theories proffered concerning the likely cause of one-sidedness, each one propounded with real authority. Briefly, the most usual reasons given are:

• The horse's brain dictates the left or right-handedness as does the human brain.
• The "curve" is decided by the way the foal lies in the mare's womb.
• The imbalance is caused by the horse's anatomy in that, for example, the diaphragm, which is one of the strongest muscles in the horse's body, is fastened further back on the left side.
• The horse is led and handled much more frequently on the left than the right side. Thus he is more practised at bending to the left.

These are four main reasons, all of which must be contributory factors, but I have known candidates and pupils who have found that the same horse is stiff to the left for one and yet stiff to the right for the other. Maybe it just could happen sometimes that the rider is not exactly as strong or sensitive on both sides. ...?

It is best in the early stages to concentrate on feeling that the horse is balanced and is working equally on both sides of his body. Any crooked-ness, such as the inner hindleg travelling along a track which is slightly inside the track made by the forefoot on the same side, should be felt and recognised as a fault by the rider.

A horse is crooked when one of his shoulders, together with the foreleg under it, is slightly out of alignment to the outside while the diagonally opposite hindleg is carried to the inside. Unless the horse is absolutely straight he cannot work truly through the whole of his body. A crooked horse resembles a bicycle which can only free-wheel due to its chain having slipped off the driving wheel. While crookedness exists, the horse cannot work in the required good form; the rider must set to work thoughtfully to rectify the error.

First the rider must check and correct his own position; he must make certain that his hips and his seat bones are correctly placed so that his weight is well distributed for the horse, the gait and the direction. Then he must ride the horse forward energetically with his forward-driving aids – particularly with both his lower legs – and he must straighten out the horse by moving his shoulders and forelegs in front of the erring hindleg. In this way the rider can ensure that each one of the horse's legs and both sides of his body take fair and equal shares in carrying and propelling the bulky mass of body weight of himself and his horse.

How to discover the stiff side

This was explained to me originally by a very dedicated but garrulous Pony Club instructor. It sounded so frighteningly scientific and complicated that I shied right off it and ignored it for the next few years. I continued to rely on an inborn feel for straightness and hoped that neither my B nor my A test examiners would mention the subject – fortunately they did not!

It was during the first civilian instructors' course at St. George's that Colonel and Mrs. V. D. S. Williams gave us a lecture demonstration on "straightening the horse" which was followed a few days later by a repetition of the same principles differently phrased by Mr. Schmidt Jensen in his practical session on "Training the Young Horse". These three experts made the whole subject so simple. Instructors please note!

PRELIMINARIES

Before the rider can begin to analyse which is the stiff or soft side of the horse he must have a quick look at the horse from the ground before he mounts. He must check that the horse stands level and square from in front and from behind and that he does not appear to have any physical defects which would affect his movement. He must check that the saddle and bridle fit well and that the horse has no wolf teeth or any mouth injury which would make the bit unacceptable.

Having assured himself that all is well the rider should mount and ride the horse for five to ten minutes while they get acquainted with each other and limber up ready for the task which lies ahead.

THE ANALYSIS

It is important that the first "enquiry" takes place at the walk when the rider and the horse are calm, the steps are relatively slow and the horse has to use all the muscles in his body in order to move his legs forward one after the other, while the rider has time to feel and analyse the horse's movement and his reactions to any request the rider may make. The rider must select a neutral work area which has no significant pulls for home or company.

The rider should ask the horse to walk forward in as good a form as possible, on a loose rein. When this has been achieved, the rider should take up the left rein, carefully and smoothly until he establishes a soft

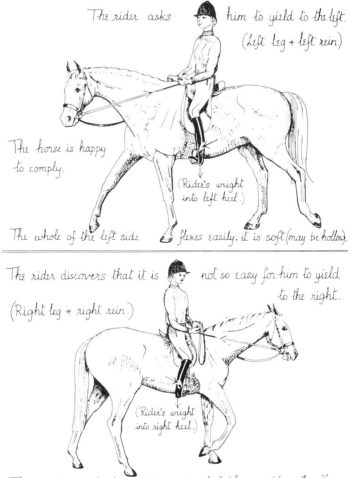

The rider asks him to yield to the left.
(Left leg + left rein)

The horse is happy to comply.

(Rider's weight into left heel.)

The whole of the left side flexes easily; it is soft (may be hollow).

The rider discovers that it is not so easy for him to yield to the right.

(Right leg + right rein.)

(Rider's weight into right heel.)

The muscles on this horse's left side do not stretch as readily as they flex.

contact with the left side of the horse's mouth; at the same time he must retain the horse's form, particularly with his lower legs. Usually the horse's reaction will be to show interest and compliance and to offer no resistance, but with a supple poll and jaw to answer the rider's request by walking on a track which curves away to the left. So far so good. The rider then eases the left rein, walks straight forward with the horse in a good form, on a loose rein before he then repeats the simple analysing procedure with the right rein. The horse may comply with the request by the right rein in the identical manner he gave to the left rein, or he may offer resistance to a lesser or greater degree.

If the horse shows any resistance the rider must not react to it but should record the finding in his memory, urge the horse forward at a lively trot, and after a suitable interval he should repeat the analysing procedure after which the original judgement may or may not be confirmed.

As the greater proportion of stiff horses are stiff to the right that will be taken as the example here.

Besides the feel which the horse gives the rider there are another two easily discernible clues. When the horse gives a left, lateral flexion, that is his head is turned to the left with his ears at a level height and a supple poll, the parotid glands protrude in a small ridge or swelling on the upper, rear edge of the lower jaw bone (the glands are squeezed out by the closing of the angle of the head on the neck). No glands will show on the right side when the horse gives a lateral flexion to the left. At the same time the top of the horse's crest gives and falls slightly to the left. If, when the same horse is asked for a right lateral flexion the rider's request meets with resistance, the horse will not willingly turn his head to the right, there is no give in the poll or the lower jaw and no sign of any protrusion of the parotid glands on the right side while the top of the crest remains upright, the horse is said to be stiff to the right.

At this juncture many riders become aggressive and unjust, attributing a cunning "malice aforethought" to the horse for his failure to give as generously to the right as he does to the left. Horses who have been reprimanded for daring to resist or who have been forced into what the rider considers to be a desirable head carriage, will react immediately with stronger resistance. Too often ignorance makes the circle increasingly vicious, leading to a contest in one-up-manship between horse and rider which continues until the horse finds himself, deplorably, having to carry both himself and his unpleasant rider while his head is strapped down by a gadget, the purpose of which is supposedly to help him use his back muscles.

The reader has only to try running round the garden with his hands tied behind his back to understand that putting the horse's balancing pole (his head and neck) out of action does not assist his musculature in any way; in fact, it hinders its use and its true development. If such gadgetry is persisted with the horse may be crippled and his muscles, gaits and performance ruined permanently.

The rider must understand the reason for the horse being soft on the left side and stiff to the right. It is, at that time, his natural way of going. Many of the muscles on the left side of the horse are less elastic than those on the right side, his resistance is physical, he is not being cleverly and deliberately wilful. Little by little his musculature must be evened up by a gradual process of thoughtfully applied physical education which is mentally easy and enjoyable as well as muscle developing and generally fittening.

At all costs, the rider must not imagine he can soften up the horse's stiff side by pulling the horse's head into "a desirable position" or by forcibly making the muscles of the left side longer through working the horse almost continually to the right.

Instead the rider should consider the horse very carefully; unless his form is good longitudinally, his top and lower lines being "sprung" yet pliant from the latent power contained within the muscles, the horse cannot be assessed nor can he be straightened.

If the horse has a stiffer side then he should always be worked on the soft side first, in this instance to the left, so that he can warm up comfortably. He should then be worked for a slighly longer period to the right, before being given a short rest and reward before he is taken to the left and then to the right again.

If the horse is markedly softer on the left side, the rider will find that he will be evasive in his acceptance of the left rein. The rider must be aware of the need to give the horse a soft but consistent contact with the left rein to the left side of his mouth, so that his forward-driving aids always work the whole horse forward on to the left rein regardless of which direction he is taking. When the horse is straight, then of course, the rider will ride in what is normally a correct way; that is, working the horse forward on to the outside rein.

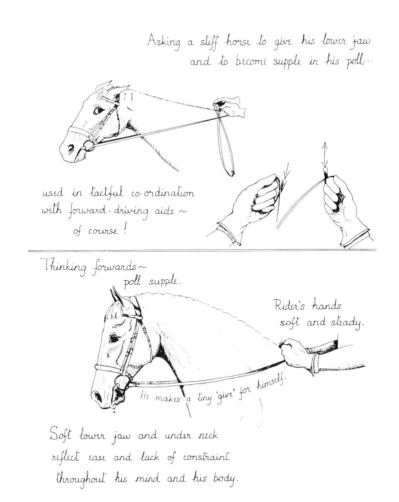

Asking a stiff horse to give his lower jaw
and to become supple in his poll...

used in tactful co-ordination
with forward-driving aids ~
of course!

Thinking forwards ~
poll supple.

Rider's hands
soft and steady.

He makes a tiny 'give' for himself.

Soft lower jaw and under neck
reflect ease and lack of constraint
throughout his mind and his body.

If, due to bad riding or training originally, the horse resists the rider's request that he should go freely forward in a reasonably good form with the top ligament and muscles of his neck stretched in order that his back muscles may be called into play, the rider should take immediate action to remedy this serious fault. The cure is relatively simple – the action must be positive.

After the rider has established a contact with the left rein he should carefully take up the right rein, keeping his hands fairly low near the horse's withers. Whilst maintaining his forward-driving aids with tact and determination the rider should begin to ask the horse to "give" his lower jaw and to become supple in his poll. It is very important that the rider continue to push the horse forward and that he does not give way with his rein aids in the slightest degree until the horse gives at the poll, whereupon he releases the pressure for himself and should be warmly rewarded with voice and a pat for doing so. The reins should not be lengthened or loosened until the horse fully understands that the rider is absolutely delighted with him when he gives in his poll and lower jaw and that he can trust the rider's hands to give him a contact which is both reasonable and comfortable.

While the rider is insisting on the horse's compliance he must be extremely careful that his posture is good, so that his seat is firm yet supple and provides a stable support to his unflinching rein aids. He must retain the forward influence and must neither raise his hands nor pull backwards.

Even horses which have become "hardened sinners" due to months or even years of bad riding will soon come to hand from this simple method. As soon as the horse has understood that he must accept the bit and give himself up to his rider's aids then the progressive gymnastic exercises will soon establish a good form and will erase the bad habits of resistance. Work over ground poles, cavalletti and small fences, turns on the forehand, circles, serpentines and leg-yielding are all excellent for this purpose – providing that they are well ridden.

In conclusion, we can list four main points:

(i) Analyse – and discover the stiff side remembering that the horse just may be straight!

(ii) Correct your own position – the whole of your seat must be perfectly balanced and poised to suit both you and your horse – with positive "vibes" but no constraint – before you can begin to correct your horse.

(iii) Ride the horse *forward* into a good form, "forward, calm and straight". Aim to get him to stride over the ground with springy steps as if he is wearing the giant's famous seven-league boots! But a *warning note*! The rider's desire for forward impulsion must never cause him to push his horse out of his natural rhythm. The rider must be very careful on this score for if the horse is pushed forward too fast then his balance and his confidence will be upset and he will scuttle frenziedly over the ground moving his feet as quickly as possible, his legs going up and down like the needle of a sewing machine with his back held rigid. Thus are "leg movers" made, for the movement cannot go through the whole of the horse's body softly and with impressive ease.

(iv) Use your head as well as your body to encourage your horse to enjoy carrying you and working forward in a good form on the bit. Make full use of your knowledge of the horse's natural instincts, and of gymnastic exercises, to encourage him to develop an equal suppleness and musculature on both sides of his body and to work forward on to the bit, both sides of his mouth offering an equal acceptance of the rider's rein aids.

MOUTHING, BRIDLING, FLEXIONS

"Mouthing", "bridling" and "flexions" are all terms of the English horse world which originate from bygone days but which are still used to describe the horse's reactions to the bit and the rider's rein aids.

These expressions can serve a useful purpose providing that they are understood and used correctly.

"Mouthing" was regarded as a stage of training when the young horse was first bridled and learned to accept the presence of a bit in his mouth. This bit was usually a snaffle equipped with smooth, hinged "droplets" of metal which hung down on the horse's tongue from the centre of the bit with the idea of giving him something to play with in his mouth, to keep it moist with saliva and to encourage him to keep his tongue under the bit. In this way he learned to move his lower jaw softly and freely and even to stretch up a little at the poll. The main disadvantage lay in the fact that the mouthing bit was often left in the horse's mouth for too long as he stood motionless or nearly so in the stable, or it was abused by adding a "dumb jockey" – a wooden contraption to which was attached two or more reins and a crupper, under the middle of which was the horse! His head and tail were raised up but his back was dropped for there were no rider's legs to suggest otherwise. Sometimes, hot and often tired young horses were left strapped up for several hours, to cool down after being lunged, in the vain hope that they would soon change into the shape of an elegant show horse, bridling or flexing and arching the neck.

"Bridling" and "flexions" came to the fore again later in the horse's training programme. When he had become balanced under the rider and reasonably fit after the first two to four months of training, the snaffle bridle would be exchanged for a full or double bridle and what was then considered to be his "proper education" would begin. In those days the concept of a double bridle was that the snaffle or bridoon would raise the horse's head while the curb bit would make him bridle or flex. The double bridle was referred to as a full or complete bridle while the varying degrees of foolishness were summed up by a cavalryman as: "There's a fool, a bloody fool and a fool who rides in a snaffle"!

Although correctly and logically a horse may be said to be flexed when the whole length of his axial skeleton bends laterally or longitudinally to conform with the track being followed, the school movement being performed or the bascule or collection required, the term flexion was then adopted to refer almost exclusively to a bending or yielding in the area of the horse's poll.

The reason for this restricted labelling is both logical and historical. In practice, any stiffness in the horse's poll will be reflected by a similar state

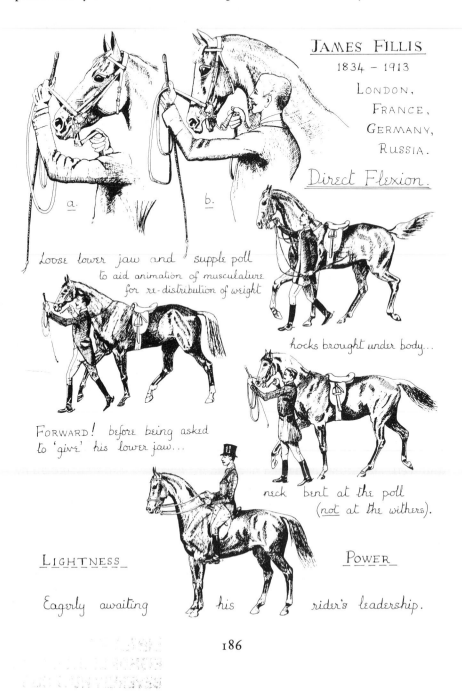

JAMES FILLIS
1834 – 1913
LONDON,
FRANCE,
GERMANY,
RUSSIA.

Direct Flexion.

Loose lower jaw and supple poll
to aid animation of musculature
for re-distribution of weight

hocks brought under body...

FORWARD! before being asked
to 'give' his lower jaw...

neck bent at the poll
(not at the withers).

LIGHTNESS   POWER

Eagerly awaiting   his   rider's leadership.

186

in his back and limbs; unless a horse is supple and can flex the joints of his poll he cannot be supple in his back and move his legs freely and actively. Past masters of equitation discovered this key to horsemanship and through the ages they devised different means to achieve this desirable flexibility at the poll. Some invented bits of increasing severity while others who were more humane and thoughtful first introduced the idea to the horse, standing by his head at the halt and on the move before they taught their horses "flexions" from the saddle. Baucher and Fillis were the two European masters who put great emphasis on flexions in their teaching and writings of the 19th century.

That flexions were accorded extra emphasis was probably due to the competitive yen for elegance. Since the days of the Stuart kings of the 17th century, artists have depicted royalty, field marshals, lords, ladies and gentlemen mounted on steeds with remarkable flexions at the poll; lovely horses of varying types from Spanish to Arab and thoroughbred, spirited, quality horses yet always under willing and absolute control – flexing most admirably at the poll and in almost every other joint besides.

Thus were generations of horsemen trained. Their eyes learned to look for a proud bearing in riding horses as well as in those who were driven; the former were ridden in double bridles with long-cheeked curb bits and the latter were strapped up with bearing-reins. It was considered essential that they should all "bridle", a national term used to describe a horse who played with his bit with a relaxed lower jaw, a supple poll and a high, arched neck.

In many ways these old-fashioned terms are closely related to the more modern requirement that a well-trained horse should be "on the bit". Old and modern terms share the same problem in that they were and are often misconstrued.

Due to bad riding such as insufficient education, an unsteady seat, heavy hands and insignificant forward-driving aids, desirable qualities too easily turn into bad habits. The horse may become "mouthy" or fussy and inconsistent, he may not trust his rider's hands or accept the bit. Also as a result of poor horsemanship, the horse may become over-bent with a false flexion half-way down his neck. These major faults brought the terms into disrepute with some instructors. However, in all ages there have been fine horsemen who have trained horses thoughtfully, kindly and well, and there have been poor riders who have had to make up for their lack of skill and understanding by substituting gadgetry for artistry.

How is the new horseman to understand all this? Perhaps the following summary will help.

FLEXION

According to the dictionary, flexion means a bending or yielding. The term was applied to horses to imply that they should bend and yield at the top of the neck. If the horse flexes at the poll whilst his head is level and faces straight ahead, that is *a direct flexion*. If the head, when level and straight, is slightly turned at the poll to one side, that is *a lateral flexion* or part of what is known more commonly nowadays as "position left or right". Flexions should never be requested by the rider's hands alone or they will be incorrect and harmful; flexions must be born of an extra lively impulsion when they are almost given by the horse to the rider who receives them gratefully, with a tactful play and harmony of all his aids.

POSITIONING AND BENDING

Before these subjects can be pursued, the rider must have the following golden rules firmly established in his brain, heart and riding:
- Form – it must be as good as possible, both the rider's and the horse's.
- Impulsion – there must be enough of it, additional, before any extra demand.
- Constraint – there should be none in his mind or body.
- Basic gaits – these must be pure, the horse being balanced, supple and physically fit; his steps should be regular and buoyant and as ground-covering as the movement of the moment requires.
- On the bit – the horse must respond willingly to his rider's requests, from his hind heels, through his whole body, to the bit.
- The muzzle end of the front line of the horse's face must always be in front of the vertical.
- His ears should be level.

Providing the rider knows and promises to remember and to apply these main rules, together with all the others which contribute to good riding, he may read on!

POSITION

A horse is said to be positioned to the right when he is in good form, on the aids and his head is turned slightly to the right at the very top of his neck. His nose should be just in front of the vertical and the tips of his ears at a level height.

When a horse is positioned correctly, the base of the neck should remain straight being "set" firmly in front of the first pair of ribs, the withers above and the sternum below. The only bend should be at the poll where the skull, atlas and axis joints "give" with a lateral flexion.

The lower part of the horse's neck remains straight, the crest falls slightly to the inside, to the right, and the rider can just see the horse's right eyelashes and the outer edge of his right nostril.

Any positioning to the left or right is entirely dependent on the rider's tactful emphasis of his forward-driving aids combined with carefully measured guiding and restraining aids, as a result of which the horse gives the required position. The horse must never be forced into an unnatural, false position by over-dominant rein aids – only a very bad rider would ever try to pull a horse into a shape.

The horse can be positioned at the halt or when he is moving. As with most ridden exercises, this work is best carried out on the move, after it has been explained, felt, recognised and understood at the halt.

The aims of positioning a horse

- To advance the rider's equestrian education. He learns to improve his ability to ride the horse straight and also to feel the good effects of a supple poll on the whole of the horse's musculature, particularly on the inside hindleg.
- His aids will be more correct and even less visible as he learns more about the influence the whole of his body can have on his horse's form.
- His riding of turns and circles and school movements will be much improved.
- This will assist the horse to give and to follow the rein smoothly.
- The horse will be loosened and freed from constraint.
- Minor faults in the horse's form may be erased.

EXPLANATION

This work should be felt as it is explained, in order that it may be understood thoroughly from the beginning. The best way to learn it is as a member of a class taught by a good instructor.

For his initial demonstration the instructor should use a mounted assistant and show him, together with the remainder of the class, the three effects the rider should seek and feel during positioning as a result of flexion in the horse's poll. He should call the demonstrator forward to stand on a line approximately 10 metres in front of the rider and sideways to them.

The instructor, standing facing the front of the horse's head, should take hold of the bit with his hands on the bit rings and outer ends of the mouthpiece, one on each side, as if he is testing to see if the bit is high

"and now to the left ~ you can see his left eye lashes and nostril, his crest lean to the left, and feel his body muscles active .....
ready to move his left hind leg forward.

enough in the horse's mouth. He should then move the bit softly and smoothly with his left hand on the right side of the horse's mouth, asking him to make a little give in his lower jaw to the right and in the two joints above, in the poll. As the horse complies and turns his head very slightly to the right, the rider will be able to see the horse's eyelashes and the outer edge of his nostril on the right side of the horse's head; he will see the crest lean over to the right as the ligamentum nuchae slides off the topmost line of the neck, to the inside, and he will feel the action from the bit go right through the whole of the horse to his right hindleg. A skilful instructor will be able thoughtfully to manoeuvre the right hindleg to make a small step forward which will really emphasise this important piece of riding training to all the participants.

The instructor then teaches the class, being particularly careful that all the horses are standing straight and square in front of him.

He tells them to shorten their reins and to urge their horses forward within themselves, on to the aids, so that riders and horses are ready – the former to ask the latter for an almost imperceptible positioning at the poll to the right.

Next the instructor explains how they will achieve this, the teaching being given as a sort of running commentary which the riders put into practice as they listen.

"Your first priority is impulsion!"

"Keep your reins short – but do not increase the pressure – *feel* a soft contact."

"Shift your weight slightly to the right."

"Ask your horse for a tiny give to the right with your right rein – keep your elbows in and turn your right forearm and wrist smoothly until your fingernails are uppermost. At the same time lower your right heel, keep your knees down and back and feel your right leg and hand working together while you guard the outside of the horse and contain the impulsion with your outside aids. Very soft with your rein aids!"

Each rider can then feel the imperceptible muscle movements affecting the whole of the horse's body; he can watch his horse's crest move or fall over to the right and he will know what to feel and look for when he attempts this same work on the move.

Before the class moves off to practise this work, the instructor must remind his pupils that as riders, they must always discipline themselves. "Before the horse can be positioned the rider must shorten his reins, increase his forward-driving aids and shift his weight slightly to the inside." He should then describe the aids to them in more detail.

The aids for positioning

These can be detailed in five points.

(i) *Both legs* add extra impulsion and keep it.

(ii) *The inside leg* at the girth, pushes the horse forward to the *inside rein* which positions the horse to the right at the poll with a light, smooth rein aid, the hand turning with fingernails upwards and the little finger towards the body.

(iii) *The outside leg* immediately behind the girth regulates the horse's form, the impulsion and the straightness in conjunction with the *outside rein* which must give sufficiently to allow the flexion at the poll whilst it also acts in a regulating manner. The outer rein keeps the bit straight in the horse's mouth, makes tiny, tactful adjustments to the height of the horse's head and carriage and, in co-operation with the outside leg, is responsible for the consistency of the horse's form.

(iv) *Both legs* maintain impulsion and keep his hindquarters in line with his forehand.

(v) *Both reins* should maintain a similar contact with the bit and keep the forehand aligned in front of the hindlegs.

The horse's body must remain straight when he is being ridden along straight lines. If the horse is not straight before being positioned he will resist the rider's request for him to flex against the stiff side and he will over-bend himself if he is positioned to the opposite side.

When he is on the move, the horse should be positioned towards the turn for all turns and slightly away from the direction of the movement in leg-yielding. At other times he should be kept straight, unless the rider wishes to work his horse with momentary positioning.

BEND

In equestrian language a bend is both desirable and correct if it affects the whole of the horse from his heels to his nose – and back again. The bend should be identical to the circle or arc of the track along which the horse is moving or, if the horse is performing a school movement, along a straight line in which his body is bent, as in shoulder-in. The bend of his central line should be uniform from poll to tail.

Riders beware! It is vital to remember that before there can be bending there must be *straightness*, *calmness* and *impulsion*!

Advantages of bending work

• To further the rider's education, feel and prowess.
• To improve the horse's form and all its mental and physical component parts.
• To help the horse to carry his rider easily as they negotiate all turns on the move in a supple, balanced manner, without strain.
• To enable him to perform correctly the many school movements which demand "a uniform bend from poll to tail".

Bending the horse to the right

Three aids are used to bend the horse to the right.
(i)   Extra impulsion and short reins!
(ii) The rider shifts his weight slightly to the right and positions his

THE AIDS TO BEND THE HORSE··· RIGHT.

Thought aids ~ plan, think and look in the right direction.
Weight aids ~ shift weight to the right early enough and sufficiently;
use right knee to keep right hip forward and to the right.
Leg aids ~ Outside leg helps to create, maintain and direct impulsion and
(Normally just behind girth) prevents hindlegs from swinging out.
(further forward controls shoulders)

Inside leg for impulsion
and it provides a 'column' around which the horse is asked to bend.
Rein aids ~ Inside rein guides, thumb part leading, free from withers.
Outside rein maintains a soft contact whilst allowing
the muscles on the horse's outer side to stretch.

Glance at his poll to pick up
his brain waves and take them on in
the direction you have planned.

Shoulders turn forehand.
(inner shoulder back)

Hips influence hindlegs
(inner hip forward)

REMEMBER ···
Both legs for impulsion,
to help the horse to keep
his BALANCE and to move
in the best possible FORM.

upper body and his horse to the right. (Left shoulder and right hip forward).

(iii) *Both legs* urge the horse forward and maintain plenty of impulsion. *The inside leg* by the girth asks the inside hindleg to come forward and works in conjunction with the *weight aid* and that of the *inner, leading rein* in asking for a give in the right side of the horse's body. It acts as a supporting column to the horse's bending body. *The outside leg* just behind the girth maintains and contains impulsion, together with the *outside rein*. They also prevent the forehand or the hindquarters from falling out. *The outside leg* also regulates and maintains the bend of the horse's body around the rider's inner leg.

FURTHER DETAILS

The depth of the bending must be governed by the horse's conformation, the standard of his training, the shape of the track on which he is working and the movement being performed.

The main part of the horse's neck should be almost straight, in line with the withers, and the horse's central line should have no more bend in the neck than is shown in the rest of his body.

The rider must avoid bending the horse too much or for too long. When the horse gives the side of his whole body as requested, the rider should not then be greedy and ask for more bending, instead he should reward his horse with a slight easing of the aids.

The work may be varied by straightening out the horse after a short period of bending work and riding him forward actively, or by bending him to the opposite side, all of which can be ridden as a continuous and fluent programme.

However, neither instructors nor riders must be "carried away" by the variations, scope and interest of this work. It must be kept in proportion, remembering that the most important, and yet also the most difficult aim in equitation, is to make the horse *straight* and in a good form, at the same time not forgetting the importance of rewarding rest periods for both partners.

Matters Arising – Advancing Technique to Improve Form

Special cautionary note

This chapter, particularly for the latter part, has described work which should be reserved strictly for trained and experienced riders. The later work should not be attempted practically by any rider until he understands fully the meaning of impulsion and knows how to obtain and contain it with correct influences. He must have the ability, as well as the desire, to increase the impulsion to a suitable degree before he makes any increase in his demand on the horse.

For example, the rider should always increase the impulsion well before he and his horse embark on a period of collected, medium or extended trot, a school movement such as a turn on the spot or half-pass, or before jumping over a fence. To "maintain the impulsion" is not enough – the rider must always ask for sufficient extra impulsion so that he and his horse have it "at the ready" before they begin any work which will require extra effort. "Later is too late": to be fair to the horse, the rider must create more energy before he asks his horse to expend it.

None of this work should be undertaken before the rider can ride a horse at shoulder-in and turns on the haunches to a satisfactory standard. If it is attempted by an inexperienced rider, without skilled tuition and supervision it could damage the horse's training as well as physique. However, an earlier theoretical knowledge will be of great assistance to every dedicated equestrian student's awareness and feel for an ever-improving form in the horses he rides, and is bound to advance his technique.

9 Developing Schoolwork

First, a controversial issue and a conclusion ... then we will begin!

Turns and lateral work

"The rider's shoulders should be parallel with the horse's shoulders and his hips should be parallel with the horse's hips", is a classical equitation directive. "Outside shoulder and inside hip forward", is the main postural aid for all turns, circles and lateral work.

A theoretical critic of some distinction has been objecting strongly for many years with a genuine concern that the equestrian "twist" is damaging to the human frame. He maintains that by instructing pupils to keep their inside hips and outside shoulders forward whenever they ride circles, turns or lateral work, the instructor will inevitably cause chronic damage to their spines; that turning their shoulders and hips oppositely is not only impossible but injurious to the rider's physique and to his general health.

I could not take these complaints seriously when I read the first leaflet three decades ago. I thought it was a joke and returned it to the sender in accordance with his own method – well-covered with my comments in red ink. I explained I had been riding for twenty-five years, using "the twist" and my spine had suffered no injury or deterioration even where I have some vertebrae fused since taking a locked six-bar gate by the roots as a child with the Whaddon Chase hunt.

I have taken my own back to be "vetted" and have explained the methods of using the rider's shoulders, back and hips in order to guide and affect the horse's movement, and have shown the complaint to eminent medical experts, as well as to a newly and highly qualified physiotherapist, all of whom passed my back as "amazingly sound" and were baffled by the critic's objections. "The human spine is built to rotate, it is good for it to do so, such exercise will help to prevent arthritis."

For the fit, active, practical horseman this can present no problems, rather it should be beneficial; ballet dancers, gymnasts, skaters, skiers and most sportsmen use far more strenuous body turns with good not ill effects. Perhaps the critic should learn to dance "the twist". As with all new exercises it should be introduced little by little but he, together with any doubters he has influenced, would soon find the dancing highly beneficial. It is a marvellous exercise for riders improving their fitness, posture, suppleness, co-ordination and senses of rhythm and balance and it whittles down their waistlines as an added bonus! After half an hour of dancing "the twist", riding a turn on the haunches at the walk will seem child's play!

Turns on the spot

These may be executed either on the forehand or on the haunches, depending on which end of the horse is the pivot of the turn. The forelegs are at the centre of the turn on the forehand, with the haunches moving on a larger circle, or a portion of a circle, around them. The hindlegs are at the centre of a turn on the haunches, with the forelegs moving symmetrically around them. Although the inside foreleg or hindleg respectively is the pivot of the turn, its foot should never actually pivot. At no time during a turn on the spot should the horse "miss a beat" in the sequence or rhythm of the gait in which he performs the turn. It is a bad fault if the horse swivels round with one of his feet stuck to the ground. The true sequence, rhythm and tempo of the gait must be maintained before, during and after the turn.

Both turns may be ridden on a small arc rather than precisely on the spot when they are being introduced to pupils or horses: this easier ground-plan will facilitate a feel for impulsion, rhythm and a true sequence of footfall before they are asked to execute a correct turn on the spot, either on the forehand or on the haunches.

Although turns on the forehand have been described fully in Book 1, I feel it would leave the reader with an unfortunate void if they were not included here. To name them but not to include all relevant details will not suffice. Usually it is helpful if an instructor goes over the same ground several times, for each time he will use different words or emphasis which aid the pupil's understanding.

Initially turns on the forehand were included in British dressage tests of novice standard for both Pony Club and adult competitions. These turns remain in tests on the continent and in many other countries. In England turns on the forehand were often poorly executed with the result that the turns themselves were castigated and fell into disrepute. Not only were they removed from British dressage tests but also their use was actually shunned by a number of riders. This negative action was a mistake for really the blame should have been attached to the riders for the inadequacy of their equestrian education. Even a few instructors had not grasped a full understanding of the gymnastic requirements and the true value of these, the first of the turns on the spot.

Turns on the forehand have remained on the list of required movements for British instructor and rider examinations, despite a short bout of opposition and their usefulness is thoroughly appreciated at all levels by all thinking riders.

Both forms of turn on the spot are extremely good exercises for developing the education of the rider and the training of the horse. The turn on the forehand is especially beneficial for novice riders and horses, and as a limbering-up or relaxation exercise for more advanced, over-tense or spoiled horses being re-trained. The turn on the haunches is more difficult, and therefore is not used until the horse is at a more advanced standard when he may be asked fairly to bend the joints of his hindlegs,

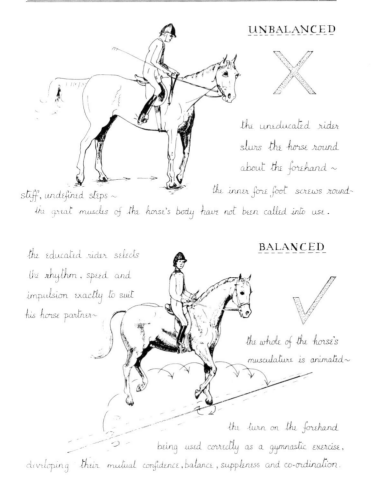

UNBALANCED

X

the uneducated rider
slurs the horse round
about the forehand ~

the inner fore foot screws round~

stiff, undefined steps ~

the great muscles of the horse's body have not been called into use.

BALANCED

✓

the educated rider selects
the rhythm, speed and
impulsion exactly to suit
his horse partner~

the whole of the horse's
musculature is animated~

the turn on the forehand
being used correctly as a gymnastic exercise,

developing their mutual confidence, balance, suppleness and co-ordination.

engage them further and use them to carry a greater proportion of his body weight.

Turns on the forehand

During a turn on the forehand the pivot of the turn is the inner foreleg, the foot of which marks time on the spot. All four feet maintain the true rhythm and sequence of the footfalls of the walk; the outer foreleg moves forward very slightly and the hindlegs move in an arc round the mobile turning-point, or inner foreleg. All the steps should be even, clear and deliberate. When the horse moves his haunches round correctly, the inner hindleg crosses over in front of the outer one; the horse has to raise and slightly arch his back in order to be able to bring the inner hindleg forwards and over. During the turning, the horse's forehand should not

WELL ridden, horse using all his muscles ~ thus improving his FORM.

TURNS ON THE FOREHAND ~

BADLY ridden, too near to the wall, hands pulling, and 'nothing moving.' N.B. Horse's right forefoot 'stuck' in the ditch --- VERY BAD.

be allowed to deviate forwards, sideways (particularly to the outside), or backwards. The inner foot should be picked up from and returned to the same place on the ground, or very near it, during each stride. Whereas the horse may advance a few centimetres, he should never be allowed to think of or move backwards.

The horse must be on the bit with good impulsion during the approach, the preparation, the turn itself and when moving straight forward in the new gait after the turn is completed. As a rule, and in a dressage test, the turn on the forehand is executed with the horse very slightly flexed or positioned in the direction of the turn. A counter-flexion to the outside may be used for corrective purposes or when the horse is ready for collection.

In an indoor school or manège, the rider should always ensure that he only asks for a turn in a suitable place. He should not be near a jump or similar obstruction, and he should never be so near to the wall that it would restrict or influence his horse. If the horse is too close to the wall, he may even be made to move backwards by it to avoid bumping his nose, or as he completes the turn the magnetism of the wall may cause him to push out his outer shoulder and he will not then move off *straight* forward. The turn on the forehand may be ridden from a square halt, or at the walk after a half-halt; the latter is often better for novice riders and horses to achieve the initial fluency of the turn. Horses should always be ridden forward energetically immediately the turn is completed.

Aims and uses of turns on the forehand

• To improve the rider's thought and feel for the horse's form and movement.

• To teach, confirm and test the use, co-ordination and effect of the rider's aids, as he learns to initiate the turn, to maintain a lively forward impulsion and then to control it step-by-step, by means of his forward-driving, sideways-moving and regulating influences.

• By developing the rider's confidence in his ability, his balance and correct posture are further established.

• Due to the simplicity of the movement, the rider will learn to avoid tensing up before, during or as he rides out of the turn which will stand him in good stead for the escalating demands of his riding career. The instructor must constantly watch for any warning signs of over-tension – even one of the rider's thumbs sticking straight out may give the game away!

• To widen the rider's understanding of the full meaning of the horse being on the bit.

• Well executed turns on the forehand give the rider an excellent foundation on which to build more advanced riding, especially in preparing him for lateral work.

• For the rider to feel clearly the arching of the horse's back, enabling the horse to cross his hindlegs over evenly and without effort whilst remaining on the bit. He can also evaluate the composite muscle work and the movement of each leg as the horse moves through his whole being, slowly and deliberately under him.

• The turn on the forehand is like a master key in the training of the horse, it opens innumerable doors so easily.

• It broadens the young horse's understanding of and then his obedience to the rider's aids, clearly yet subtly co-operating together.

• It teaches the horse to respond to his rider's sideways-moving aids.

• It is one of the finest loosening exercises which the rider may use to limber up his horse, to supple him and to release excess tension – it is the simplest way of removing constraint.

- It improves the horse's form and the elasticity of his gaits by proving a first-class physical training or gymnastic exercise. The horse has to stretch and contract all the relevant muscles in his body, to lift his middle slightly and round his back in order that he may cross his inside hindleg over in front of the outside one, evenly and effortlessly whilst remaining on the bit. This improves the horse's top-line as well as the quality of the gait which is ridden immediately after the turning is completed.
- It prepares the horse for lateral work, the first step of which will be leg-yielding.
- If any horse resists his rider's demand for the rein-back, a portion of a turn on the forehand will work like a tin of 3-in-1 lubricating oil; it will ease his mind, muscles and joints and enable him to move backwards willingly with good, clear, easy steps, entirely without constraint.
- From the practical viewpoint the turn on the forehand is often useful even in such mundane exercises as opening and shutting gates.

The aids to turn on the forehand to the right

(a) The rider must first make a plan. He should choose a sensibly convenient place where he may ride a turn without interruption or risk of disturbing other riders. The spot chosen must be sufficiently far ahead to give him time to make correct preparations.

(b) As the rider approaches the selected spot he prepares by:

    (i) Using his forward-driving aids to increase the impulsion as necessary to make the turn in a good form.

    (ii) Thinking and co-ordinating for a turn on the forehand to the right.

    (iii) Making a half or full halt. (Correcting his own position and the horse's balance and form).

    (iv) He shifts his weight slightly inwards to make it easy for the horse to turn.

(c) He then rides a turn on the forehand to the right, smoothly and evenly, looking at, thinking and feeling for his horse as well as looking ahead as he turns.

(d) The horse should be kept as straight as possible, between the rider's aids as he moves his hindquarters over to the left; he may have a very slight bend at the poll to the right. The turn is executed mainly from the sideways-moving influence of the rider's inside leg supported when necessary by the inside rein and regulated by the outside leg and rein.

Using the aids

PREPARE

The rider animates the whole of the horse's musculature with his forward-driving aids whilst carefully containing the impulsion with tactful restraint. He sits vertically upright with a soft and supple ease as he calls upon the horse's muscles to lift and move his hooves forward and over. The rider should not ask the horse to move his feet until the whole of the horse's body feels vibrant and ready under the rider's seat.

TURN ON THE FOREHAND ~ TO THE RIGHT.

The rider thinks & uses both legs, to prepare his brain and his muscles. *Both legs for impulsion!*
Right leg asks horse to soften his right side and to move his hind legs forward & to the *left.*

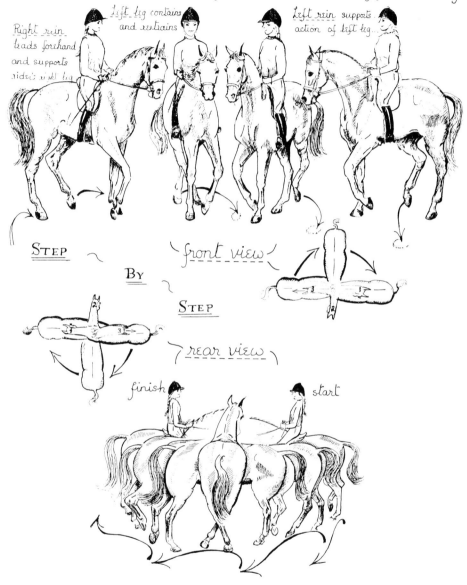

Left leg contains and restrains

Left rein supports action of left leg

Right rein leads forehand and supports rider's right leg

STEP

front view

BY

STEP

rear view

finish   start

THE RIDER'S WEIGHT

Is shifted imperceptibly to the right with the inner hip and seat bone forward to invite the horse to commence the turn with his right hindleg and to facilitate its crossing over in front of the left hindleg during each stride of the turn.

THE RIDER'S INSIDE LEG

The right leg in this instance is the governing aid. It is applied just behind the girth to move the hindquarters over, or on the girth to maintain the impulsion, as is required to maintain the horse's form as he carries out the movement.

THE RIDER'S OUTSIDE LEG

The left leg regulates the movement, ensuring that the turn is made step-by-step, and that the sideways movement is arrested when the turn is completed. The rider uses his outside leg at the girth to maintain the horse's balance and form or just behind the girth to control the hindquarters, or forward on the girth if he wishes to control the horse's shoulders, and in order to maintain impulsion.

THE RIDER'S INSIDE REIN

The right rein indicates the turn, asks for a very slight flexion to the right and leads the horse in the direction of the movement; it also supports the action of the right leg if necessary. To apply the inside rein for these purposes the rider should turn his hand at the wrist, softly and smoothly, to turn the fingernails uppermost (thumb leading the way).

THE RIDER'S OUTSIDE REIN

The left rein regulates the flexion and the movement, and safeguards the straightness of the horse; it works softly towards and together with the left hip.

BOTH LEGS

The rider's legs are responsible for maintaining increased impulsion, keeping the horse on the bit so that the movement passes through and involves the whole horse, ensuring that he neither thinks nor moves backwards.

BOTH REINS

Have a slightly restraining effect to prevent the horse from stepping forwards. The left rein supports the left leg and the right rein supports the right leg. The rider must not bring his inside hand (right) in towards the horse's central line; he must never exert a strong or backwards pull on the inside rein nor must he lose a smooth regulating contact with the outside rein.

It is very important that the turn is executed mostly by thought, weight and leg aids and not by the hands which should merely keep a smooth contact in a supporting role.

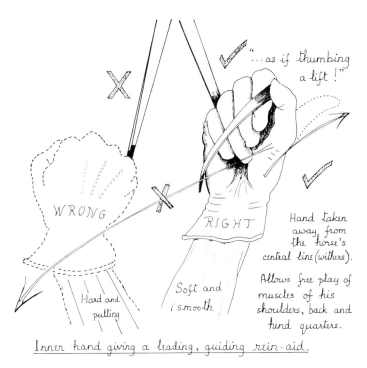

"... as if thumbing a lift!"

X X

WRONG

RIGHT

Hand taken away from the horse's central line (withers).

Allows free play of muscles of his shoulders, back and hind quarters.

Hard and pulling

Soft and smooth

Inner hand giving a leading, guiding rein-aid.

All the aids must be used with tact and harmony so that they co-operate well and are invisible.

From the beginning, instructors must warn their pupils that they must conclude a turn on the forehand with the horse's inside forefoot almost exactly on the piece of ground on which it trod when the turn was commenced. It is a turn on the spot. Any horse who moves outwards as he completes the turn reveals both a poor quality of instruction as well as a lazy rider.

After riding a turn on the forehand the horse should be straightened and kept well *forward* on the bit, mainly by the rider's outside leg which is used actively, forward by the girth, to urge the horse forward at a lively pace.

Common faults

The most common faults made during a turn on the forehand to the right are:
• The preparations are poor, especially those of the ground-plan and of the horse himself. He must have a fair chance and all possible help to organise his large and unwieldy body mass before he is asked to make a turn.
• The co-ordination of the rider's aids is insufficient, causing the horse to lose his form, to side-step awkwardly, to go above the bit and to hollow his back.

In this case the instructor must reduce the demand to suit the capabilities of rider and horse. He must explain that as a major riding principle it is always best to do a few steps well and that to continue with any exercise after the horse has lost his form can only be destructive to that horse's training and harmful to his physique. The rider should make good preparations and then ride only two, three or four strides of a turn before riding straight forward at a lively trot, rewarding the horse as he goes. It often helps the rider if he counts each step of every stride; this relaxes his mind as well as his whole seat and makes it easier for him to think and to feel the horse's movement under him.

• The rider fails to keep the horse in a good form, on the bit before, during or after the turn.

This fault is usually due to a misunderstanding concerning the sideways-moving aids when the operative action is thought to be exclusively sideways. The instructor must remind his pupil that when a rider asks for his horse to move sideways, simultaneously he must increase his forward-urging influence. Unless the rider tones up his forward-driving aids when he applies sideways-moving aids, the greater demand of the work will cause the horse to become either baffled, sluggish or tense and he will lose his form. "Think forward and over".

• The rider's inside aids are too severe: the horse runs away from the pressure of the rider's inner leg resulting in a turn which is erratic, hurried and irregular, rather than being performed comfortably, step by step. As a result, invariably the horse's form and movement deteriorate, the exercise loses its value – and its good name. To correct this fault the rider must improve the tact and co-ordination of his aids; possibly the influence of the rider's outside aids should be increased to regulate the movement and to contain the impulsion, but he must be on his guard to keep his horse on the bit and straight between the aids so that his form and movement are correct.

• If the horse is bent laterally too much and steps to the side with his forelegs as well as his hindlegs so that his outside shoulder falls out, the rider must cease the exercise at once, straighten the horse and ride him straight forward on to the bit, after which a new turn may be ridden, thoughtfully and with care.

To prevent the forehand falling out, the regulating outside leg (the left one) should be moved forward and used on the girth, supported by the outside rein, if necessary. The instructor must make sure that the rider's inside hand is not stiff, heavy or exerting too strong an influence. The rider must remember that the horse's fault is invariably due to bad riding.

• The rider allows the horse to think and even to move backwards – this ia a major fault. If it occurs the turning must be ceased immediately and the horse should be ridden forwards vigorously. The time and the place for the next attempt at a turn on the forehand must be chosen with care. The horse must be absolutely calm and the turns should be made towards home or other horses. If there are any further signs of worry, an assistant with a reward bag will provide the best solution.

TURN ON THE FOREHAND ~ *to the right.*

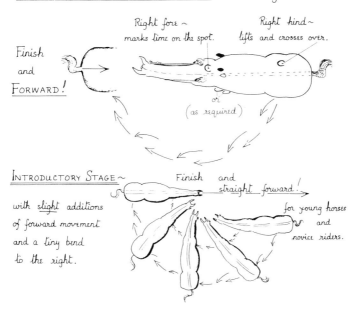

Right fore ~
marks time on the spot.

Right hind ~
lifts and crosses over.

Finish
and
FORWARD*!*

or
(as required)

INTRODUCTORY STAGE ~

with slight additions
of forward movement
and a tiny bend
to the right.

Finish and
straight forward!

for young horses
and
novice riders.

MORE ADVANCED ~ COLLECTING.

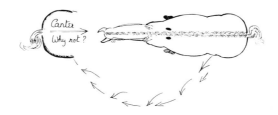

Canter
Why not?

When he corrects all the above faults, the instructor must be tolerant, remembering that all human beings have differing levels of the ability to co-ordinate and that remarkably few have a natural talent in this respect. Any impatience on the instructor's part will be reflected doubly in his pupil and the situation will deteriorate. He must help his pupils and lead them to feel and achieve correct turns.

A turn on the forehand to the right can also be made when the horse is flexed to the opposite side, in which case the labels "inner" and "outer" are exchanged to match the horse's bend.

Thus, when riding a right turn the outer (right) leg moves the horse's hindquarters sideways to the left, and the horse has a very slight flexion in the same direction. During the turn the horse is kept well forward on to the inner rein to retain his form and to prevent him from stepping backwards.

This method of turning on the forehand, to the right with a flexion to the left, is useful:

- To practise the rider in the use of diagonal aids and to increase his knowledge and appreciation of the co-ordination and harmony of his aids.
- To straighten the horse, particularly if he has been incorrectly trained, and has been allowed, or even encouraged, to push out his outer shoulder when positioned slightly towards the turn.
- To prepare the horse for the collection which will be required in the more advanced school movements.

Turns on the haunches

A turn on the haunches – half or demi-pirouettes – at walk is a comparatively demanding movement for a horse; it does not enter his training curriculum until half-way through the work programme for lateral movements.

When he turns on the haunches the horse's inner hindleg is the pivot of the turn: it is picked up, turned and treads again on the same spot. The outer hind foot steps closely around the pivot and the forefeet describe an arc around it. The outer foreleg crosses over in front of the inner foreleg, the hindlegs "mark time" on the spot as they turn, they do not cross over. The rhythm of the walk and the sequence of footfall should be regular and well defined. The horse should be positioned in the direction of the turn and be well on the bit before, during and after the turn. Due to the activity and the bending of his hindlegs the horse's croup should be somewhat lowered and the turning although difficult should appear easy.

Aims of the turns on the haunches

- They are particularly good exercises for educating the rider about the influence that the positioning of his body can have on that of his horse. By

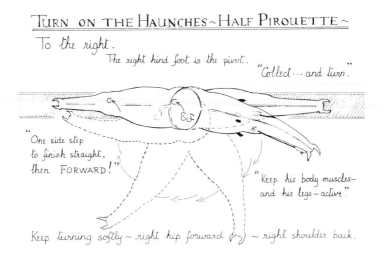

Turn on the Haunches ~ Half Pirouette ~

To the right.

The right hind foot is the pivot.

"Collect ... and turn."

"One side step to finish straight, then FORWARD!"

"Keep his body muscles – and his legs – active."

Keep turning softly ~ right hip forward (↻) ~ right shoulder back.

a definite but supple moving forwards of his outer shoulder and his inner hip he can effect a corresponding positioning in his horse. If any reader doubts the efficacy of this influence let him put it to the test, together with his partner the horse.

• They provide an excellent physical exercise for the horse. Turns on the haunches develop all the muscles involved in collection, that is to say those muscles which enable the horse to carry more of his own and his rider's weight on his hindlegs and which lighten his forehand.

• They educate the rider's feel. By these turns he learns to have a feel for collection, as the horse expands his back muscles, "filling out" the rider's seat, in order to engage his hindlegs to carry most of their combined weight.

• They improve the rider's co-ordination and equestrian tact; they further the education, use and harmony of his aids. By carrying out turns on the haunches, riders learn to measure and blend the forward-driving aids with the sideways-moving and the restraining aids in an effective yet tactful manner.

• They clarify the use of the diagonal aids to the rider and the horse.

• They loosen, or limber up, the horse.

• They encourage the horse to bring more of his weight back on to his haunches and thereby to improve his balance and carriage and the light-ness and freedom of his movement when carrying and working with his rider.

• They improve the horse's execution of smooth turns.

• They prepare the horse for collected work.

• They develop his musculature, his fitness and his form.

Warning note

Riders must not overdo these turns on the spot. Because their respec-tive lists of aims and accomplishments are both worthy and lengthy the reader must not be led to imagine that if he asks his horse to make thirty turns on the spot in each lesson he will have a Grand Prix horse at the end of a week. In reality he would have a horse on his hands who was a mental and physical wreck!

Four to ten turns on the forehand, dispersed at intervals within the first half of his daily lessons will help younger horses to build, and school horses to keep, their form. Gradually, as the training standards of riders and horses improve, turns on the haunches can be introduced after the horses have been limbered-up well. Little by little both varieties of turns on the spot will have wondrous effects on both partners – providing that they are well ridden.

The aids to turn on the haunches to the right – at walk

(a) The rider must make a plan and then good and thorough prep-arations. He must establish a good medium walk with the horse straight and evenly on the aids. The horse must be confident, balanced and walk with regular, determined strides. From this medium walk the rider can ask for a few steps of collected walk with his forward-driving aids into softly containing rein aids – not by pulling. The rider should use half-halts as may be necessary.

(b) When he feels the horse is ready the rider should shift his weight to the inside and keep the horse well forward on the bit with both legs maintaining a lively impulsion and a regular rhythm.

(c) He then positions the horse to the right. The object of this positioning is to help the horse to make the turn easily and comfortably. If the horse's poll is flexed softly in the direction of the turn, he can see and understand where he is going and the suppleness at his poll will be reflected throughout the whole of his body, down to his hinds heels – and up again! Thus horse and rider are ready to co-ordinate together to make a right turn on the haunches.

Using the aids

PREPARE

The rider's weight is shifted and remains slightly to the right so that the rider-burden is nicely balanced for the horse. The rider's loins must be supple so that his seat bones do not get "stuck" and cause the horse to miss a beat with one or both of his hindlegs; he should think of "growing tall ears" so that he sits on the saddle with a supple poise. The rider's inner hip should be well forward and the legs stretched down to keep the hip joints open and supple and the seat stable to the inside.

The rider must employ the whole of his being to measure and preserve the horse's balance. With a fine blending of boldness and caution he must encourage vibrant work within the horse as well as the regular walk sequence of his footsteps.

THE RIDER'S INSIDE LEG

The right leg is applied close to the girth to engage the horse's inner hindleg, to prevent it from stepping out to the side, to maintain impulsion and form and to govern the speed at which the horse turns within each stride; this last is dependent on a tactful co-ordination of the inner rein.

THE RIDER'S OUTSIDE LEG

The left leg is applied behind the girth and assists the inner leg in maintaining impulsion. Above all, it is kept "on guard" to prevent the hindquarters from swinging out.

THE RIDER'S INSIDE REIN

The right rein retains the positioning and leads the forehand step by step round the inner hindleg.

THE RIDER'S OUTSIDE REIN

The left rein acts close to the horse's neck. It contains the horse's impulsion and form, restrains as necessary and supports the rider's outside leg.

The rider should move his outer shoulder forward to turn the horse's forehand and to ensure that his upper body moves well with the horse's turning. The hands then relate to the positioning of the rider's shoulders: they position the horse and indicate the turn, the inner rein leading the way. At the same time the rider must sit well to the inside with an easy poise to be in perfect balance with his horse. The rider must keep his inner hip well forward – softly, not stiffly – inviting the horse to use his back muscles freely to engage his inner hindleg and thus maintain the true sequence of footfall as the hindfeet mark time on the spot.

The rider must look where he is going and think and feel for the fluency and rhythm of the horse's movement under him.

The rider must be careful that his knees do not rise in the excitement of his endeavours to make a good turn. Any such posture fault will detract from the suppleness of his seat and influence on his horse. The rider must discipline his posture here as always. It is important that his legs are stretched down in order to keep the angle of the hip joints open and to retain suppleness throughout the whole of the rider's seat, particularly so that his seat bones can move well with the movement of the horse's back muscles.

After the turn is completed, the horse is straightened and ridden well forward on the bit.

If at any time during the turn the horse should show any inclination to step backwards, the rider must immediately ride him forward before starting another turn.

Common faults

The most common rider faults in turns on the haunches are:
- The rider fails to make preparations which start early enough and are sufficiently well ridden.
- He does not position the horse correctly before and during the turn.
- The rider forgets to shift his weight to the inside early or well enough to warn and invite the horse to make the turn and to stay in perfect balance with him as he is turning.
- Due to the foregoing fault, the rider's seat slides out which causes the horse to follow suit!
- The rider's outside aids are too weak or they may be forgotten altogether; in either case, again, the horse's hindquarters will swing out and the turn will no longer be "on the haunches".
- The rein aids are too strong – the rider's hands are heavy – the horse feels forcibly restricted and thinks or even steps backwards. This is a major fault, caused by bad riding.
- The rider forgets to keep applying his forward-driving aids. As a result the horse loses impulsion, his form deteriorates and he may resist the rider's request because to continue the turning without sufficient impulsion is difficult and possibly painful for him. It is up to the rider to encourage the horse sufficiently with his forward-driving aids, to create

more impulsion in order to enable the horse to meet the extra demand of the turn.

The rider's forward-driving aids must always be of a considerably greater proportion than those which move his horse sideways. This third "horseman's commandment" should always be obeyed but it is often forgotten.

The sequences of this major rider fault are always apparent in the horse. If the impulsion is not maintained:

- The horse may resist what are now unfair demands.
- He will not be on the bit and as his hindlegs are not engaged, he may hollow his back.
- He will think or even step backwards.
- He may raise his head and set his jaw with a stiffness which will be apparent also in his poll, his back and his hindlegs.
- The regularity of the gait will be impaired and the sequence of footfall may be broken as he "misses a beat" or screws round on his inside hind foot.
- The tempo is changed; if the horse is tense he may swing round too fast or, alternatively, he may drop the front of his trunk and plod round with slow, laboured steps.

If any of these dressage faults occur, the rider must be humble enough to realise that it is up to him to improve his horsemanship; he must find and analyse his own faults in order that the horse is able to carry out these difficult turns correctly, with an easy yet proud bearing.

Often it is helpful for riders who have lively imaginations to conjure up a practical situation such as:

Imagine you are riding along a precipitous mountain path; you are hundreds of feet up with a sheer drop down to the valley on your right. As you walk along with great care, you see that a landslide has completely blocked your path; you will have to turn around and retrace your steps along the narrow path. You must ask your horse to make a very good turn on his haunches to the right – help him to use all the muscles he possesses to keep his balance and move his feet carefully and precisely as he makes a neat and nimble right about turn, keeping his hindlegs marking time on the spot.

(Well done! That was a marvellous turn – see how easy it is?!)

Introductory work for turns on the haunches

Initially, inexperienced riders and novice horses should turn on an arc such as they will meet when riding well into and through a corner. When they are competent at these turns, they may progress to turns which are based on very small half-circles inwards, and return at walk with the

... you must ride a turn on the haunches to the right...

horse's hind feet tracing an even smaller half-circle, the rider thinking of riding it in half-pass or travers, or they may ride small squares with quarter turns, nearly on the spot at each corner.

The purposes of these early, wider turns are:

• To give the horse and rider time to co-ordinate together as they attempt a new movement.

• To clarify the shifting and use of the weight aid and the uses of the different areas of the rider's seat from the top of his head to the soles of his feet.

• To feel and practise the co-ordination of the inside and the outside aids.

• To improve the horse's collection whilst retaining his confidence; the demand is not too great too soon.

• To introduce short turns to horses and riders, bearing in mind that these may have practical uses as well as being required in dressage tests at elementary level.

The aids to make a turn on an arc were described fully in Book 1 and of course they should be practised at every corner in the manège as soon as the riders and horses are fit and able. A corner which is cut reveals slovenly riding and a schooling opportunity missed.

TO RE-CAP

Hoping to inspire riders to make better use of corners.

As the horse approaches the corner-to-be, the rider makes a half-halt, keeping his inside hip well forward.

He shifts his weight to the inside to prevent his seat from sliding out and to remain in balance with the turning horse. The outer shoulder must not be allowed to fall back, rather it will be required to move forward to lead the horse's forehand round the turn.

Both legs urge the horse forward; the outside leg regulates the body's bending round the rider's inside leg and prevents the hindquarters from swinging out. The inside leg urges the horse to step well forward with his hindlegs so that they come under the horse's body and he engages his hocks to carry the weight – especially the inner one. The rider's inside leg also prevents the horse from moving his hindlegs inwards stiffly, thereby avoiding engagement of the hocks to carry the weight of rider and horse through the turn.

The rider's inner rein positions the horse ready for the turn and leads him into the turn, while the outer rein prevents the horse's body from over-bending in the neck, shoulders and ribs and regulates the size of the arc. Both hands follow the slight turn of the rider's upper body but they should not move inwards so much that the outer one crosses over the horse's central line at the front of his withers. Of course, the rider's hands should never be moved to the outside while riding a turn, a corner or a circle.

After the turn has been completed the horse must immediately be allowed a slight easing of the aids as an unspoken, "Thank you, well done!" The rider should straighten the horse by using his outside leg at the girth to put the horse's shoulders in front of his propelling hindlegs and he should ride forward in the new direction.

The Lateral Movements

General principles

Lateral movements (work on two tracks) are those in which the horse moves forwards and sideways simultaneously. The horse's forehand and his hindquarters move on two separate tracks. As this work is relatively difficult for the horse it must be introduced and developed sensibly. The rider must understand the true aims of this work, particularly concerning the improvement of the musculature of the whole of the horse in order to

Early turns ~ the horse's hind feet moving on a small arc.

To the Right.

Collect

STRAIGHTEN
& FORWARD.

Think right and of all his muscles ~ glance right ~ weight to the right.
Inside hip and outside shoulder forward ~ both legs urge for impulsion.
Left leg just behind the girth ~ right leg at the girth, co-operate bending the body.

Later!
The hind feet mark   time ~   the turn on the haunches
                                         is On The Spot.

increase his strength, athleticism, and stamina, as well as the beauty of his
form and movement. The criterion of well executed lateral work from the
rider or the dressage judge's point of view is that the work should be of
excellent quality throughout the whole of the horse – it should appear to
be effortless and the horse should look even more proud. It is wrong to
allow petty details of the footwork to over-influence the assessment.

The Family Tree of the Lateral Movements.

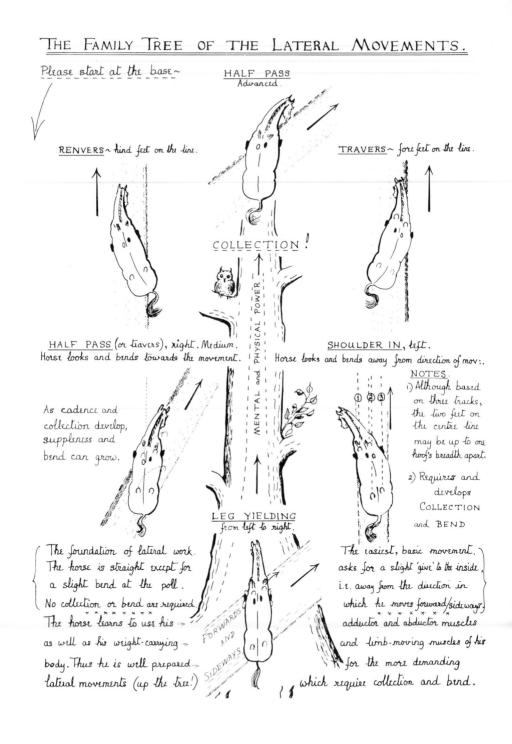

Please start at the base~

HALF PASS
Advanced.

RENVERS ~ hind feet on the line.

TRAVERS ~ fore feet on the line.

COLLECTION !

MENTAL and PHYSICAL POWER

HALF PASS (or travers), right. Medium.
Horse looks and bends towards the movement.

SHOULDER IN, left.
Horse looks and bends away from direction of mov:.

NOTES.
1) Although based
on three tracks,
the two feet on
the centre line
may be up to one
hoof's breadth apart.

2) Requires and
develops
COLLECTION
and BEND

As cadence and
collection develop,
suppleness and
bend can grow.

LEG YIELDING
from left to right.

The foundation of lateral work.
The horse is straight except for
a slight bend at the poll.
No collection or bend are required
The horse learns to use his →
as well as his weight-carrying →
body. Thus he is well prepared →
lateral movements (up the tree!)

FORWARDS
AND
SIDEWAYS

The easiest, basic movement,
asks for a slight 'give' to the inside,
i.e. away from the direction in
which he moves forward/sideways.
adductor and abductor muscles
and limb-moving muscles of his
for the more demanding
which require collection and bend.

Whether the legs cross to a lesser or greater degree or whether the feet point straight ahead or turn slightly to the left or right is of little or no consequence compared with the manner in which the whole of the horse moves and carries his rider during the lateral movements – the feet are the end result of all the major factors such as whether the horse is on the bit, with sufficient impulsion and collection, whether he is balanced, supple and unconstrained, whether the gait remains regular and whether the movement is started, carried out and finished, all with apparent ease.

The lateral movements' "family tree"

LEG-YIELDING

The most basic and easiest of all the lateral movements. The horse is not required to be collected; he is kept straight, with a *very* slight bend at the poll, away from the direction in which he is moving. He learns to use his abductor and adductor muscles and they become stronger and his shoulders more free in their movement. Thus leg-yielding can be regarded as the foundation stone for all the more advanced and difficult lateral movements.

SHOULDER-IN

The horse is collected and uniformly bent round the rider's inside leg, from the poll to the tail, away from the direction in which he is moving. During shoulder-in, the horse moves on two tracks, his shoulders and forefeet having been brought inside the original track or line of progression. The tracks of the outer forefoot and the inner hind foot merge on to a common, central line and thus the movement is often referred to as being "on three tracks".

In a dressage test a rider may need to show a little more angle to make it clear to the judges that he is riding his horse in shoulder-in. In this case he should limit the distance between the two feet on the central track to the breadth of one horse's hoof.

Although shoulder-in of a sort is included in dressage tests of elementary standard, it is really more of a preliminary stage which prepares the rider and the horse for the true shoulder-in as required in advanced dressage tests where the degree of collection and of bend are far more pronounced.

HALF-PASS

The horse is collected and bent towards the direction in which he is moving. As he moves forwards and sideways, the horse's outer legs cross over in front of the inner legs. Although the horse should bend through his whole body, from the poll to the tail, the bend will be more apparent at the poll and in his neck, especially in the preliminary stage.

The difficulty or standard of the half-pass is decided by the acuteness of the angle at which it is ridden. The more acute the angle the greater is the demand on both the rider and his horse. In the preliminary stage and up to tests of medium standard, the degree of collection and of bend will be less than that required in the advanced dressage tests.

TRAVERS

A very close relation, almost an identical twin to the half-pass in its advanced stage. The horse is collected, uniformly bent from the poll to the tail towards the direction in which he is moving and his forefeet travel along the track of the centre line or parallel with (but not too close to) the wall.

RENVERS

Another close relative! The horse is collected and uniformly bent from poll to tail towards the direction in which he is moving, but in this movement his hind feet travel along the track of the centre line or parallel with the wall.

COUNTER-CHANGE OF HAND

A series of alternating half-passes to the left and the right; these may be of medium or advanced standard. The number of counter-changes and the length of the half-passes to be fitted into a given area prescribe the angles at which they are ridden; these factors combine to determine the degree of difficulty of the whole movement. Counter-changes of hand are an excellent test of a horse's collection, balance and suppleness.

Aims and uses of lateral movements

For the horse

All work on two tracks demands more balance, mental and physical endeavour and co-ordination from the horse than does work on a single track. Thus the purposes of lateral movements are:

- To improve the horse's sensitivity and obedience to the rider's aids, particularly those of his thought, weight and legs.
- To supple all parts of the horse, both longitudinally and laterally, by increasing the freedom of his shoulders which enables him to move his centre of gravity further back, as his training progresses.
- To develop the horse's abductor and adductor muscles together with all the muscles of the horse's forehand, back and hindquarters.
- To improve the horse's physique, his form, agility and fitness.
- To straighten faulty action such as dishing and plaiting.
- To activate and develop the haunches, thus increasing their power and carrying capacity, thereby lightening the forehand and eventually leading the horse to true collection.
- To develop and establish the elastic band and its play between the horse's hindquarters, his back, his neck – from its base at the withers, up to the poll – his lower jaw, his mouth and thence to the reins.

In order to achieve the objectives of any movement on two tracks the rider must do his best to ensure that the horse maintains his balance and form, his impulsion and a correct position or bend and that he moves forward with an eager willingness, submissively on the bit, at a regular and rhythmical gait and without any sign of tension in his mind or body.

For the rider

- All lateral work, from the preliminary turns on the spot, through the easy leg-yielding, to the more advanced, collected lateral movements, provides excellent opportunities for the rider to practise and develop his "feel" and the harmony of his aids. It will greatly improve his ability to use his co-operating aids in a sensitive, well-timed, thoughtful and correct manner.

- When riding on two tracks it is easier for the rider to feel how the different parts of the horse's body work. He will learn to feel and enjoy sitting on a horse that is moving well (free, light and active); he will be able to discern which part is not working in a correct way, and he will then be taught how to eradicate the faults in his own riding. Later he will learn how to correct horses who have been badly ridden and who have lost their confidence, fluency and gaits.

- From an everyday, practical point of view, correct education in lateral work teaches the rider how to position or place his horse as he wishes. For example, at ground level it enables him to open, close and fasten gates skilfully when mounted. Later, when riding spoiled or wayward horses, he can use his knowledge of lateral work to parry their evasive movements or resistances with dexterity rather than force.

Rider using some steps of shoulder-in to parry his horse's natural wish to shy into the middle of the road.

. . . . with dexterity rather than force . . . .

- The rider must be humbly aware that all lateral work presents a greater challenge to his riding. He must think and feel with even more consideration, and he must preserve the correct poise and positioning of his seat. He must check that his inner knee is low and stable on the saddle, for the rider's inside leg should provide a strong yet supple column round which the horse's body will be bent. A lowering of the inner knee and heel will keep the hip bone above them straight, forward and its top edge level with that of the outer hip bone; the foundation of the whole of his seat will remain correct with an easy poise, ready to be used as the rider wishes in order to develop the horse's movement.

Desirable qualities

These are what the rider should feel and the judges hope to see.
- Every movement on two tracks should be ridden to a well thought out plan and after correct preparations.
- Before, during and after all lateral movements the horse must be on the bit and in good form, the gait must be free and regular, maintained by a constant impulsion, yet remaining supple, fluent, balanced and cadenced. Too often the impulsion is lost because of the rider's preoccupation with the horse's bend or footwork, or of his need to reach the correct marker in a dressage test.
- During lateral movements, the forehand should always be very slightly in advance of the hindquarters. If the hindquarters lead, even fractionally, the exercise loses its value – the movement no longer goes through the whole of the horse.
- The correct sequence of footfall and the rhythm of the gait must be maintained and the tempo should remain metronomically consistent before, during and after the lateral movement.
- An exactly similar flexion at the poll and or bend throughout the horse's body and angle with the line of progression should be shown to either hand. The horse's mouth and his ears should be level at all times.
- It must be remembered that any lateral flexion at the poll, or bending in the horse's spine affects the movement throughout the whole horse. In all lateral movements the horse shows a flexion or a bend in the direction in which he is looking. While this flexion or bend is barely perceptible in leg-yielding and only slightly so in the easier half-passes, it is more evident in shoulder-in, travers, renvers and the advanced half-passes of Grand Prix standard. These last four are the most collected movements; they are also the most difficult and should never be asked for until rider and horse are sufficiently educated.
- In the more difficult collected lateral movements, the horse should appear to be majestically full of contained power as he carries his rider with a consummate ease which gives an elegant quality to their performance.

Additional notes

Initially, lateral movements should be taught and felt at the walk to allow the horse time to work out the movements of his feet, and the rider to sort out, feel and apply the aids. However, as soon as the aids, feeling, timing and understanding are correct, work should be carried out at the trot when impulsion and the horse's forward-thinking are more naturally and easily maintained. With well-trained horses and riders, all work on two tracks may be executed at a canter.

Movements on two tracks should only be ridden for short periods, leg-yielding in a slightly shortened gait, and the more advanced movements at a collected gait. During the early and middle standards of training this work must always be interchanged with riding forward on a single track at an energetic forward-going gait. Later, it may be used as a "key" to improve upward and downward transitions. For example, for extension, the horse's shoulders being more loose, and to encourage soft halts.

During all work on two tracks, the rider must think and feel that the tempo is exactly right for the individual horse to keep his balance and manoeuvre his feet easily. The horse must not be forced to move too quickly, nor be allowed to dwell slowly and laboriously, for in neither of these two extremes is it possible to be supple or collected, and the turn loses its value as a schooling, gymnastic exercise.

With correct, subtle interchanges of the outer and inner aids the rider should be able to control the horse's forehand and hindquarters. Eventually, as the horse's training progresses and his musculature develops, the change-over from the basic leg-yielding to the more advanced lateral movements can be made easily and virtually invisibly.

As his pupils gain experience and proficiency in their riding of lateral work, the instructor should teach them how to use their schooling whips correctly in that the rider should carry his schooling whip in the hand towards which the horse is working.

For example, the rider will carry and use the whip discreetly in the right hand for leg-yielding from left to right, for left shoulder-in, for right half-pass or travers or renvers to the right. For, in all these movements, if the horse is asked to bring his right hindleg well forward, actively, underneath his body to make a good support, then his left hindleg will have to bend well in all its joints and be equally active in order to cross over in front of the right hindleg and it will be comparatively free to do so. If the rider is taught to think, feel and to ride lateral movements in this way, particularly shoulder-in, then gradually the engagement of the horse's haunches will improve and collection will develop.

Before introducing lateral work into the young horse's training programme he must be physically fit, balanced and obedient to the lateral and the diagonal aids; he should be capable of good, smooth and obedient turns on the forehand, and quarter turns on the haunches. Young horses should only be ridden in lateral work by experienced riders.

Warning

If the more demanding (collected) work on two tracks is introduced too early, before riders are sufficiently educated or horses fit and trained, invariably more harm than good will be done. For example, it is irresponsible to ask pupils to ride shoulder-in before both riders and horses are capable of maintaining a fair degree of collection.

Common faults

- The pre-planning of the movement and its approach are poor.
- The rider's preparations for the horse are slipshod or missing altogether!
- He must shorten his reins sufficiently – unless he does so he cannot keep an even, soft feeling on both reins, from his shoulders through supple "tidy" elbows, to hands which are well-carried with the thumb part of the hand turning smoothly outward, well clear of the withers. Neither hand must be allowed to interfere with the horse's two "elastic bands".
- The rider must correct his position frequently, making it as nearly perfect as possible so that he and his horse are balanced and are ready to perform the movement in harmony together – and so that they stay that way consistently.
- He must use half-halts, of exactly the right size to achieve this balance and to improve the quality of the gait, before commencing the lateral movement, and as may be necessary during the movement itself.
- He must purposefully remove excess tension from his seat, for this will inevitably have unfortunate repercussions in other parts of his body. For example, he may hold his breath; one or both of his hips and seat bones may get "stuck" into the horse's back muscles, preventing him from bringing his hindlegs forward under his body. Stiff knees and ankles will inhibit the rider's use of his lower legs, his back, neck, shoulders and/or arms may become stiff. As always, any one of these faults, or any excess movement of the rider's upper body, will be reflected in the horse's way of going – he cannot move fluently, actively and with confident ease unless the rider has a well-poised, supple seat and strong yet tactful forward-driving aids.

The instructor must remind his pupils of these riding points frequently for they are essential not only to the preparations but also to and during the lateral movement itself.

- The rider's seat may be faulty or not yet established well enough to withstand the greater demands imposed by the riding of lateral movements.
- The rider's knowledge and understanding of the aids may not be sufficient. He may even have misunderstood or have learned incorrect signals. He must not imagine that he has only to press one button for leg-yielding, another for shoulder-in and yet another for half-pass. It does not work that way at all.

"My horse is so stiff in half-pass to the right...."

How can the horse understand or move laterally to the right with such a rider-burden ~ and such a confusion of aids?

There is a current instructor-chant which runs, "One aid, one answer." Of all the glib gimmicks that surely takes the prize! Riders must be encouraged to think and feel that they are trying to communicate mentally and physically with a partner who has a mind of his own, to say nothing of three hundred bones and seven hundred muscles to reorganise in order to move himself and his rider in an extraordinary forward and sideways movement. One aid can *never* produce an answer – the rider must consider all the possible chords of the keyboard and play those which suit the horse, the exercise, the movement, the mood and the moment.

- The rider's sense of timing is weak: this will mar the co-ordination of his aids, his feel for the horse's balance, and the suitability of the tempo of the gait in which the movement is being performed.
- The rider either forgets or loses the rhythm himself, and the horse follows suit.
- Sometimes the horse moves, or is made to move, sideways too much, so that his legs interfere with each other as they cross over. The horse will bang the back of his knees, or other joints, and hurt himself; tension will result, the forward thinking and impulsion will be lost, the natural, smooth and rhythmical movement of the feet will be upset and the horse may damage his legs. In this case, the instructor must admonish the rider for he must urge the horse to bring his leading hindleg further forward underneath his body, and he must concentrate on riding the horse *forwards* more than sideways.
- The rider may be greedy, thoughtless or over-ambitious and continue the lateral movement for too long. The instructor must remind the pupils that it is far better to do a few steps which are really good and to use the improvement in the gait to create a similar improvement in an ensuing movement – for instance, some lengthened strides or transitions.
- The rider may apply his aids in an awkward or forceful manner. This is a very serious fault as the horse will become tense, the experience will become painful while fluency and harmony will be lost.

- The rider may seem to lack sufficient "feel" for the work. This is quite a common fault and presents a worthwhile challenge to the instructor. He must "think positive" and, even if it is a long process, he must lead his pupil with encouragement, and praise the slightest response and improvement. Nothing smothers "feel" more quickly than negative criticism, disapproval or even doubt.

Possible variations of exercises

Those which contain lateral movements are legion, a few examples have been outlined in Book 1, and the details of further exercises follow. When using any of these exercises for the training of riders or horses, the instructor must be quick to correct the faults listed above and he must emphasise the following *plus points*:
- The rider should move his horse over forwards-sideways, step-by-step, in a movement of consistent power, rhythm, ease and enjoyment.
- He should ask for only a few good strides, rather than prolonging the movement at the risk of its deteriorating into a valueless "soft shoe shuffle".
- The rider must always be generous in his heart, and quick to reward good work with a pat and a walk on long reins, or a halt and a titbit of apple or carrot.
- During all lessons involving lateral work, the instructor must encourage his pupils to gain a deeper understanding of their own and their horse's physiology, so that they realise which muscles are used and can be developed in order that the horse may move in a more advanced form, having the ability to lighten his forehand and carry his own weight and that of his rider with strong, engaged haunches.

Leg-Yielding

General principles

This subject has already been described in Book 1. That leg-yielding, or side-stepping as it is often called, was not accepted with alacrity when it was reintroduced in England in the 1960s is an understatement – typically British, in every way!

However, the whys and wherefores, misunderstandings and general furore are now history, and were touched on in Book 1, together with full details of how to teach leg-yielding to novice riders. What follows is a "re-cap" for more experienced riders, together with some additional thoughts.

It is worth delving much deeper than those early, superficial criticisms, for more constructive thought about leg-yielding could lead to a major improvement in the standard of British equitation.

Firstly, leg-yielding is more related to the shoulder-in, not to the half-pass, for in both movements the horse is bent away from the line of

LEG-YIELDING.

The foundation stone of all the lateral movements.
The horse learns how to use new muscles when carrying his rider;
the rider learns how to coordinate his thoughts, body and aids as
he asks his horse to move both forwards and sideways.
The riders below are riding leg-yielding to the left~
i.e., from the right leg. Introduced at walk, then better at trot.

KEY   a = adductor (towards body) muscles.
       b = abductor (away from body) muscles.

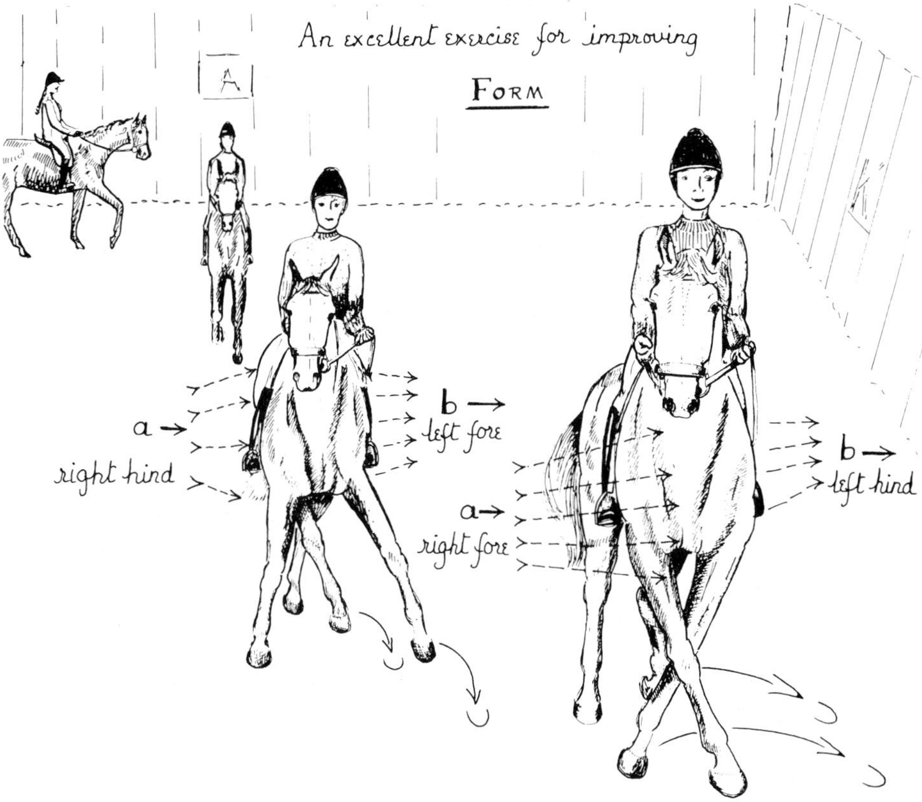

An excellent exercise for improving

FORM

A

a →
right hind

b →
left fore

a →
right fore

b →
left hind

progression. Leg-yielding is an easy preliminary exercise which can be used in comparatively early stages of the horse's training, and which will prepare him for the more advanced, collected exercise of shoulder-in. On the other hand, the earlier (Medium) half-pass with less bend and collection, is a junior version of the more advanced (Grand Prix) half-pass, travers and renvers. In all these movements the horse is bent towards the line of progression.

Leg-yielding is easier for the horse than half-pass. Thus, if instructors leave out the two most important preliminary gymnastic exercises of turns on the forehand and leg-yielding in their teaching of riders and training of horses, it is not surprising if the horses' gaits suffer and they lose marks in dressage tests for "stiff and tense backs and rigid mouths".

Instructors must think far more deeply about how their pupils ride and how the horses move and carry themselves and their riders, rather than whether the horse can be directed along the prescribed ground-plan of a dressage test. The purity of the horse's gaits, his form, his being on the bit correctly, his mental and physical development, and the visual proof that his training has produced a horse who is calm, supple, loose, confident, attentive, willing and eager to please – these should be the criteria. A dressage test is merely a means of displaying the horse's training and of obtaining a judgement on it.

Re-cap

No section on lateral movements can be complete unless it starts at the beginning with leg-yielding, for it is the most basic of all the lateral movements. Leg-yielding is the rider's best means of making a horse supple and unconstrained, of developing a true acceptance of and contact with the bit, of improving the freedom, elasticity and regularity of his gaits, of increasing his form. Leg-yielding is also an invaluable exercise for the progressive training of the rider introducing him to a correct feel for lateral work, particularly that he makes correct preparations and then influences his horse with his weight and leg aids, supported by rein aids, rather than the other way round.

The horse should be on the bit, straight and well balanced as he moves freely forward and sideways in level, rhythmical strides, his inside legs passing and crossing in front of his outside legs. His head should be very slightly bent at the poll away from the direction in which he is moving; his mouth, ears, shoulders and hips should all be level.

In an arena, leg-yielding can be performed on any diagonal line, with the horse's body almost parallel with the long side of the arena, or down the long side, with the forehand to the inside and always very slightly in advance of the hindquarters. The former is the better exercise. Leg-yielding should not be ridden with the horse's head towards the wall as this suppresses the horse's natural forward urge.

Although leg-yielding is included in official international dressage tests for junior riders it is not included in official adult advanced dressage tests which require a high degree of collection.

When introducing leg-yielding to a new class or pupil for the first time, the instructor must be absolutely clear, concise and painstaking with regard to detail, to ensure that his pupils not only apply their aids correctly, but that they achieve a correct belief in and feel for this new and important work.

Frequently when instructions are given, if a variation of slant or phraseology is introduced the result will be an even better absorption and understanding by the pupils. Although the aids for leg-yielding and the method for teaching the movement were described fully in Book 1, the aim of this book is to serve as a guide for more experienced riders and instructors. For these reasons, the aids are given below in paragraph rather than note form.

Aids for leg-yielding – from left to right

(a) First the rider prepares himself. He maps out a sensible and inviting ground-plan. He checks that his reins are short enough, improves the posture of his upper body, and ensures that there is no constraint in his pelvis as he sits correctly and softly on his two seat bones.

(b) With the horse in a lively, well-balanced working gait, the rider makes a half-halt and slightly shortens the horse's steps. He then uses his left leg by the girth to move the horse over to the right. With young or half-trained horses this leg may be used on or just behind the girth, depending on whether the rider wishes to influence the horse's shoulders or his hindquarters. The rider's right leg urges the horse forward and prevents him from falling out with his right shoulder; it may be used on the girth, or slightly further back to prevent the horse from moving sideways too much or too quickly if he gives way too readily from the rider's inner leg.

(c) The right rein leads the forehand to the right with the thumb part of the hand turned smoothly, lightly and slightly out to the right. The left rein supports the action of the other aids, particularly that of the left leg, when necessary, and maintains a barely perceptible bend to the left at the poll, so that the rider can just see the horse's left eyebrow and the edge of his left nostril. To use his rein aid the rider applies a smooth pressure, by moving his left hand towards his left hip, keeping the thumb turned slightly outward and the fingernails nearly uppermost. He should never pull backwards towards his stomach, nor press the rein against the horse's neck.

(d) Both legs must co-operate well to maintain impulsion. The rider's weight should remain central, with the body upright and neither in front of nor behind the movement, but inviting and going with it. Both hips and both seat bones should be well forward: if either one of them is allowed to slide or set backwards it will impede the forward activity of the horse's hindleg on that side.

(e) The timing, measurement and mixing of the rider's aids are of the greatest importance, also a feel for rhythm, balance and movement – all the qualities which combine in equestrian tact.

The Aids for Leg Yielding to the Right.

THOUGHT AIDS.

THINK ~ plot ground plan. FEEL ~ analyse the horse's form. THINK ~ connect with his mind.

WEIGHT AIDS.

Organise your seat with supple poise to help your horse with his balance and action.

LEG AIDS.

Inside (left) leg ~ sideways moving; impulsion; activating body muscles; softening inner side.
Outside (right) leg ~ containing and maintaining impulsion and regulating as necessary.
(whip encouraging forward activity of outer hind leg.)

REIN AIDS.

Inside (left) rein ~ co-operates with and supports action of inside leg.

Outside (right) rein ~ leads horse to right & co-operates with other aids, mainly + outside leg.

OVER AND FORWARD

Left hand acts towards left hip as + when necessary.

VOICE AID.

Helps to harmonise thoughts and movements of rider and horse, to translate, to aid rhythm, to encourage and reward, spontaneously, kindly and quietly.

A FEW GOOD STRIDES···

THEN

FORWARD···

226

(f) The horse should yield to the leg and be influenced as little as possible by the rider's hands. He should maintain his balance, form and rhythm as his left legs cross over in front of his right legs.

(g) The rider should ask for only a few good strides, at any one time. As the last step is made he should then align the horse's shoulders with the hindquarters and ride straight forward at a lively pace with a definite action of his outer leg well forward on the girth. This will supple the shoulders and activate the haunches and thus improve the horse's impulsion and his strides – the rider having the feeling of popping a pea out of the end of a pea-pod!

(h) When the horse understands what the rider is asking for and moves easily on two tracks, then the rider must ensure that the right hindleg is active and is moved well forward under the horse – for this reason, the schooling whip should be held in the rider's right hand and used with great tact, delicacy and a fine sense of timing to activate the right hindleg.

Additional notes

When the rider understands the correct feel, has confidence in the application of his aids and the horse obeys the inner (lateral) aids willingly, they are ready to learn the next step in their education: discreetly, the instructor may now introduce and teach an increase in the use of the outside aids, until, little by little, both rider and horse will be prepared for further bending and collection, the more advanced collected lateral movements.

Leg-yielding can be used to great advantage in all stages of training, both for pupil and horse, but is of particular benefit in developing a rider's feel and the co-ordination of his aids. It is an invaluable exercise also in the training of young or spoiled horses as it dissolves constraint and gives freedom to their shoulders, thus encouraging the horses to carry their riders confidently with strong and pliant backs and improving their form and movement.

Whether leg-yielding is ridden to, from or across the centre line, horses must be kept moving well forward, and the instructor must always ensure that they are kept straight and that their outer shoulders do not fall out, nor should their hindquarters lead. This, obviously, he can see best from the front.

Leg-yielding may be preceded or followed by circles of 7 to 10 metres in diameter. The direction of the circle will depend on the quality being tested or developed: if a left circle follows leg-yielding to the right the instructor or dressage judge looks for a smooth joining of the two movements, with the horse yielding from the left leg, yet with the shoulders and hindquarters well under the rider's control making the negotiation of the circle balanced and easy. When schooling, however, the instructor may ask for a circle to the opposite side, using the change-over to test and educate his riders, to improve the horses' obedience to the riders' weight and leg aids, and to further loosen and supple their shoulders, and improve their elasticity and balance.

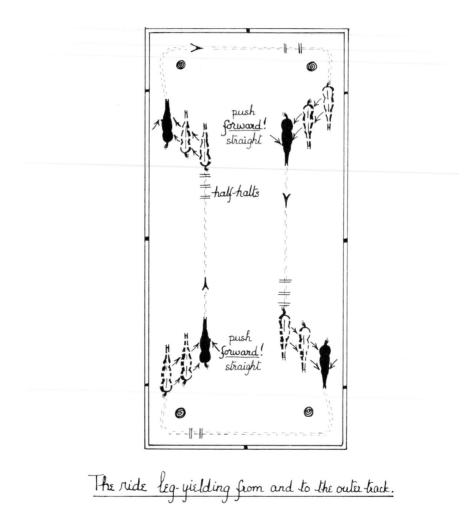

push
forward!
straight

half-halts

push
forward!
straight

The ride leg-yielding from and to the outer track.

Leg-yielding may be followed by a strike-off into canter, and the rider will find this exercise invaluable in improving the smoothness of the transition. Here again the choice of the leading leg will depend on the object of the exercise: to develop smoothness, it will be most natural and easy for both rider and horse if a left canter depart (strike off) follows leg-yielding from left to right, but to improve the rider's feel and ability and the horse's obedience to the aids, a right canter depart would be a greater test.

When riders and horses are sufficiently advanced in their training, leg-yielding can be ridden down and across the centre line. Between every change of direction, in this counter-change of hand in leg-yielding, the horse must be ridden straight forward for a few steps, and during the whole exercise the central line of the horse must remain parallel with the long sides and the centre line of the arena.

GYMNASTICS IN THE GYMNASIUM.

LEG –YIELDING···

TO THE RIGHT~

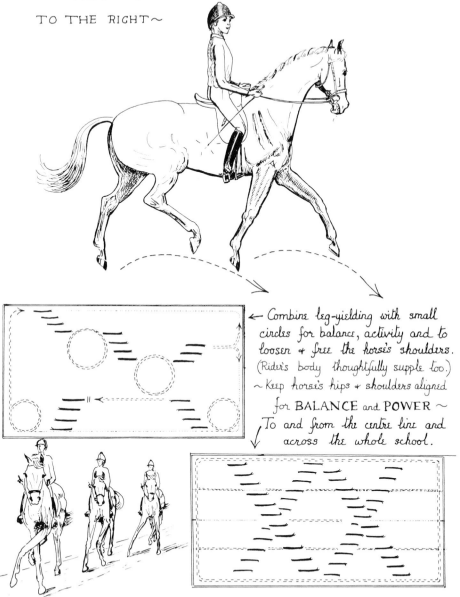

← Combine leg-yielding with small circles for balance, activity and to loosen & free the horse's shoulders. (Rider's body thoughtfully supple too.) ~ Keep horse's hips & shoulders aligned for BALANCE and POWER ~ To and from the centre line and across the whole school.

Leg-yielding on a circle should only be attempted by well-educated riders and horses, as the horses may easily be bent too much, in which case they will avoid working forwards on to the leading rein. A wrong form of "leg-yielding" with swinging hindquarters on small circles must be avoided at all costs, as this eliminates the horse's natural desire to go forward and can also endanger his legs and joints.

Common faults

In addition to those listed in Book 1, the most common rider faults for instructors to correct in a class, or with riders carrying out any exercise involving leg-yielding are:
- Careless lack of preparation – of the plan and of their riding (reins are too long, knees rising, etc.).
- The riders may think mostly of the crossing-over movement of the hindquarters, forgetting that to "loosen" the horse's shoulders is of paramount importance. Therefore, they should think more of the fore-hand yielding smoothly to the leg.
- They often forget the preparatory half-halt or embark on the exercise at too fast a pace for the horse to manoeuvre himself forwards and sideways with ease.
- They think merely of moving their horses in a general sideways direction rather than of maintaining and improving the quality of the horse's form, freedom, balance and cadence as he is ridden forward and sideways, step-by-step.
- A rider may use the inner, lateral aids too continuously and exclusively, especially if the horse is a little slow to react. If the rider persists in asking for too many steps, the horse goes away from the rider's aids with his shoulders leading (outer shoulder falling out), and bending the whole of his neck instead of being *straight*. Worse, he will stop thinking and move *forwards*, the movement then bearing no relation to leg-yielding, and being detrimental to the horse's training.
- Less experienced riders will often bend the inner side of their bodies, a fault sometimes referred to rather inaccurately as "a collapsed inner hip", so that their seats are pushed outwards or they lean in, putting too much weight on the horses' inner sides thus making the movement more difficult for them.
- Some riders are slow to feel the exact second when the horse gives, and they retain what is then an unnecessary or even harmful support to their inner leg with their inner rein, instead of rewarding his compliance with a tiny give of the inner rein.
- Impatience or over-ambition.

Incorrect aids

The most usual faults in this respect are:
- The reins are too long, making co-ordination and balance difficult – if not impossible!

- The rider uses too much inside rein (almost exclusively), and no outside leg at all.
- The hands are not carried and turned smoothly and correctly; instead they are awkward and heavy.
- The hands are used too strongly, impeding the horse's movement, especially if the inside rein is also pressed against the horse's neck (cowboy fashion!), or is being used to support the outside rein rather than the inside *leg*.
- Inactivity of the rider's outside leg, it may even be stuck out, away from the horse's side, instead of maintaining the impulsion.
- The rider's hips, seat bones and/or weight aids are stiff or displaced, thus blocking the freedom of the horse's lateral movement.
- Excess tension in the rider – impeding the flow of breathing, thinking, feeling, timing, co-ordination and rhythm, and causing similar tensions in the horse.

Conclusions

Leg-yielding is an excellent, simple exercise whereby the pupils can learn to feel and to understand how to work their horses from the inside

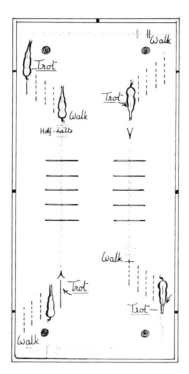

Use leg-yielding and ground poles
to improve transitions.

aids on to the outside aids, in order to make them straight, supple and active. It is important that they are clearly warned of the two major faults which may occur if they ride carelessly, particularly with regard to the outer aids:

(i) The horse throws out his outside shoulder – his impulsion then literally "escapes" through it.

(ii) The hindquarters swing out beyond the rider's control.

If either of these two bad faults are allowed to occur through inefficient supervision, a good basic suppling exercise will quickly degenerate into thoroughly bad and harmful work. The *straightness* of the whole horse is of paramount importance in leg-yielding.

Although when the movement is being ridden in a dressage test, a slight bend at the poll away from the direction of the movement must be shown to the judges, when schooling, the rider may choose to make the "almost imperceptible bend" towards the movement, as if in a preliminary form of half-pass. The instructor should teach his experienced pupils to use this latter variation to correct a horse who is bending too much in leg-yielding and is thus avoiding working correctly, on two tracks with a straight body. Leg-yielding is one of the easiest and best exercises by means of which the rider can parry and correct any crookedness to the bit.

As the horse becomes more athletic in his movements, due to the suppling effect of leg-yielding, he will become more responsive to the influence of the rider's outside leg. This will encourage greater activity in the haunches and better engagement of the hindlegs, forward under the horse, so that he becomes straight and more forward going, his bearing and schooling improve and he is led towards collection.

More Advanced Lateral Movements

Shoulder-in

INTRODUCTION

Shoulder-in is an excellent suppling and collecting exercise in which the horse is bent round the rider's inside leg and looks away from the direction in which he is moving. The bend is uniform from the horse's poll to his tail and his inside legs cross in front of his outside legs, the crossing of the forelegs being more apparent than that of the hindlegs.

The horse's hindlegs follow the outer track of the arena or the centre line with the forehand about one step to the inside, so that his outside forefoot and inside hind foot are more or less on the same track and the angle of his curved body with the line of progression is approximately 30°. An exactly similar bend and angle should be shown on both reins.

The horse should have been well prepared by leg-yielding exercises, and be athletically competent, confident, balanced and supple when ridden in them. He should have been started in work towards collection before shoulder-in is introduced into his curriculum.

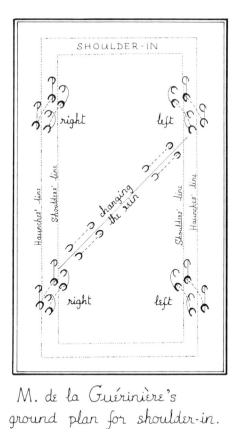

SHOULDER-IN

M. de la Guérinière's
ground plan for shoulder-in.

Although shoulder-in may be ridden at walk when riders are learning
how to ride the movement, to give them more time to organise themselves
and their aids, it is most usually ridden at collected trot. It may be ridden
at canter by experienced riders when training horses to advanced standard.

The aids for shoulder-in left

(a) The rider makes all necessary preparations well in advance: the
plan, his position in the saddle, his horse's form, the quality of the gait,
the tempo, the horse's balance and so forth.

(b) Riding at collected trot, the rider makes a half-halt, he then bends
the horse slightly to the left, and brings the forehand about one step to the
inside of the track, with the aids he would use if he were starting to ride a
circle.

(c) He makes another half-halt to increase the collection slightly and
moves the horse over, forwards and sideways, using his left (inside) leg at
the girth and thinking of riding the horse's hindlegs forward along the
track.

(d) The horse is bent round the rider's left leg with the help of the right (outside) leg just behind the girth and the left rein. Thus the left leg moves the horse sideways, supported when necessary by the left rein which also helps the right leg to maintain the bend.

(e) The rider's right leg prevents the horse's hindquarters from swinging out and, together with the left leg, maintains the forward impulsion.

(f) The right rein tactfully leads the horse in the direction of the movement, supports the right leg, contains the horse's form, and regulates the amount of bend.

(g) The rider's weight should remain in the centre of the saddle; his seat should be carefully poised to lead, blend and go with the movement. His shoulders and hips should be parallel with those of his horse.

(h) He should look ahead over his horse's right ear, proudly yet without a vestige of tension or apparent effort. He must think and feel how his horse is feeling and moving as well as guiding him accurately along the line of progression.

Additional notes

It is the greatest importance that the rider pays enough attention to his own position, his feel and his aids, for shoulder-in is a difficult exercise to ride well. Not only must the rider think about the horse's form and his collection, he must also think in two opposite directions at the same time, for the horse is bending to the *left* while he is moving forwards and to the *right*. He must remember that the rein aids only assist those of his legs and that, therefore, his legs must be in the correct position for him to be able to use them to the best advantage for his horse.

The left knee must be low and secure on the saddle, providing a support for the hip above and the leg and foot below – so that the lower leg's signals may be steady yet supple – and suitably strong to maintain the bend in the horse's body. The right knee and thigh should be softly on the saddle for they must not restrict the movement of the horse's muscles as he uses them all to make each step better than the last. The rider must ensure that he uses his right leg sufficiently to control the hindquarters, to assist the bending and to aid impulsion.

The rider's outside leg must be active as it is responsible for asking the horse to engage his right (outside) hindleg forward under the mass of his body. This causes the horse to bring his left (inside) hindleg even further under his body with a consequent increased bending of the joints of his hindleg, a lowering of his croup, and a stretching and strengthening of his back and loin muscles; his shoulders are further "loosened" and freed and his collection develops. If a whip is carried it should be held in the outer hand and may be used to strengthen the rider's outside leg aid if necessary.

Concluding shoulder-in

The three best ways to conclude a shoulder-in exercise are:

The Aids for Right Shoulder-in.

Thought aid ~ Plans, feels, analyses, leads and helps horse's mind and body.
Weight aid ~ Always in harmony with rider's and horse's BALANCE.

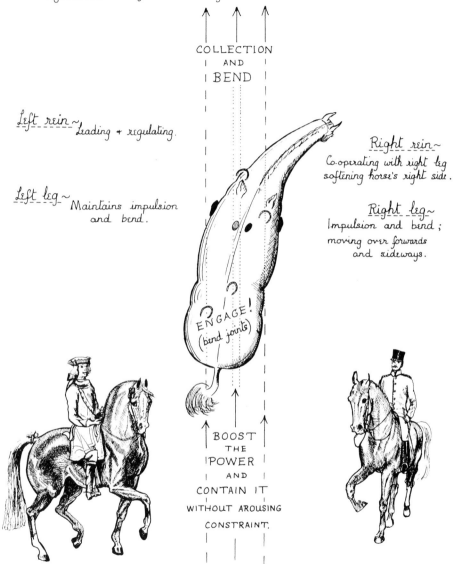

COLLECTION
AND
BEND

Left rein ~ Leading & regulating.

Right rein ~
Co-operating with right leg
softening horse's right side.

Left leg ~ Maintains impulsion
and bend.

Right leg ~
Impulsion and bend;
moving over forwards
and sideways.

ENGAGE!
(bend joints)

BOOST
THE
POWER
AND
CONTAIN IT
WITHOUT AROUSING
CONSTRAINT.

(i)   A small circle and straight ahead, or continue once more in shoulder-in – this is an excellent way to improve the balance and the bend of the shoulder-in.

(ii)   Straight forward on a diagonal or large circle line, at medium trot – this is especially good for the horse's forward urge and will improve the horse's medium trot.

(iii)   Straighten the horse on to the track by moving the forehand over a step, to the right from left shoulder-in, so that the shoulders are aligned in front of the hindquarters – at which moment the horse should be ridden forward at an active or perhaps a medium trot. This last is the more difficult and should not be used until the shoulder-in is of a good quality; it will then test the horse's responsiveness, balance and agility as well as testing the tact and harmony of the rider's aids.

Possibly the easiest and best way to learn shoulder-in is from leg-yielding along the side, from which the shoulder-in can gradually be built by increased influences of the rider's aids particularly that of his *outside*

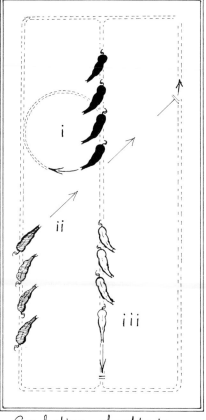

Concluding shoulder-in.

GROUND PLANS FOR SHOULDER-IN.

<u>Increasing the circle</u>   <u>on two tracks.</u>

First in the easy form   of leg-yielding.

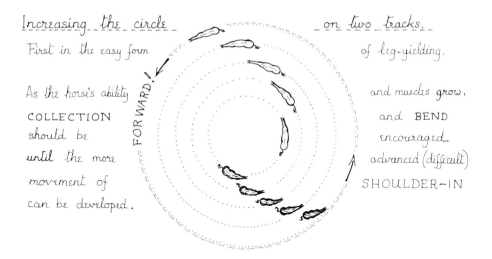

As the horse's ability   and muscles grow,

COLLECTION   and BEND

should be   encouraged

until the more   advanced (difficult)

movement of   SHOULDER-IN

can be developed.

(FORWARD! written within circle diagram)

<u>Over circle side points</u>··· <u>On the centre line</u> ··· <u>From and to small circles.</u>

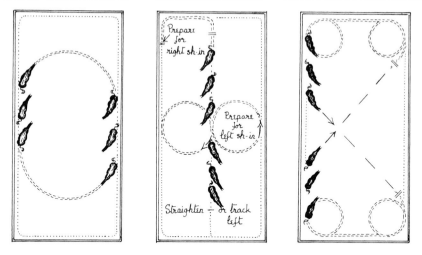

(Labels in centre diagram: Prepare for right sh-in; Prepare for left sh-in; Straighten — or track left)

Riders remember··· all collected work is very demanding,
both mentally and physically, for your horse-partner ~
Ask him for a few strides of shoulder-in and then ride FORWARD.

237

leg. If the rider feels any tension in his horse he must ride forward immediately and return to the easier leg-yielding exercises for a while, to re-establish calmness and the quality of the gait. Alternatively, shoulder-in may be led into from an 8 metre circle. As soon as a few good strides of shoulder-in have been completed, the 8 metre circle and the shoulder-in may be repeated and/or the horse should be ridden forward at a medium gait.

As soon as riders and horses understand the shoulder-in, it is usually better executed slightly inside the outer track or down the centre line, as the rider has then to control the horse solely by the correct use of his aids, rather than by relying on the wall to provide a substitute for his outer leg.

As riders and horses progress and become more correct and confident in this work they may be instructed to decrease and increase the circle on two tracks. When increasing the circle this may now be ridden at a collected gait at shoulder-in.

It is very important that the horse preserves his natural, eager willingness to go forward, that his general elasticity is improved and that his top line becomes markedly rounder as his musculature develops. All these will be improved by combining lateral movements with an interplay between lengthened and shortened strides and many direct but smooth transitions. Such programmes must be thoughtfully planned and ridden, with a certain amount of "dash and dare" but absolutely no hurrying.

Each lateral movement should be thought of as part of a continuous skein of movements within an exercise period which is composed especially to improve all the qualities desired in the riding horse. Each movement should be carefully linked into the next one with a thoughtful regard for how it may be used to develop each ensuing piece of work.

The instructor should place himself in a position which is well in front of his class or pupil in order that he may view the movement and his pupils' aids from the best vantage point as they work towards him, down the centre line, or at the corner at the end of the long side down which the horse is advancing.

Common faults

- Insufficient preparation by the rider, of the plan, himself and the horse.
- Insufficient impulsion and collection – due to weak or fading forward-driving aids, or to the horse's impulsion and movement being stifled by a faulty position or incorrect aids.
- Reins too long: the rider's inner hand moves in towards the horse's withers and cramps the freedom of his shoulders. The movement is then prevented from coming through the whole of the horse.
- Too fast a tempo – the horse cannot keep his balance and loses the cadence and even the rhythm and regularity of the gait.
- The rider's seat is displaced to the outside with the result that the inner side collapses and upsets weight aid, load distribution and balance. Probably his inside knee is neither lowered nor secure. This weight

displacement usually causes the horse to tilt his head in an effort to retain his balance.

• The rider's inside hip joint and seat bone are not eased forward to allow the horse's inside hindleg to come forward and the movement to go through the whole horse. This fault will show iself by the horse's tense back and uneven steps, the loss of forward fluency, and by a tilting of his head.

• The rider has too strong an influence with his inside rein, even hanging on it, or he may move his inner hand across the withers, towards his outer rather than his inner hip. In both cases the horse will be bent in his neck too much, if not exclusively; he will push out his outer shoulder, thus evading his rider's aids, his impulsion will fade and he will no longer be truly working on two tracks.

• The angle of the horse's body with the track or the line of progression may be too wide; this makes the whole movement into a gymnastic "tussle" whereby freedom and impulsion are stifled and the regularity and harmony of the gait are jeopardised.

• The rider's inside leg is placed and used too far back: this will push out the hindquarters instead of encouraging elevation of the trunk up through the shoulders, a bending round the rider's inside leg and engagement of the haunches.

• The rider forgets the importance of the outside aids; he fails to use his outside leg just behind the girth, to maintain the impulsion, the collection and the bend. Only if the rider uses his outside leg sufficiently will he be able to ask the horse to bend in his body, round the rider's inside leg and the gait will remain lively, retaining a good cadence.

• The rider's outside hand is heavy – due to the heel of the hand and the elbow leading the way, rather than the thumb-part of the hand. The horse will usually show resistance in his mouth and/or will tilt his head. He will lose the bend and the cadence of the gait which can become a quick "knee-snapping" scramble which is far removed from shoulder-in.

• The angle between the track being ridden and the horse's body varies during the movement or between left and right shoulder-in. Both faults are attributable to the rider who must be consistent with his aids and must not ask for more bend on the hollow side than the horse can give with ease on the other side, towards which he is more stiff.

• Excess tension! Often due to the rider trying too hard, even to the point of not breathing. Riders must remember to ride with music in their hearts.

Half-Pass

Half-pass, travers and renvers.

These are very closely related: all three are lateral movements in which the horse looks and is bent in the direction in which he is moving. The half-pass is a variable relation to travers and renvers: in its more advanced form it is identical to them.

Half-Passes, Renvers and Travers.

(a composite picture to facilitate understanding
by comparison.)

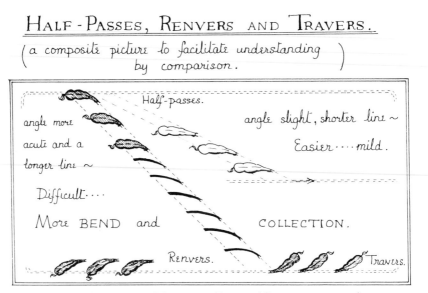

Whereas a half-pass is ridden on a diagonal line, travers and renvers are ridden either down the centre line or near to and along lines which are parallel with the wall. The most usual faults are listed collectively at the end of this subsection.

Introduction

That the half-pass is a lateral movement of more flexibility than it is usually accorded is an ambiguous statement. It is made purposefully, of course, to arouse thought and to awaken realisation that there are, in fact, half-passes and half-passes. There are early, easy ones, and, following a gradual build-up of education and collection, there are later, more difficult ones.

The half-pass is executed on a diagonal line, across or partly across the arena. The horse should remain as nearly parallel as possible with the long side of the arena, with his forehand, however, always very slightly in advance of his hindquarters.

The difficulty or demand of the half-pass can be varied by differences in the angle of the line of progression with the centre line. For example, the angle is much less acute in dressage tests of Medium or Prix St. George standard, and therefore considerably less collection and bend is required in them than is necessary for the more difficult half-passes demanded in tests of Grand Prix level. In the latter, advanced half-passes, the horse must be extremely well collected and uniformly bent from his poll to his tail, as is required in travers and renvers.

As the horse performs the half-pass he should remain on the bit with a lively impulsion, and display all the required qualities of form and gait before, during and after the half-pass. The general picture should be one of suppleness, a calm ease and a reasonable degree of collection, commensurate with the standard of the horse's training.

The aids for half-pass – to the right

(a) The rider makes adequate preparations – the plan, himself and his horse.

(b) He improves the quality of the gait and collects his horse appropriately, using as many half-halts as may be necessary.

(c) Having established a trot (or canter) of suitable collection, well before the point at which he intends to commence the half-pass, the rider makes a further half-halt, and bends the horse to the right round his right leg, at the girth, as if he were starting to ride right shoulder-in.

(d) The rider moves the horse over, forwards and sideways to the right, using his left (outside) leg just behind the girth, supported by a leading right (inside) rein, and as necessary, a lightly containing left rein.

(e) Both of the rider's legs maintain the forward impulsion, especially the right leg which also helps to balance the horse, supports the bending and prevents the hindquarters from swinging too far to the right, in advance of the forehand.

(f) Both reins support the action of the legs: they contain the impulsion and form and regulate the bend, preventing any deviations from the line of progression or of the bend within the horse's body.

(g) The rider's weight should be placed slightly to the right with supple hips. The right hip and knee should be low and secure on the saddle, and the hip and seat bone above it should be kept straight and well forward. His upper body should be vertical and should go well with the horse as he moves forwards and sideways. He should look ahead, tactfully considering the direction as well as his horse's reactions and work.

(h) He should "ride a good finish" – the last steps must be as good as all the others have been – hopefully! Additionally, he must be ready to straighten the horse and go forward or to change the bend, as may be required, as the half-pass is terminated.

Additional notes

Pupils and horses must be well-prepared: they must be confident and competent in their work when performing turns on the spot (on the forehand, or on the haunches) and in leg-yielding.

The half-pass should be introduced at the walk, the instructor explaining and demonstrating the movement and the rider's aids.

The ride should be lined up on the quarter line, facing the long side, along which the instructor will demonstrate the exercise several times so that they can see and understand the ground-plan, the commands, the movement itself and the aids, with particular regard to the fine interplay and harmony of the latter.

The easiest way to teach the half-pass or to improve those which are badly ridden, is to prepare by using a small inwards half-circle and to use the magnetic effect of the wall to help the horses and riders to return forwards and sideways towards their "beloved" outer track!

Introducing the Half-Pass.

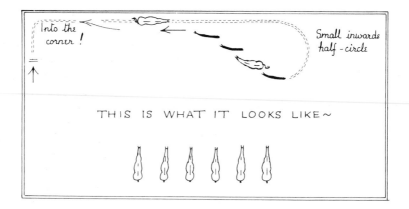

Into the corner !

Small inwards half-circle

THIS IS WHAT IT LOOKS LIKE~

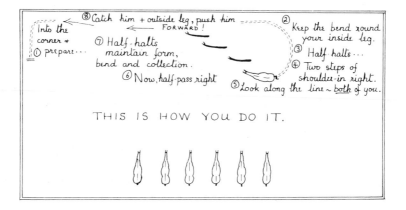

③ Catch him + outside leg, push him FORWARD !

② Keep the bend round your inside leg.

Into the corner + ① prepare...

⑦ Half-halts maintain form, bend and collection.

③ Half-halts...

④ Two steps of shoulder-in right.

⑥ Now, half-pass right

⑤ Look along the line ~ both of you.

THIS IS HOW YOU DO IT.

The exercise can be ridden collectively in open order, and is often better carried out in this way, as a friendly team spirit overcomes individual nervousness, the riders ride naturally and the horses go *forward* extraordinarily well.

The instructor should warn the riders that he requires all the half-circles to be of 8 metres exactly, that they must be preceded by a preparatory half-halt which must be repeated as required before and during the half-pass, and that every rider must leave the outer track together on the final word of command, "Whole ride half-circle and return in half-pass – inwards half-circle, *now*."

They should be commanded to trot as the majority reach the outer track, after which they should be brought to a walk with good dressing which they must organise for themselves. The exercise can then be repeated on the other rein.

In order to perfect this introductory stage as quickly as possible the instructor must note any faults displayed by members of the class. Faulty positions can be corrected and overcome while the ride is on the move but if any rider is confused, lacks effectiveness, fluency and confidence, the instructor should line up the ride on the quarter line so that he can ask each member of the ride for a question or comment and can use this opportunity to demonstrate the wrong and the correct methods to them. He must be careful to question the whole ride, from left to right or vice versa, in order to preserve the nerves and dignity of the less confident members – although probably they made the worst mistakes. It is an easy but bad instructing fault to single out the lesser riders first.

As soon as the ride has accomplished half-passes to the right and to the left successfully at the walk, the movement should be taught at the trot, following the same ground-plan. The instructor must remind his pupils to make full, discreet use of half-halts, to ride well-rounded 8 metre half-circles, and to preserve the bend created by the correct riding of the half-circles as they ride the half-pass. He should encourage them to reward their horses instantly whenever they comply willing and give their riders a good feel.

Later this exercise may be used again in a more advanced form, on inner rectangles or "little squares" which are ridden 1 metre inside the outer track. This is the preferred format because it is much better for the horses' training that they are not allowed to go right out on to the outer track at the end of their half-passes where their impulsion and straightness may so easily be inhibited by the wall. In this later exercise the riders "catch" their horses with their outside aids and make a definite transition, straight forward into medium trot for several strides before returning to collected trot or whatever may be commanded.

When the riders and horses are proficient in the easiest of the above exercises, as a variation they may be worked down the centre line, from which they ride in half-pass, nearly out to the quarter or three-quarter line. Each rider then straightens his horse before riding a half-circle outward, on to the outer track, or points his horse back on to the centre line, depending on his horse's requirements and on the space available. The riders must be alert and work well as a team. As a general rule at the end of the centre line every rider should take the opposite rein from the rider in front of him; this is best for training both riders and horses and will preserve an equal number of horses on each rein, all equally spaced as they work together in the arena.

From the first lessons in the half-pass, instructors must stress the importance of the use of the inside leg – the rider's right leg in the right half-pass. Only if this is used sufficiently attentively with the knee low and firm and the lower part applied strongly at the girth, will the horse lift up and bring forward his right hindleg, which in turn will cause him to engage his left hindleg even more in order to cross it over in front of his right, forward stepping, hindleg. In this way the horse's shoulders and

Exercises to Improve Half-Passes.

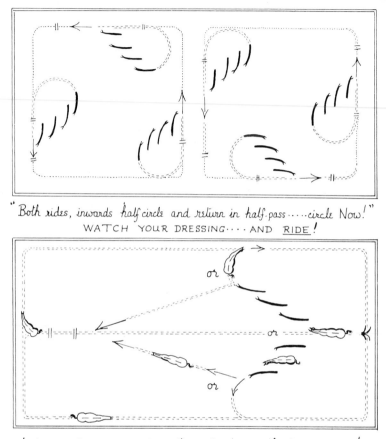

"Both sides, inwards half circle and return in half-pass .....circle Now!"
WATCH YOUR DRESSING···· AND <u>RIDE</u>*!*

Individual variations from the centre line ~ thinking riding!

middle part are lifted, his hindquarters are actively engaged and his form and collection will improve. The riders should carry their whips in their inside hands to strengthen the inner leg aid if necessary.

The instructor should watch his pupils collectively from the side during the first exercise at walk and trot. In later exercises he should observe them from behind where he can best see the position and influence of their weight, hips and legs, and from the front to check the riders' rein aids, their positions, the horses' general form and the correct qualities and fluency of the movement. From both viewpoints he must encourage the use of the inner leg and a soft, elastic pressure on the inner stirrup iron; he must help his pupils to evaluate the feel of good work for themselves, impressing upon them that they should be content to settle for a few good strides rather than risk a deterioration of the movement by prolonging the half-pass. He must get each pupil to think of, and need to use, the outside leg well forward as they ride the last step of the half-pass, so that they push the horses' shoulders in front of their hips, and then ride their horses straight forward, parallel with the outer track, at an active gait.

Travers

Introduction

Travers (head to the wall, or to the line of progression) is a collected and comparatively advanced suppling exercise on two tracks in which the horse is bent round the rider's inside leg. The bend is uniform from the poll to the tail, and the horse looks in the direction in which he is moving. The forehand follows a line inside the outer track, or down the centre line with the hindquarters about one step to the inside. The horse's outside legs pass and cross in front of the inside legs; the inside forefoot and the outside hind foot are more or less on the same track, and the angle of the horse's body with the line of progression should be approximately 30° but never more than 45°.

The aids for travers to the right

As the aids are so very similar to those for the half-pass to the right, the aids and the method are here combined into one paragraph.

When riding on the right rein at collected trot the rider makes a half-halt. He then uses a volte or thinks of a quarter pirouette to the right to prepare, position and bend the horse before he rides him in travers down the centre line or just inside the outer track. He keeps the horse's hindquarters about one step inside the line being followed by the forehand, using his left (outside) leg just behind the girth to move the horse over, supported if necessary by the left rein. The horse is bent round the rider's right (inside) leg, which is on the girth, and the right rein leads the forehand to the right; the horse moves forward and sideways on two tracks. Both of the rider's legs maintain the forward impulsion, and both reins contain the form and collection, support the legs when and where necessary and regulate the bend. The rider's right leg asks for the horse's inside hindleg to come forward under the horse, and it prevents the hindquarters from swinging too far to the right. The rider's weight should be placed slightly to the inside with a soft, elastic pressure on the inner stirrup iron; he must be supple in his hips with his inside seat bone slightly forward, the upper body stays softly erect and must go with the movement and the rider must look ahead tactfully. As in the half-pass it is of great importance that the rider pays enough attention to the right (inside) aids, especially to his right leg, because an increased engagement of the horse's right hindleg also makes the horse engage his left hindleg so that it crosses over further underneath his body, and this, in turn, gradually increases the horse's collection and improves his form.

When the travers movement is finished the horse should be straightened and moved forward at an active gait. When training riders and horses in travers it is often advisable to finish with a circle or volte on a single track after which they ride straight forward, or repeat the travers again.

Additional notes

Although the ground-plan, the feel and the aids may be introduced by asking pupils to ride their horses just inside the outer track at the walk, this method should not be prolonged beyond the first lesson as this advantage cannot outweigh the disadvantages of restriction and lack of "room" or scope for the desired impulsion and collection.

To prevent the horse from the bad habit of "leaning" his outside shoulder against the wall, travers should be ridden on the centre line or on other lines parallel to it, or on a short diagonal line across the arena and always well clear of the track along the wall. Thus, although the movement is often described as being "head to the wall" this is the one place where it should not be ridden, or at least, never with the forehand moving along the outer track and the horse's outside shoulder virtually pressed against the wall, for this would effectively block all his natural forward impulses.

"Ovening and closing the camera lens"

This is the label Major Boltenstern attached to one of his favourite exercises for introducing and developing a fluent feel for lateral work in riders and horses. In 1962 when we first heard this novel name, it gave a familiar exercise a better meaning with consequent improvement in our understanding and riding of "decreasing and increasing the circle – on two tracks."

The horse is ridden in travers to decrease the circle and in shoulder-in to increase it again, the rider being very careful to preserve the bend of the horse's body around his inner leg – applying his outside leg also behind the girth while keeping his inside hip joint and seat bone well forward and his inside shoulder back. The horse's collection and bend remain unchanged throughout this exercise as does the positioning of the rider's aids. Thus it is very easy and natural for both partners to devote more time and thought to developing the major desirable qualities of the gait and of the horse's form. Above all, the rider is given a wonderful opportunity to think and feel how he influences his horse through his own position on his horse's back and by soft yet meaningful aids.

The engagement of the horse's hindquarters, so necessary for this work, may be encouraged by the following exercise:

"The little square"

Inside the track and with the aid of preliminary half-halts, a little collection can be asked for as each corner of the square is ridden, followed

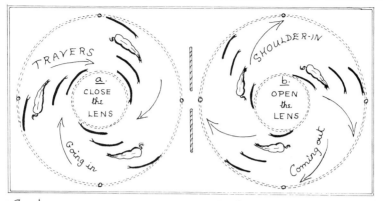

Six horses and riders can be instructed together .... as a team ~
Friendly rivalry between the riders on A. circle and those at C. adds spice!

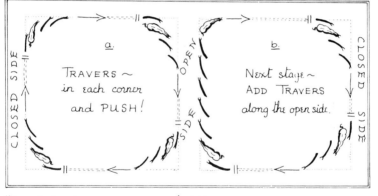

"Don't forget HALF-HALTS! To improve your seat and ....
your horse's balance, his co-ordination and his IMPULSION.

by a push with the forward-driving aids straight into a more active gait, so that the square is ridden to the directive "Straighten, half-halt, weight, turn and push."

The next stage is for the two corners on the open side of the square to be ridden in collection, working towards travers after the first corner, with a slight bend round the rider's inside leg while the outside leg holds the hindquarters on a slightly inner track. After the next corner the horse is ridden straight forward energetically with an active outside leg on the girth, on the line of the square.

Renvers

Introduction

Renvers (tail to the wall, or to the line of progression), is the inverse position to travers, with the hindquarters instead of the forehand following a line inside the outer track, or down the centre line. In renvers to the right the horse looks and is bent to the right round the rider's inside leg. The horse moves on two tracks with his body at an angle of approximately 30° and not more than 45° with the line of progression; his left legs pass and cross in front of his right legs. Except for the position "tail to the wall" as opposed to "head to the wall", the aids and the general principles are identical to those required for travers.

The aids for renvers to the right

As for the travers described above, the aids and method are condensed here into one paragraph.

The rider begins on the right rein, he collects his horse, and just before he reaches the far end of the long side, he makes a half-halt, and then rides as nearly as possible, a half-pirouette to the right. Before this movement is quite completed – that is where the horse's body is at an angle of approximately 30° with the wall – the rider applies the aids for the renvers which are identical to those for travers, described above, and he rides on two tracks with the hindlegs just inside the track along which he had previously ridden and with the forelegs following an inner track.

Common faults

The faults listed below are common to riders executing the half-pass, travers and renvers – to the right.
- Insufficient preparation.
- The horse is not truly on the bit.
- Fading impulsion – rider not using both his legs sufficiently.
- The rider makes too few half-halts to improve the horse's balance, collection and the quality of the gait before or during the half-pass. If the rider says, "Steady – forward, steady – forward", under his breath to himself and his horse, this will often prove to be of considerable help to the consistency of the horse's balance, impulsion and rhythm, and to his suppleness and collection.
- The horse may tilt his head or appear unlevel; in both cases the rider must be told to check and improve his own position in the saddle and then to push the horse forward on to the bit so that his haunches may be engaged in a way which allows him to work through his back to the reins. A displaced seat is the most common cause of head-tilting in the horse, especially if this is combined with a stiffness in the rider's hips, and in this case, if the right seat bone is back, "blocking" the forward movement of the horse's right hindleg and the play of his back muscles.
- Too fast a pace and too little collection – ease and harmony are replaced by worry, awkwardness and irregularities of form and gait.
- The rider asks for too much bend in the horse's neck, he fails to achieve any bend at all, or he rides his horse with a wrong bend. All of these are indicative of faulty riding: the rider's education does not yet match the movement he is trying to ride.

- The horse loses the almost parallel position of his body with the centre line; his hindquarters either "lead" or "trail"; the movement becomes valueless.
- The rider asks the horse to move sideways at too acute an angle, which destroys the fluency and value of the whole movement. When this fault occurs in a dressage test it is usually due to thoughtless, inaccurate riding, the rider having failed to prepare in the previous movement. He makes a late start into the half-pass and forces his horse along an almost impossibly angled line of progression in order to avoid overshooting the next marker in the test.
- Resistance – any sign of evasion or resistance is a fault. This may be due to lack of equestrian tact or education in the rider or of training in the horse, or to pain in the horse's mouth, trunk or limbs.
- Rider faults – these two words can cover a veritable multitude of sins! Much as the pupil will blame the horse, and dressage judges have to, the instructor must apportion the blame where rightfully it belongs. His first priority is to ensure that his pupil's position is as near to natural perfection as his physique will allow, and that his application of the aids with his horse is technically correct, clear yet smooth and soft, and that there is a good rapport and harmony between the rider and his horse.

Rather than finishing with a negative string of the main rider faults, it is more helpful to conclude with an example of some of the instructions which can be given to a class riding half-pass, travers or renvers – in this instance, to the right.

"*Steady the pace* – you must improve the quality of the gait."

"*Shorten your reins* for a light contact – and keep them short."

"*Think* where you are going, and how your horse *feels*."

"*Relax your seats!*" (Maybe this is technically incorrect, but it is a short phrase which conveys a vital message quickly, and simply, whereas, "remove the excess tension in your back, pelvis and thighs" or an injunction to decontract the same could confuse the issue – as well as the tissues – and certainly would miss the moment.)

"*Keep your horses on the bit!* – ask them to move in a better form."

"*More legs* – especially the inside one."

"*Shoulders* – correct your posture!"

"*Half-halt!*"

and "*Well done!*"

"Remember your upper arms belong to your body and your elbows belong to your hips – *keep your elbows in*, lead with your right thumb."

"*Keep your knees down* – as if your knee-caps are looking at your horse's elbows!"

"Use a small circle or a volte to prepare your horse – *establish the bend round your right leg*."

"*Look where you are going* – make it easy for your horse and watch out for each other."

"*Sit to the right*."

"Keep your right hip forward – and your right knee firm."

"Count the rhythm – to your horse – and keep counting in your whole being. Softly, fluently – keep it going – *forward!"*

"Well done!", whenever and providing it was well done.

All the above instructions should be repeated at frequent and regular intervals.

These and other similar corrections will soon effect an improvement in the horse's performances. It is not necessary for the instructor to label each correction with a pupil's name, it is much more generally effective if he does not do so, in order that all pupils can benefit. The exception to this is the phrase, *"Well done!"* If praise is directed individually to "Mark" or "Erica", the pupil's spirit will soar and the rest of the class will try a little harder hoping to earn similar acclaim for their good horsemanship.

Most of the faults apparent in the horse's performance can be laid fairly and squarely on the rider's doorstep. If he is to succeed, the rider must be big enough to appreciate his inadequacy and that he needs help. This, of course, is where the instructor plays a vital part in every equestrian competitor's riding life, for success can only be achieved through constructive and constant criticism and correction – as rider, horse and instructor strive together for perfection.

As soon as the foregoing lateral movements can be accomplished to the satisfaction of the rider, the instructor, the judge – and the horse – the rider should learn how to put them together into a sequence which is logical, interesting, stimulating and artistic.

Lateral movements are for the horse what a dancer's, swimmer's or keep-fit enthusiast's daily routine is to a human. Thus, just as it is better

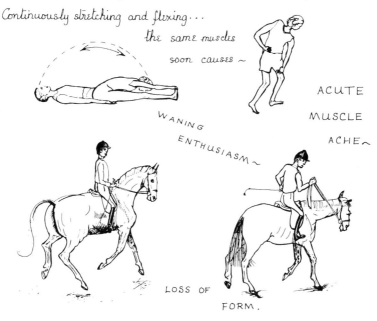

Continuously stretching and flexing...
the same muscles
soon causes ~
ACUTE
MUSCLE
ACHE~
WANING
ENTHUSIASM ~
LOSS OF
FORM.

for a human being to work methodically through a variety of exercises rather than wearing out one set of muscles – stretching and flexing the same muscles for half an hour – so it is with the horse. He should never be expected to go round and round the school in travers – just think of the muscle ache – which would be enough to dampen any horse's enthusiasm, diminish his form and destroy his impulsion, suppleness and collection as well as his gaits. Lateral movements should be created piece by piece, ridden for short stretches only with well measured reward and interspersed with easier forward-going work. When riders and horses are confident and proficient at all the various movements, these may be put together so that each exercise leads into and improves the next one, the rider thinking and directing the horse's movements and the horse following his rider's thoughts and responding with gymnastic enthusiasm to his every indication.

Ground-plans and lateral movements which are accurately, and correctly ridden can provide the basis for scores of work or dressage programmes, whereby the smooth interplay of the movements is reflected in the balance, suppleness and developing musculature of the horse; the rider's aids become further refined and the horse becomes increasingly responsive.

Counter-change of hand

Introduction

A counter-change of hand is the term given to a series of two or more half-passes in alternate directions; the angle of the track of the half-passes will depend on the number of half-passes to be accommodated in the given space. The number of counter-changes to be fitted into a given area and the angle at which they are ridden combine to determine the degree of difficulty of the whole movement; the greater the number, the more acute the angles and the more difficult are the half-passes.

In each half-pass, the forehand must lead very slightly and the transitions must be absolutely smooth and perfect. At every change of direction, the horse should display a willingness as well as a fluent suppleness through his body; he should follow his rider's leadership without question or resistance – the rhythm, tempo and regularity of the gait should remain constant!

As he makes each change of direction, the rider must think of riding the beginning of a quarter pirouette, to ensure that the hindquarters will not lead in the new direction.

A *zig-zag* consists of a series of short half-passes, for an equal number of metres or steps on either side of the centre line; the distance covered at each step must be consistent. These exercises not only test the quality of the half-passes themselves, but also the horse's obedience, suppleness, balance and general acceptance of the aids will be revealed by the fluency

ONE COUNTER CHANGE

*Easy angles,
short lines.*

MORE SEVERE.
*angles more acute,
both lines are longer.*

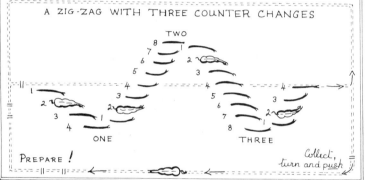

A ZIG-ZAG WITH THREE COUNTER CHANGES

TWO

ONE   THREE

PREPARE *!*   *Collect,
turn and push*

and regularity of the exercise as a whole. The movement should be symmetrical, calm and effortless from beginning to end.

Counter-changes of hand are fun to ride and are an excellent means of advancing the horse's training, but . . . they are also extremely testing of a rider's ability. He can only succeed in these exercises if his seat is well-established, poised and supple and his aids are tactful and correct – he must lead his partner mainly with his "thought, weight and thumb" – as always!

Changing from one lateral movement to another

In the early stages of lateral work, when changing from one lateral movement to another or changing direction, the rider should ride the horse forward for one or a few steps before commencing the next exercise. Later, with more advanced horses and riders, these changes can be made without such an interval as long as the whole performance retains high degrees of fluency, balance, collection and ease.

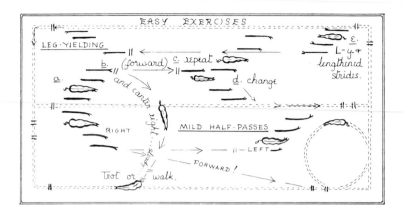

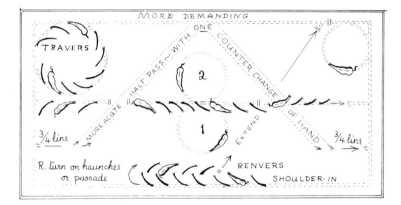

These changes, with or without interval, greatly improve the horse's suppleness, and increase the rider's feel and ability to change and use his aids correctly, tactfully and fluently.

If the rider wishes to change from shoulder-in to travers, it is best if a small circle or a volte on a single track in the direction towards which the horse is bent, is interposed between the two movements. Thus the order becomes, "shoulder-in left, volte left, travers left" – the volte provides extra time and room for the re-direction of the horse.

To change from travers to shoulder-in the same principles are followed as described above, except that this time, the change-over may be made directly, omitting the volte. In this case the bend is retained, the horse is ridden forward by both of the rider's legs, as if on a single track on a small circle, for one or two steps as the hindquarters come to follow the forehand. The horse is rebalanced with a half-halt and is then ridden in shoulder-in.

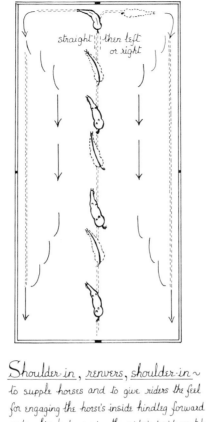

straight then left
or right

<u>Shoulder-in</u> , <u>renvers</u>, <u>shoulder-in</u> ~
to supple horses and to give riders the feel
for engaging the horse's inside hindleg forward
under his body, under the rider's inside seat bone.
"Inside hip <u>forward</u> !"
Later this may be developed to include (and improve) the half-pass.

When the rider changes from shoulder-in to renvers, he makes a half-halt and turns, thinking of a half-pirouette, and then returns in renvers inside the track in the opposite direction, the horse's oblique position, bend and impulsion being carefully maintained. If the movements are being ridden down the centre line, shoulder-in left is followed by a volte left at X, both being on the left side of the centre line. After X, renvers left is continued with the horse's forehand to the right side of the centre line, the whole sequence being artistic and fluent for the horse and rider.

If a pupil were to ask, "What are the main considerations for me to keep uppermost in my mind when I ride my horse through a work programme which incorporates lateral movements?" I would reply:
• You must think for and with your horse, through every step of the programme – making sure that he is on the bit and in good form all the way.

• Guard your horsemanship! Analyse, criticise and improve your balance and body control as well as the manner and mode of your communication with your horse.

• Your thought and weight aids are major influences in this as in all other work; their invitations must be exactly right in timing and amount.

• Pay great attention to how you are going to ask the horse to carry out each movement and to change fluently from one movement to the next so that the work is easy, interesting and yet a little testing; aim to improve his balance and co-ordination and aim, above all, to develop the mighty muscles of your horse's body.

• Be dextrous rather than dogmatic with your aids to encourage a more lively gait and a greater flexion of the horse's hindlegs. To increase the carrying capacity of his hindquarters, ask him to bring each hindleg further forward and in, under his trunk's central line and the weighty mass of his body – topped by his rider!

Very rarely is it advisable for a rider to put one of his legs aside, passively resting, out of action. Certainly he cannot afford to do so when riding any of the lateral movements.

• Give extra thought to the application of "the other leg", the outside leg for leg-yielding and shoulder-in and the inside leg for half-pass, travers and renvers.

For example, in *shoulder-in* the rider should time and use his outside leg positively and effectively, just behind the girth, to contain and increase the horse's impulsion. Additionally this outside leg should encourage the horse to bring his outside hindleg well forward; consequently he will have to make an even greater bending and forward reach with his inside hindleg to bring it across in front of the outside hindleg.

In *half-pass, travers and renvers* the rider should use "the other leg", his inside leg, at the girth, quite actively and with careful timing, to encourage the horse to bring his inside hindleg well forward under his body. The horse will then have to organise himself and motivate the great muscles of his trunk to bend both hindlegs particularly well in order to lift the outside hind foot across, in front of the forward-placed inside hindleg.

Thus you can see that "the other leg" is largely responsible for producing the desired bending and collection of the more advanced lateral movements – which themselves do so much to improve the horse's form.

○ The Double Bridle

So what about the double bridle? Should we never use it? The answer to that double question must surely be, "Yes, of course you may and should use it, from time to time, when your pony or horse is ready to wear it. The former should be well-trained, on the bit and confident, capable of carrying out his school work and general tasks in a good form. You, the rider, must have a seat which is well-balanced, supple, educated and secure, completely independent of the reins. Both partners should be taught how to go in, and how to use, a double bridle. It is not difficult but it is very important that you should learn correct methods so that fitting, action and rein-handling become a natural but correct facet of your riding."

Riding in a Double Bridle

First, the bridle and the bits must fit and be suitable for the horse concerned. The general principles of the fitting and action of a double bridle were described in Book 1.

Every rider should make a point of checking that his saddlery fits well before he mounts. He must be especially particular if the horse is wearing a double bridle because there is more to check and there is a greater risk of damaging the horse's mouth if any part of this bridle is incorrect.

The bridlework should fit in the same way as a snaffle bridle:

• The whole bridle should be of a type suitable for the horse's head and for the purpose for which it will be used. Although very thin leather work may be preferred by some exhibitors at horse shows it is impractical for all other purposes.

• The browband should not be so short that it pulls the headpiece forward to pinch the base of the ears, nor must it be so long that it loops down over the horse's brows.

• The order of the headpieces at the poll should be:

  (i) The broad, bridle headpiece lies on top; it includes the throat-lash and supports the curb bit.

  (ii) The bridoon or snaffle headpiece lies immediately under the main headpiece; the buckle lies on the right or off side of the horse's head.

  (iii) The noseband headpiece lies under the other two headpieces and rests on the horse's mane at the poll; it is buckled on the left or near side.

  Thus there are always two buckles on each side of the horse's head.

• The noseband should be of a plain, cavesson type. It should be fitted under the other cheekpieces and lie comfortably around the horse's jaws, two fingers' breadth below the lower edge of the zygomatic ridge or facial crest, and when the noseband itself is fastened it should allow two fingers' breadth between its front and the horse's nasal bone. If it is done up more tightly then the training is at fault.

• The bridoon bit should be fitted exactly as if it were a snaffle (which it is!). It should be the correct width for the horse and have a mouthpiece which is essentially comfortable for him. The rings of the bridoon are smaller than those of an ordinary snaffle so as not to be too cumbersome. The bit should be pulled up high enough to make a little smile but not so high that it forces a grimace!

• The curb bit should be of a correct width, type and proportion and should lie just below the bridoon in the horse's mouth. The height of the curb bit must be right for the comfort of his chin groove as well as his mouth. Great pain can be caused if the bit is fitted too high, so that when the curb reins move the lower ends of the bit's cheekpiece backwards, the upper ends lift the curb chain above the chin groove and on to the sharp, bony prominences of the back of the lower jaw.

• The curb chain should remain snugly in the chin groove and act when the cheekpieces are drawn back to form an angle of 45° with the line of the closed lips.

Fitting the curb chain

The links of a curb chain are designed so that when the chain is twisted to take up the slack, the links then present a flat yet supple and strong bearing surface.

The rider should stand on the left side of the horse and make all adjustments from that side, working under the lower jaw and between the snaffle and the curb reins. This is the most efficient stance unless the right hook is too much closed for the curb chain links to slide readily on and off, in which case the rider may have to move round to the offside and make adjustments there.

The curb chain should be twisted until it lies flat, then with the loose or "fly" link in the centre hanging down, the chain is attached to the right hook on the offside of the horse's curb bit. The inner bearing surface of the chain should face downward when it is being lifted on to the hook on the right or offside and the chain should always be given an extra clockwise half twist to bring the bearing surface uppermost before it is fitted on to the left or nearside hook.

This rule applies to the end links which are always put on the hooks first as well as to the subsequent links which are added to adjust the curb chain to fit the horse's chin groove.

There should be no more than two links on either hook, that is, the end link and the second, third or fourth link.

The chain should be adjusted as evenly as possible on both sides and not more than one link's difference between the two sides. It must not be too tight or too loose. The mouthpiece and the curb chain should act together on the horse's lower jaw when the cheeks of the bit form an angle of 45° with the line of the horse's mouth.

THE CURB CHAIN.

Incorrect ~ untwisted.

Right hand hook.

Incorrectly twisted ~ anti-clockwise.

Correct.

Correct ~ taking up on the right side, last link on first, then the required link. Thumbnail up both times!

Left hook.

Correct ~ last link on first, then the shortening link ~ Thumbnail down both times, for a neat and comfortable fit.

Correct ~ Twisted clockwise.

tightening at an angle of 45.°

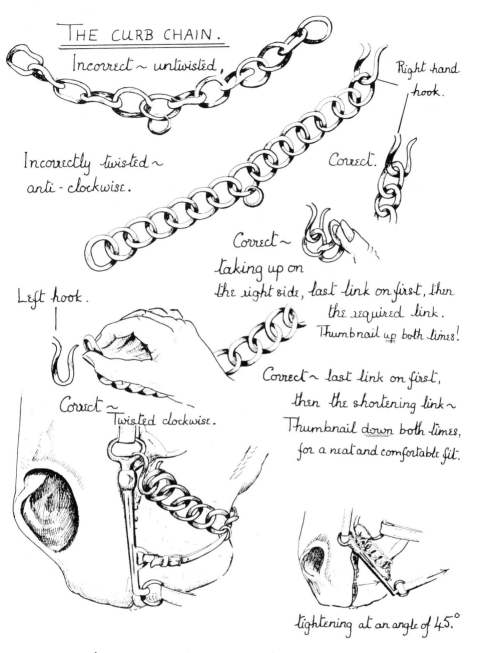

Adjusting the curb chain.

If the curb chain is still slack when adjusted to the fourth link on each side, then it is too long. It is advisable to ask the blacksmith to cut off one or more links from each end.

Whereas it is comparatively simple to hook the links on to the right hook and to keep the bearing surface of the chain flat on the horse's chin groove, it is the last part of the operation which provides the test – the left hook is the one which tries or proves the horseman! Often it is difficult to give the chain the extra half twist needed to keep the chain flat, especially when putting on the second, adjusting link. If the hand is above the chain and the thumb is on the outside of the chain and is always stationed on the outside, the problem will be solved quite easily: "thumb-nail downwards" is the infallible rule, for the end link and the adjusting link.

If the chain is not given this extra half twist, it will be partially unravelled and the top edge of the curb chain will dig into the delicate structure and tissues of the horse's lower jaw.

A lip-strap should always be worn as its fulfils three important functions:

(i)   It prevents the horse from immobilising the curb bit by catching hold of one of the cheeks with his corner incisor teeth.

(ii) It prevents the curb bit from becoming reversed if the horse throws his head up and down violently, which he may do if he is startled or upset.

(iii) It prevents the curb chain from being lost, and for this reason it should be fastened before the bridle leaves the saddle room.

The severity of a double bridle depends on the length and proportions of the cheekpieces, the height of the port and the tightness of the curb chain, as well as the temperament, hands and education of the rider handling the reins. It is not a bridle for young horses, however high-mettled they may be, nor is it for inexperienced riders for, if it is incorrectly used, a double bridle can ruin a horse's confidence as well as his gaits.

Action of the double bridle

THE BRIDOON

This acts on the tongue, bars and lips of the horse's lower jaw and the rider uses this snaffle bit to convey his light, smooth rein aids at all times; thus he guides, regulates or restrains as required with the bridoon reins.

THE CURB BIT

This acts on the bars of the horse's mouth and perhaps slightly on the tongue, combined with a leverage supplied by the curb chain on the horse's chin groove; there is also very slight pressure on the poll due to the forward tilt of the top of the curb bit. These combined actions encourage the relaxation of the lower jaw and make the horse's response, in this respect, to the rein aid, quicker, lighter and more sophisticated. The bridoon rein speaks – the curb rein adds refinement to the speech!

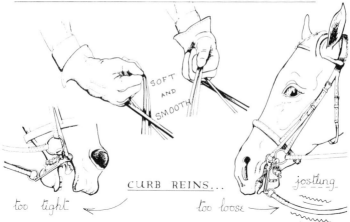

SOFT AND SMOOTH

CURB REINS...   *jostling*

too tight ←   *too loose* →

Holding the reins

There are several good methods of holding the reins of a double bridle. Having tried most of them I can recommend one I have found best, and which is simple and effective and causes least change and upset to the rider's trained, subconscious habit and reactions.

The rider holds the bridoon rein where he usually holds the snaffle rein, between the little and the ring fingers, with the curb rein brought inside, under the bridoon rein, to be held between the ring and middle fingers.

The thumb lies mainly on the bridoon rein where it lies over the middle of the index finger. The curb reins must never be too tight nor yet too loose, for then the slackness of the reins will make the curb bit jostle in the horse's mouth.

The aims of riding in a double bridle

These are to further the horse's advanced dressage work, increasing the alert and light response to his rider's aids and adding grace, contained power and elegance to his form and movement. In addition there are three practical reasons:

(i) To show a horse to his best advantage. A show horse will often move in better self-carriage when wearing a double bridle always providing that the rider is skilled enough to allow him to do so. Knowledgeable show or conformation judges will, however, always recognise and commend the long-term training policy of a rider who shows his four-year-old horse in a snaffle.

(ii) To accustom the horse to a double bridle when he may have to wear one for competition purposes – dressage tests of Medium standard and above, or show classes.

(iii) To accustom the rider to the correct handling of the reins and the use of a double bridle, to enhance the sensitivity of his aids.

For riding in a double bridle – all indicating bad training methods – the following false reasons should be avoided:

- "To improve the horse's head carriage – to bring his nose in." An incorrect assumption: the horse's head carriage must be a result of correct forward riding, so that the impulsion comes from active hindlegs, through the horse's back to the bit. Thus the young horse must go correctly in a snaffle before he wears a double bridle.
- "To stop the horse – a double bridle, or a pelham, gives me better brakes." A long-term fallacy. Eventually the horse will stiffen his back, neck and jaw against the pain in his jaw, which reduces the length and buoyancy of his strides and his mouth will become sore, hardened and even calloused. The horse must be schooled in a snaffle and trained to go smoothly, obediently and in balance in this bit, if his form, his gaits and his mouth are to improve rather than deteriorate.
- "It's rather smart to ride in a double bridle." The worst reason of all!

Pelhams – a word of warning!

Fortunately for horses pelham bits are not as popular as they were even a few years ago and their use is more or less confined to the polo field and to children's ponies.

The pelham was often presumed to be a simple, mild bit because there was only one bit in the horse's mouth. It was thought to have "just a little more braking power than a snaffle", and to be far milder than a double bridle for the latter, "filled the horse's mouth with ironmongery". In fact the pelham is a relatively severe bit due to the complications of its actions.

First, let us consider the mouthpiece. A snaffle with one or two joints lies reasonably snugly and comfortably round the horse's tongue and on the sides of his mouth, and the action of either or both reins is simple, direct and can be very smooth. A straight mouthpiece is more harsh, acting on the tongue on which it lodges. An action on one end of the bit has a dislodging action on the other end as the mouthpiece is rigid, being all in one piece.

The bridoon of a double bridle is a comfortable jointed snaffle and is the principal bit with which the rider works when he rides his horse in a double bridle.

The pelham has only one mouthpiece and herein lies the snag. Usually the mouthpiece is straight and thus it can never have the soft and supple action of the snaffle.

Theoretically the rider should use *either* the top rein of the pelham which lifts the bit and curb chain up in the horse's mouth so that the chain is lifted above its correct position in the chin groove, and the bit action is that of an unbroken snaffle, *or* the lower rein, when the curb chain sits and acts correctly, the bit action being that of a curb.

In practice both reins are often used together, with a dead hold so that the horse learns to lean on the bit and to pull, or to over-bend and pull.

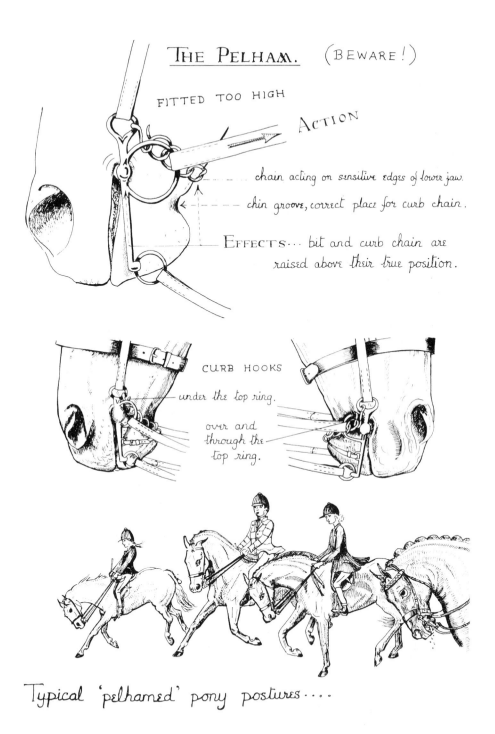

THE PELHAM. (BEWARE!)

FITTED TOO HIGH

ACTION

chain acting on sensitive edges of lower jaw.

chin groove, correct place for curb chain.

EFFECTS... bit and curb chain are raised above their true position.

CURB HOOKS

under the top ring.

over and through the top ring.

Typical 'pelhamed' pony postures....

The bars of the horse's mouth soon become calloused and ossified, and the horse "loses his mouth". Once the sensitivity is lost in this way it can never be regained.

The secondary risk is that the horse's reaction to a pelham often has an adverse affect on his balance, form and action. He goes more and more on his forehand, leaning on the rider's hands, with a stiff body and a stifled movement so that all his gaits become awkward and concussively short-striding.

On the other hand, every horse or pony that has been well-schooled in a snaffle will go well in a double bridle for special occasions providing that it has been introduced carefully and correctly.

11 Advice to Intermediate Instructor's Examination Candidates

Although this chapter is written with the main object of helping Assistant Instructors to prepare for the Intermediate Instructor's Examination it is also aimed at a wider field. It is hoped that all horsemen will glean some help from the information given under the several sub-titles of these examinations.

The principles are similar for every standard of test or examination, from Pony Club B Test to the B.H.S. Fellowship, but as it is always wise to walk before learning to run, the B.H.S. Intermediate Instructor's Examination will be used as an example – that for the Fellowship will be tackled a little later!

The Intermediate Instructor's Examination is composed of two entirely separate parts. The first part is a test of the individual's personal standard of horsemanship and of stable management or horse care. In England there is a wide variety of riders and/or horse owners; many are members of the B.H.S. some of whom have their own horses while others do not. There are also riders who join a local Riding Club or Pony Club. In order to avoid unnecessary duplication of examinations, and also in an endeavour to unite all the different groups within the national training and examinations system and to keep their standards level, any one of the top proficiency certificates will be accepted as the first leg of the B.H.S. Intermediate Instructor's Certificate. These highest awards for proficiency are:

- The B.H.S. Stage IV
- The Riding Club, Grade IV
- The Pony Club A Test.

The second leg is taken as a separate examination and is that for the Intermediate Teaching Certificate.

The two legs may be taken in either order; when both have been passed, the student is awarded the full Intermediate Instructor's Certificate and is qualified to give lessons without supervision and to take a certain amount of responsibility in and around the yard.

Dealing with the examination leg by leg:

The First Leg

For this, as listed above, there are three options. The choice for each student is usually quite easy. If the student has been studying at one of the B.H.S. approved riding schools, in all probability he will already have taken one or more of the B.H.S. stage examinations as well as that for the Assistant Instructor, in which case he will sit the B.H.S. Stage IV examination. If, on the other hand, he is a long-established member of the Riding Club or of the Pony Club then he will sit the Grade IV or A Test.

The syllabi for all three examinations are similar in content as well as in the standard required for a pass. Although the syllabi may differ in their wording, in small details, or the order of their respective requirements and in the day's format, the pass standard of the skills of the horseman's craft are parallel in all three examinations.

The requirements are listed under two main headings, equitation or riding, and stable management or horsemastership; they may be summarised as follows:

- Equitation. Candidates must be educated horsemen, riding well on the flat and over fences and being capable of training horses up to the standard necessary to compete with success in Novice horse trials or dressage events at Elementary level.
- Stable management. This subject is wide and is tested both practically and orally.

Candidates should understand the reason for maintaining a correct posture when riding and their influence should be unobtrusive yet effective as they ride their horses to improvement with logic and tact both in the manège and out of doors.

They should know the qualities desirable in a riding horse and have at least a basic understanding of the following terms: balance, good form, free forward movement, rhythm, calmness, suppleness, impulsion, straightness, submission, on the bit, cadence, extension and collection.

They should have a sound knowledge of school figures and their uses; they should be able to ride trained horses in the school movements required at Elementary dressage standard, including turns on the spot, simple changes of leg, counter-canter and the easier lateral movements.

They should understand the action and fitting of the more usual types of saddlery, appreciate the disadvantages of using the various gadgets on the market, and be experienced in the correct use of a double bridle.

They should be capable of making clear, sound appraisals of a variety of horses.

They must be able to ride over a course of fences which will include changes of direction, gait and speed, the fences being of various types and of heights up to 1.05 metres.

They should understand how to correct basic training faults, both on the flat and over fences.

They should ride all horses to improvement with an obvious poise, tact and harmony.

They should understand the principles of training the young horse from his early days as a foal up to Novice horse trial or Elementary dressage standard. Although this last section is tested orally, candidates must speak from obvious practical experience to back up the theory.

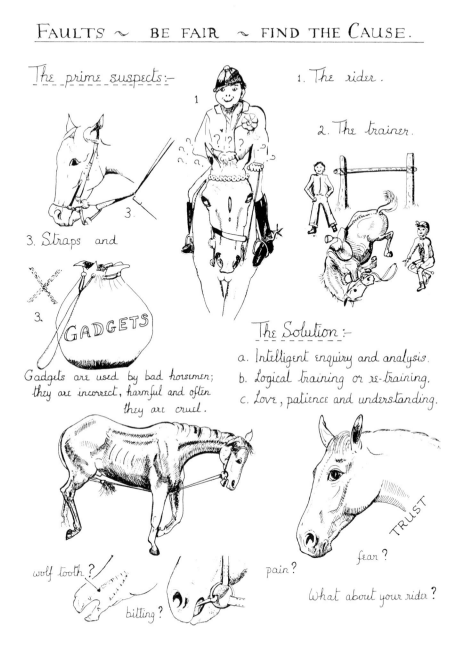

The prime suspects:—

1. The rider.

2. The trainer.

3. Straps and

3. GADGETS

Gadgets are used by bad horsemen; they are incorrect, harmful and often they are cruel.

The Solution:—

a. Intelligent enquiry and analysis.
b. Logical training or re-training.
c. Love, patience and understanding.

wolf tooth?

bitting?

pain?

fear?

TRUST

What about your rider?

Although the standards of the three alternative examinations for the first leg are parallel their format may vary slightly. Where there are differences, the objectives are still identical: to preserve the confidence, form and soundness of the horses so kindly loaned by the examination centre.

The following notes are for general guidance rather than being applicable only to one of the examinations.

Oral theory of equitation

All riders should understand the theory and the logic on which their ridden work for this standard is founded. The following is a list of subjects from which examiners may select a few; the candidates should have clear explanations for all of them supported by reasons and objectives in each case.

School figures – of all shapes and sizes.
Form, and the manner in which the horse should carry his rider.
On the bit – as opposed to accepting the bit.
The basic gaits.
Balance.
Suppleness.
Straightness.
Rhythm.
Tempo.
Cadence.
Transitions.
Lengthening and shortening.
Half-halt.
Turn on the forehand.
Leg-yielding.
Shoulder-in.
Half-pass.
Rein back.
Turn on the haunches, half or demi-pirouette – synonymous terms for the movement. (There are two turns on the spot, which are recognised school movements, a turn on the forehand or a turn on the haunches (or half or demi-pirouette). It is incorrect to speak of a "turn about the forehand". This latter is not a school movement, it is a mongrel term – the dam being an introductory turn on the forehand at the walk and the sire being the last part of the command to a class, "Turning on the forehand to the left, whole ride halt ... and about turn, *now*.")
Counter-canter.
Simple change of leg or of canter lead.
General principles of training young horses and older ones.
Work with ground poles and cavalletti.
General principles of jumping fences, including training young horses, gymnastic jumping distances, cross-country fences, show jumps.

Stable management

The practical yardstick of this section is that candidates should be capable of taking sole charge of horses or ponies, stabled and at grass, not more than two of each, for a fortnight.

Candidates' explanations and demonstrations at this standard should be confident, adequate and competent, providing clear evidence of sound, practical experience rather than superficial theoretical knowledge.

They will be tested on most of the following subjects:

Handling horses and ponies; stable buildings, hygiene and health, bedding – varieties and management; watering and feeding; grooming, care of the feet and of the teeth; clothing, clipping and trimming; fitting and care of saddlery; conformation and identification; identification of common, minor ailments, together with treatment, under veterinary supervision when necessary. Care of horses and ponies at grass and at special events, competitions, hunting, long-distance riding, etc.; routines, including daily yard maintenance; repairs, ordering and storing supplies; exercise and work for fittening.

"You name it – they'll test you on it!" It is almost like that but, in fact, if a candidate has been involved with horses for many years and he has an enquiring mind, he will have learned most of these facts and practices. Providing he has been taught, he will have formed correct habits of carrying out all his stable management tasks methodically and in the most efficient manner.

Stable management examiners can vary tremendously; some are over-zealous, even officious, and seem to delight in grilling candidates for hours on end while others, the more experienced, are essentially practical. The following are true life examples of each variety.

The first, who might be referred to as "the nasty examiner" asked two questions of a Pony Club A Test candidate, "What do you think of this stable?"

As the small, dingy, loose box in question belonged to a well-known B.H.S. approved riding school, but clearly was not one of its best stables, the candidate assessed it as, "Quite nice."

Obviously, more was expected, so she added that the grooming tools would be better kept in a bag rather than lying about on the bedding (which was very dirty, but she did not like to add that.)

"What about the ventilation?"

"Oh, it's all right – providing the top door is always left open."

"How many cubic feet of air space does a stabled horse require?"

"Good gracious – quite a lot I should think."

The examiner cast his eyes skywards and fired the next question. "How much food would you give to a thousand pound horse?" The candidate brightened up at this. "Ah! well that would all depend on the animal, for it could be a small show pony, a ride and drive cob, a young eventer or a hunter. Any one of those could cost £1,000 or he might point-to . . ." at this she petered out for the examiner seemed likely to explode.

"A thousand pounds in *weight*, you stupid girl."

"Oh, I am sorry – how awful . . .", she said to the departing figure of the examiner who left in a hurry to catch his train.

The second, ultra-practical, examiner came to Talland. Again the examination was a Pony Club A Test. At lunch-time he told us he had had a splendid morning. He had only had three candidates – they'd all been first-rate.

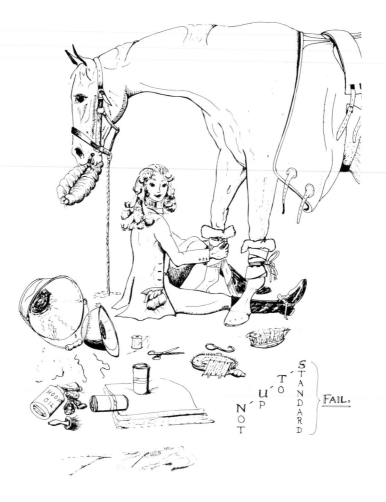

"The best of the lot was a boy: as soon as I saw him flatten the straw round the horse's foot I knew he had done that job hundreds of times so I let him off the bandaging and we talked about the Beaufort hounds instead. He was tip-top with all the other sections too."

How right he was. That boy went on to be a stalwart member of the British three-day event team.

Equitation

Riding in or working in, appraising or judging the horse and his performance. These two practical tasks are invaluable facets of every horseman's career. Both are tested at this level and at the more senior examinations yet to come. However, to date, equestrian textbooks have omitted to advise readers on either of these procedures and it is hoped that the following paragraphs may bridge the gap.

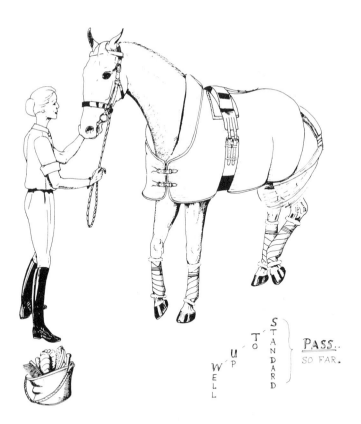

WELL UP TO STANDARD } PASS.. SO FAR.

Initial investigation

It is always invaluable to form a quick first impression of the horse. The eye and expression may reveal something of the character and the size, colour, sex, age and type should be noted as well as good and bad points of conformation and soundness.

Riding in or working in

When a rider mounts any horse for the first time at the commencement of a period of work he should ensure that the horse stands absolutely still, this whether the horse is a stranger or a familiar friend. The rider should complete the preliminaries of introduction, then adjust his stirrups, check his girths and shorten his reins before he puts his horse on the aids. Only then, when all the preparations are completed should he move the horse forward from the halt.

he should not move or slouch off ~ before the rider is ready and until they are both

IN GOOD FORM.

The Rider Should Get Acquainted··· at the Walk.

The rider should get to know the horse at the walk before limbering him up at the trot and canter. This is the riding in period and may last for four to ten minutes.

During this period the rider should have these main goals:

• To build up a rapport with the horse so that he is calm, confident and listening.

• To give the horse a chance to accommodate the rider's weight and to get used to the way this particular rider-burden sits on his back.

272

- To undergo a mutual discovery of each other's signals; to set up a communications system. It is worth remembering that all horses will respond readily to thought and weight aids even if they have not been mentioned previously in the horse's training programme. On the other hand, horses who are used to being ridden with invisible aids will resent the rider moving or brushing back his outside leg when he asks for a canter depart. Many well-trained, sensitive horses will buck or kick at the rider's boot if it is moved back too far.
- To make a preliminary investigation of the horse's training, form and gaits, his fitness, ability and talent. This research may include jumping and a short gallop if fences are available, the footing is good and there is sufficient room.
- To ride with consideration for other riders as well as for the horse and the land on which they ride.

The horseman's love for his horse

is a wondrous thing~

it must be taught,

fostered and cherished~

it must never be lost, or even dimmed.

Appraising the horse and his performance

This is a subject of considerable size and scope; it is one that must be taught and developed from the earliest lessons.

Any improvement in a horse's form and in his performance must depend on the continuous and accurate appraisal of that form and performance by his rider. If the horse is not being improved then the odds are that he will slide in the opposite direction, down the slippery slope of deterioration, due to no fault of his own.

The rider must be trained to become a sensible, knowledgeable analyst who has been educated by instructors, by innumerable ponies and horses and through his own enquiries and diligence. Every rider should be a family doctor, psychologist, detective, physiologist and advocate all rolled into one, in order that he may make true yet lightning quick analyses of his own performance and that of his horse. "Forward, calm and straight." "Are we working that way – if not, why not?" Action, reaction, counter-action, reaction and then better action!

This rich harvest may only be gleaned by thoughtful riding, a genuine love for the horse and soft, smooth, invisible aids. The rider employs his brain, his heart and the whole of his seat, from the top of his head to the soles of his feet to influence his horse. His aids stem from a correct but easy posture and are timed and measured to the finest degree.

Only if a rider is capable of true and continuous appraisals can he be worthy of the title "horseman", and only then is he ready to sit a horse knowledge and riding examination of Stage IV standard.

It is sad that the lure of commercialism, or of selfish ambition, tends to encourage riders who are "cash-happy" or fired with competitive aggression rather than the less flamboyant, genuine horsemen. Of course, some horses are lucky, they are ridden by good or even talented horsemen but an increasing number have to suffer from their riders' shortcomings. Then drudgery or force and gadgetry are used in place of horsemanship and horses' happiness and life-spans are shortened senselessly.

The appraisals which a rider has learned from his first stable management and riding lessons are applicable at Stage IV standard – and above.

The young rider will have learned to determine the sex, height, colour and type of ponies and horses. He will have learned how to age a horse and how to look and test for signs of unsoundness and ill-health. He will have been taught the order in which a horse treads with his feet at the three basic gaits and to feel and think as he rides. The rider will have been encouraged to analyse the horse's muscle use and power as he carries his rider and moves over the ground. He will understand the meaning of form and of all the other qualities which are desirable in a riding horse. These judgements will develop in speed, accuracy, depth and value with further education, application and experience.

Although the foregoing paragraphs might satisfy a qualified examiner they are but a beginning for a learning rider or a prospective candidate. They need more detailed guidance.

An appraisal programme

Usually a candidate is given an imaginary situation to guide him. For a Pony Club A Test candidate the story might be, "A friend of mine has heard of a horse for her daughter to hunt and perhaps to compete with locally. I want you to try this horse for me for ten minutes. When I call you I want you to come back to me and give me your report as if I am on the telephone. You must imagine I cannot see even what colour he is – he might be a skewbald Shetland pony! Your report, though concise, must give me as much information as possible."

The objects of the story-technique are numerous: it starts a rapport going between the examiner and the candidate and encourages one to evolve between the rider and the horse. By guiding him it steadies the candidate's nerves and encourages him to think ahead positively.

THE PREPARATORY, DISMOUNTED APPRAISAL

Thorough but quick. First the rider must appraise from afar. He should take a stationary "snap-shot" view of the whole horse, the sex, the general outlook, symmetry and type, asking silently, "For what job is this horse most suitable?" and "Does the saddlery look comfortable for rider and horse?"

Then the rider should approach the horse, saying, "Hello" in horse parlance, before checking:
- His teeth for age, conformation and care.
- The fitting of his bits, bridle and saddle and that they are in good repair.
- That his limbs appear clean with no undesirable lumps and bumps.
- That his feet are good, being cool, well shod and that he stands level and square.

THE MOUNTED APPRAISAL

The rider must tune in to the horse, quickly but with great tact.

The initial stages of the mounted appraisal are identical with those for riding-in with the additional factor of that "report" for which the examiner is waiting.

As soon as the horse has accepted the rider and they have agreed on a code of signals the rider should formulate a plan of work which suits the horse, the situation and, hopefully, the examiner.

By the time the rider has reached a standard which is slightly above that required for Stage IV, Grade IV or Pony Club A Test, he will have composed hundreds if not thousands of schooling plans based on classical movements and correct school figures. These he should use now and be seen clearly to do so whether he is riding in a large field or in an indoor school. He should adapt the work, using the scope of the field or the walls of the school to advantage. The horse will only give a good performance, or even improve, if the rider is sufficiently educated and skilled; the examiner can only judge the education if he is shown it!

If the rider is riding out in the open, he should use easy school movements such as turns on the forehand, leg-yielding and transitions to

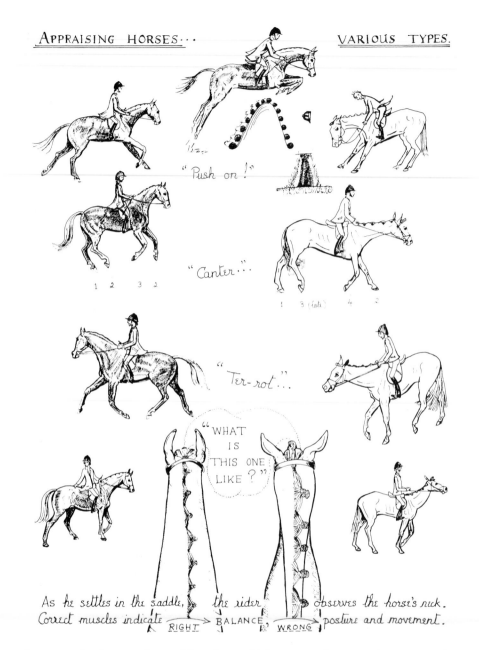

"Push on!"

"Canter.···"

"Ter-rot.···"

"WHAT IS THIS ONE LIKE?"

As he settles in the saddle, the rider observes the horse's neck.
Correct muscles indicate RIGHT → BALANCE ← WRONG posture and movement.

improve the horse's form, his gaits and his responsiveness. As soon as the rider has formed an evaluation of the horse's gaits, his balance, straightness and suppleness in a short workout on the flat, he should test the horse's reactions and style over one or two simple fences. Providing the going is good, the rider should find out if the horse has a turn of speed and can gallop well. It is not necessary to make two or three circuits round the entire field to do this – no owner wishes his valuable horses to be galloped

276

and jumped hard by one candidate after another. A horse's ability for general purpose levels can be appraised easily over a few fences and quite a short distance at gallop.

The rider should finish his riding outside by selecting a short course of fences to find out more of the horse's attitude to jumping and to show a fluent performance after a well selected and ridden track. If a horse is a good athlete he will invariably enjoy jumping and give the rider a good, bold feel. Horses are like humans in this respect!

The rider must let the horse down gradually and thoughtfully as he returns to the examiner to report on his findings. The report must have a basic plan, such as:

- General description ... sex, height, colour, type, age and work for which best suited. (Don't forget to mention sharp or wolf teeth if they exist.)
- Temperament ... willing, calm, responsive, obedient or lacking confidence, sluggish, nappy.
- Conformation ... overall impression supported by a few specific details, good points first followed by defects.
- Gaits ... walk, trot, canter and gallop, evaluate each one.
- Suitability for ... the friend's daughter or whatever applies to the briefing.
- Future work programme, to develop the horse mentally and physically and thereby improve performance and value.

Appraisal of schoolwork

On the flat, in an enclosed manège, in or out of doors. In this situation the horses will be of varying types schooled to a reasonable standard of dressage. They may wear a snaffle or double bridle and dressage saddles as opposed to general purpose or jumping saddles.

The initial stages of the previous appraisal programme will again apply. The candidate should feel his way to compressing these preliminaries into a shorter period if this is acceptable to the horse. For example, in the dismounted appraisal, it is quicker to run eyes rather than fingers over the horse's limbs and the riding in period should not exceed four minutes. Thus more time is available for the rider to explore the horse's training and to ride a progressive programme of the school movements required by the briefing.

Whenever they work horses in a manège riders should use the school as a gymnasium and this they must do especially well at an examination of this level. They must ride correct corners, circles and other school figures with thought, feel accuracy and, of course, exercising courtesy to each other. Not only must they look good on a horse but they must be effective with aids which are acceptable and invisible and which are evidence of good training.

Candidates will be told to exchange horses after a specified interval;

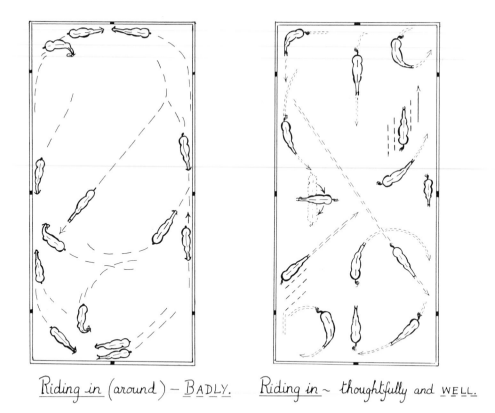

Riding in (around) — BADLY.   Riding in ~ thoughtfully and WELL.

they should have an appraisal report ready on each occasion, although it may not be asked for every time.

Sample briefs
- Evaluate the horse's basic gaits at working and medium paces and also his response to your aids through the transitions.
- Show me your plan of work for counter-canter.
- You have been offered the ride on this horse in a dressage competition at Elementary level in two weeks' time. Evaluate his work at that standard, tell me of any problems you encounter and how you will improve his work.
- Show me your progressive programme to develop shoulder-in.
- Neither of the turns on the spot, nor leg-yielding, half-pass or rein-back are in current British Elementary dressage tests, yet all have a practical as well as a gymnastic value and they are in the syllabus for this examination. Pick any of these school movements and use them to complement each other in your work out. (Or the examiner may specify movements.)
- Ride in for a few minutes and then ride a short reprise similar to a free-style dressage test, containing work at the three basic gaits as well as most of the school movements.

Appraisal of work over fences

This phase may have been included already or it may be a separate part of the examination. The candidate should show an efficient and effective approach; he should ride each horse boldly yet with tact and he should show practical horse sense in his selection of the fences available as well as good style in his riding. If the courses are not predetermined he must choose and ride a track which is fluent and inviting to the horse yet imaginative enough to reveal his skill. He must display equestrian harmony based on positive thinking and positive action!

The Second Leg

This is the intermediate teaching examination. Candidates are tested in their ability to teach a class lesson and two private lessons – one to a pupil

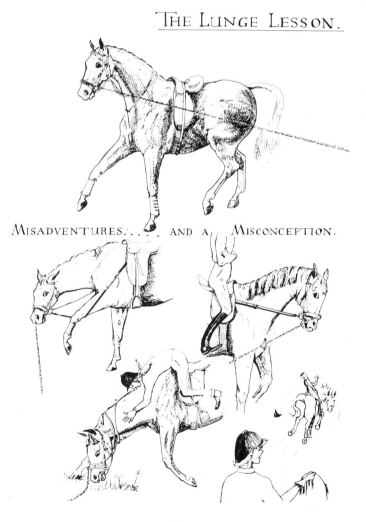

THE LUNGE LESSON.

MISADVENTURES.... AND A MISCONCEPTION.

working to Elementary standard of dressage, and another over fences as a preparation for Riding Club or Pony Club horse trials. Candidates then give a lunge lesson, answer questions on safety, equitation and lungeing theory, give a five-minute lecture and join a discussion on stable management.

As with all teaching connected with the horse there are several different methods and varieties of method for carrying out every lesson or task. The basic principles remain but little changed over the years though some small details do vary from country to country. These are all British examinations but in the British Isles we probably have a wider variety of horse than exists in any other country and that is the crux of the matter. The method demonstrated must be safe, efficient, suitable for both horse and pupil and it must prove its worth by being seen to produce improvement.

The lunge lesson will provide a good example. Whether to use the side reins provided or not will depend on the horse, the lunger's ability and his need, and the standard at which the pupil is riding. Whereas some cold-blooded or excitable horses may lunge better with side reins to help their form or control, many warm-blooded or thoroughbred horses with equable temperaments will maintain a better form and give a better feel if they are lunged without – providing that the lunger is sufficiently skilled.

A British compromise of fairly loose side reins may help a novice rider to gain a feel for form and to appreciate the necessity for still hands. Side reins are also a necessary safety precaution if the footing is of luscious grass! The horse must always be watched whenever side reins are fixed to ensure that he does not get tied up in them. Unless the horse is extremely reliable and the side reins are relatively loose, they should be unfastened from the bit and clipped on to a "D" on the front of the saddle before a rider is allowed to mount or dismount.

WARNING

A horse should not be lunged in side reins over ground poles or cavaletti. Only a fool would lunge a horse over a fence in side reins or in any restrictive gadget: this is an ignorant and cruel practice which can do irreparable harm to the horse's mouth, his confidence and his natural style of jumping. Invariably he will hit the fence with one or more legs which may also suffer serious injury. A skilled trainer will use the design and construction of the fence itself to encourage the horse to improve his bascule for himself – naturally.

"Never jump a horse in side reins" is one of a very few inflexible laws, the breaking of which would cause a candidate to fail a B.H.S. examination.

Other causes of failure include:
• An incorrect manner, whether it be unco-operative, overbearing, timorous to the point of being dangerously "wet", or discourteous, abrupt or rude. In fact, by now, candidates should have acquired most of the qualities of the good instructor, as listed in Book 1.

Now try jumping *that* with your hands and arms out of action!

- Allowing pupils to ride without the protection of a well-fitting hard hat, or while wearing plimsolls or other unsuitable items of clothing.
- Carelessness – allowing a horse to kick or tread on another horse or to get away.
- Failure to observe any of the safety rules when teaching in the stables or when pupils are handling or riding horses.
- Giving a lesson which is negative, depressing or boring, or which has a detrimental effect on the training of both horse and rider.

The lunge lesson itself should be of good quality, the candidate striking up an immediate and strong rapport with the horse and the pupil – and not entirely forgetting the examiner! The candidate's lungeing technique must be both safe and correct in all respects – handling the equipment, working the horse and improving the pupil. He should be quick to diagnose major riding faults and to teach relevant corrective exercises in order to erase the bad habits and to develop the rider's feel for his own and his horse's posture and movement. The content of the lesson should never overtax either horse or rider, the emphasis being on *feel, thought and harmony* rather than physical endurance. The pupil should be encouraged to comment on, question or discuss his feelings and discoveries in order that a strong team spirit may prevail to the maximum benefit of the pupil and the horse. These principles of educated yet kindly and ever-deepening understanding should be the core of every riding lesson.

Examination preparation

This must be thorough and it must be complete to enable the candidate to have sufficient confidence to cope adequately with himself, the examination, its format, a strange environment, strange horses and perhaps even stranger examiners, as well as all the many unexpected eventualities which may occur and put extra strain on the candidate's resources.

Students should study current copies of all four syllabi; each one may contribute a little extra clue with regard to the requirements. Both theoretical knowledge and practical prowess must be of a high standard. Whereas in previous examinations "workmanlike" has been the chief yardstick, now further knowledge, poise, purpose, efficiency, ease and style should be present, all of which must be well established if they are to withstand the tensions of an examination day.

The candidate must be well prepared over a reasonable if not considerable period of time. The examiners are too wise and experienced to be hoodwinked by training and experience which are scant and superficial. Candidates must remember that "Rome wasn't built in a day"!

The Intermediate Examination Day

General notes

All the points previously mentioned concerning examination days apply to this – even more so, for the programme is more compact and concentrated, the timetable allows for no dilly-dallying and thus it tests the candidate's efficiency of mind and body as well as the standard of his training.

Candidates must be quick to establish a good and genuine rapport with every pupil in the opening stage of each of the five phases of this examination, in order to inspire the pupils to give of their best and thereby reap the richer rewards of real learning and improvement. It must be remembered that for these riders the day is a hard one – sometimes it is deadly boring, if, for example, they are taught by a string of nervous, indeterminate and uninspiring B.H.S.A.I.s.

Each candidate must resolve to provide a highlight in these pupils' day, for they are an invaluable group of people. Without their co-operation the day could not exist. So, be grateful to them and in your gratitude teach well!

The increasing pressure of the examination must not extinguish the preliminary half-halts labelled safety. The inspections of the pupils' clothing, the horse tack, the equipment, footing and fencing must be quick but not cursory. All corrections must be tactfully phrased – candidates must not lose pupils or examination centres. Remarks such as, "This saddle is dreadful", or, "Of course, the horses are useless", are not conducive to co-operation from any party nor will they yield the desired result of a pass mark from the examiners.

B.H.S. examiners are trained not to be rigid in their own personal likes and dislikes nor to criticise petty details in which a candidate's work may differ from their own favoured method – they are reminded frequently of the second motto concerning Italy's capital city, "Many roads lead to Rome". It is the general picture which is borne in mind and which earns a pass. The candidate must show that he is a genuine and a reasonably knowledgeable horse lover, that his work is founded on and bounded by practical commonsense, as well as proving himself to be competent in his execution of the tasks allotted to him. Examiners are trained to look for the good, to encourage candidates to show what they know and never to petrify them with scathing looks or comments concerning the gaps in their knowledge. Although examiners have to guard against instructing, they can and should build up a rapport with each candidate, thereby enabling him to give of his best.

Of course, examiners differ tremendously: some are anxious not to appear too trivial and manage to look gloomy and forbidding, some try to explain their questions so clearly that an excess of detail confuses everyone, while others sound short and sharp, if not disgruntled. Others again are so jovial that they seem to have forgotten that it is an examination day. One thing is certain and that is that all the examiners are doing their best in their own way to make fair assessments of the candidates before them – theirs is a long and arduous day. Examiners undertake these tasks due to a genuine desire to maintain the nation's standards in horsemanship, for only if they are so tested will the skills survive. Examiners are also very busy people with full lives of their own; a commitment to examine away from home for the whole of one day can call for the reorganisation of a complete week's work. Neither examiners nor centres are paid realistic fees so that the charges to the candidates are not excessively high; thus the time and effort contributed by examiners and the facilities offered by centres are given to the sport.

If candidates realise this they will understand that examiners are human and, on the whole, generous individuals, quite apart from their roles as trained and experienced horsemen and examiners.

The centres are generous too, for their work-programme will invariably be turned upside down for an examination day. That they lose income from outside riders may be a minor problem compared with horses lamed for days or weeks by the end of the examination.

The examinations at this standard have one major change in their format: candidates may not take either leg of the examination at a centre at which they have been training for any period during the month prior to the examination. This rule ensures that the test is the same for all candidates in that they are all unfamiliar with the environment and with the horses. It also encourages students to widen their horizons by going to centres in new parts of the country. An additional advantage is the exchange of "news and views" and increases of uniformity and unity between those B.H.S. approved riding schools which are examination centres.

Let us return to the candidates themselves. As with all examinations, prospective candidates must be self-motivated: they must research, study, revise and consolidate; they must try to establish the qualities of an instructor, listed in Book 1, before they sit the Intermediate Teaching examination. Sound knowledge, training and experience will provide the candidate with skill and confidence both of which will withstand the stress and strain of the examination day. A correct mental attitude is most important: "Train to *pass* the examination".

Candidates must be bright and cheerful, willing and eager, positive and assured, thoughtful and aware. All of these qualities are needed, tempered with courtesy and the degree of humility necessary to admit a mistake but not to cause diffidence or slow reactions.

Tips

• Be sure you have entered the correct date in your diary and that you possess the prerequisites necessary for the examination you are about to take.
• Ensure that your transport is organised – and roadworthy.
• Know your exact destination and allow enough time to reach it.
• Although you may have a better night's sleep at home, it is foolish to contemplate a long journey early in the morning before a taxing examination.
• Check that all your riding clothing and equipment is complete, clean, neat, comfortable (*not* new boots!) and in a good state of repair.
• The candidate should wear a plain shirt, with a neat collar and a quiet tie, well pinned in place, breeches or jodhpurs which are "easy" – not skin-tight, a tweed hacking jacket which is long enough with only one badge on its lapel, together with a hard hat. For girls, one or two hairnets to wear under the hat and a head scarf to cover the hair when carrying out the stable management tasks. Take gloves, spurs (the latter removed for lungeing and both removed for stable management) and two whips (shorter for jumping, longer for working on the flat). If the weather is cold take one or two jerseys and an overcoat or tidy anorak.
• Take a thermos or two of hot soup, coffee and/or tea and a selection of "tasty morsels" to eat; nerves can become frayed if they have to contend with the pangs of hunger as well as the strain of the day.
• Aim to arrive at the examination centre at least half an hour before the examination is scheduled to begin. If journeying from home, allow time to have and fix a puncture – do not arrive in a flurry and a fuss or, worst of all, late. *Never* be late – arriving under a quarter of an hour before assembly-time is "late"!
• On arrival, report to the centre's office, secretary or person in charge, so that they know you are there. Study the day's programme on the notice board and get yourself ready. You may offer to help – with a clean job. An examination day always presents the centre with a heavy workload – a little two-way appreciation can work wonders for everyone's morale!
• It is customary for the examiners to meet and decide on various aspects and duties concerning the running of the examination with the centre's chief instructor and amongst themselves. This is a very necessary part of their preparation for the day which is to follow – they are not conspiring

together to fail all the candidates. In fact, every examiner I know starts out hoping to pass every candidate.

Treat the examination day as one of life's new experiences – learn all you can from it. If you enjoy the day you are far more likely to succeed. For many candidates it is best to treat the day as a trial run for the next time; this helps to dispel excess tension and anxiety – and perhaps the next time will not be needed after all!

- It is not the end of your career if you fail. This is where resilience is required. Like a cork in a bucket, rise to the surface and learn from your failure. As the results for these examinations are given verbally it is essential for your further training that you take a notebook with you to jot down the examiners' constructive criticisms.
- If you pass – well done! Don't rest on your laurels, there is much to be done. Go out and practise what you preach – study and learn, and when you have tucked sufficient practical experience under your belt and recorded it in your log-book, then will be the time to prepare for and pass the next examination for the full B.H.S. Instructor's Certificate.

The briefing

Before the examination commences the chief examiner collects his team of examiners together with all the candidates, the latter in numerical order so that already he can start to fit names to faces. He gives them a comprehensive description of the programme and the examiners' expectations of the candidates during each phase.

A sample of such a briefing follows, together with notes for candidates added at the end of each section.

The class lesson (18 minutes each)

One of the pair of candidates will ride the spare horse, as leading file of a ride of four or six pupils, while the other candidate teaches the lesson. At the end of the first lesson the two candidates will exchange roles. At the end of the second lesson they will move on to the next phase – quickly, for time is short.

The object of this phase is not to prove that the candidate could have a second string to his bow as a sergeant-major on a parade ground, drilling his troops, but that he can teach a group of riders how to improve their horsemanship through the correct use of school figures. The candidate should have clear authority, use recognised commands and exercise safe controls as he works the ride in an open order or in more closed order, for example, for double ride work. His manner should be good and his eyes quick as he teaches and uses the school figures to improve the riders and their horses. He must use changes of gait and of exercises to suit the horses and his pupils, to educate them to improve their form and to arouse their interest.

Examiners wish to be shown candidates' knowledge and understanding of school work: for this phase, position corrections are a bonus,

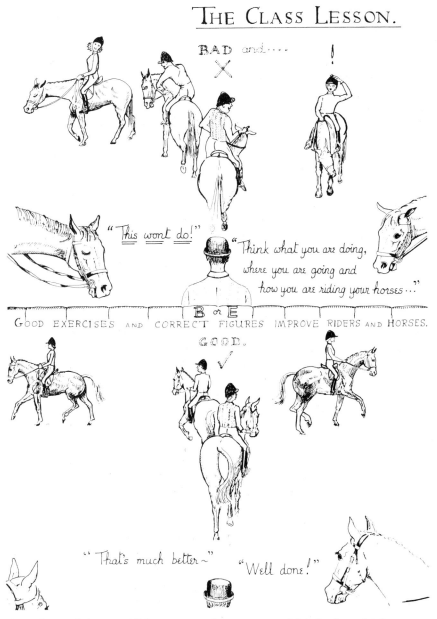

THE CLASS LESSON.

BAD and....

X

!

"This won't do!"

"Think what you are doing,
where you are going and
how you are riding your horses..."

B or E

GOOD EXERCISES AND CORRECT FIGURES IMPROVE RIDERS AND HORSES.

GOOD.

✓

"That's much better~"

"Well done!"

though candidates will be expected to correct rider faults which prevent the horse from going in a good form.

Ground poles will be available if a candidate wishes to use them.

NOTES
• In the first line-up, the candidate should place his fellow-candidate at one end of the line; he should be asked to align himself and his horse squarely with the wall they are facing and the rest of the ride should be

287

CORRECT FOUNDATIONS. SCHOOL FIGURES

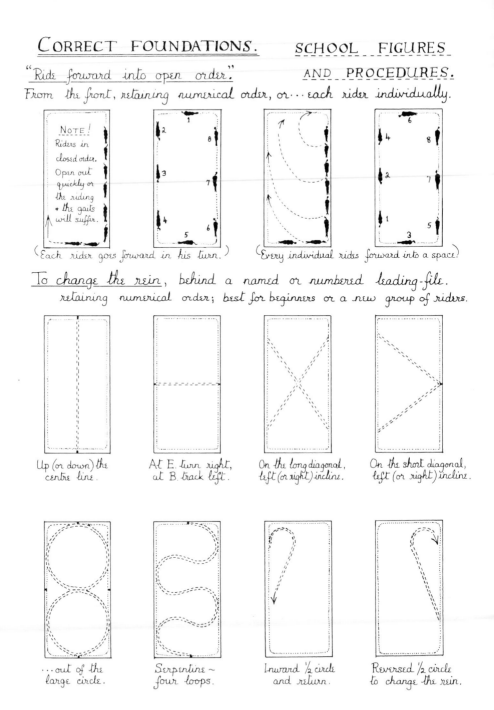

"Ride forward into open order." AND PROCEDURES.

From the front, retaining numerical order, or... each rider individually.

NOTE!
Riders in
closed order.
Open out
quickly or
the riding
+ the gaits
will suffer.

(Each rider goes forward in his turn.) (Every individual rides forward into a space.)

To change the rein, behind a named or numbered leading-file.
retaining numerical order; best for beginners or a new group of riders.

Up (or down) the
centre line.

At E. turn right,
at B. track left.

On the long diagonal,
left (or right) incline.

On the short diagonal,
left (or right) incline.

...out of the
large circle.

Serpentine ~
four loops.

Inward ½ circle
and return.

Reversed ½ circle
to change the rein.

Some Ground Plans for Class Lessons.

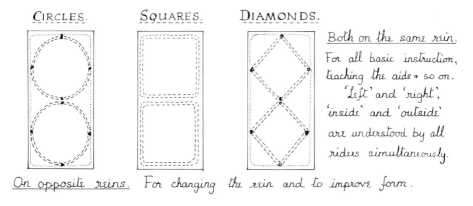

CIRCLES.   SQUARES.   DIAMONDS.

Both on the same rein.
For all basic instruction,
teaching the aids & so on.
'Left' and 'right',
'inside' and 'outside'
are understood by all
riders simultaneously.

On opposite reins. For changing the rein and to improve form.

HALF CIRCLES ACROSS THE SCHOOL.   SMALL CIRCLES IN THE CORNERS.

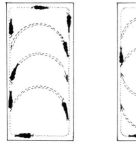

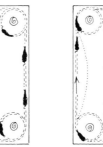

PAUSE ~ for rewarding rest, questions, comments, discussion and demonstration.
FORM A RIDE ON THE C. CIRCLE DIAMETER LINE (in numerical order).

Achieve a high note
then trot (or walk)
on long reins,
in a good form,
ride into line ~
in balance, straight
and THOUGHTFULLY.

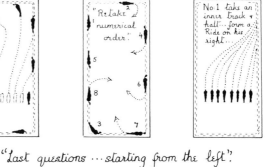

"Retake
numerical
order". 4
5
8   6
3   7

No 1 take an
inner track &
halt... form a
Ride on his
right...

To FINISH ~   "Last questions ... starting from the left".

289

told to take their dressing from him. If there is a young horse present or one who is better at the rear of the ride, he should be at the other end of the line.

- The pupils' names should be listed, either by memory or on to a small card, and their clothes and tack inspected. Each pupil should be regarded as an interesting individual and names should be confirmed before the ride is moved off, the leading file leading, of course! The original order should be restored for the final line-up as this makes school work easier for the class to follow and displays the instructor's tidy mind and his training.

- If the riders are more novice than anticipated, the candidate should give them simple exercises such as two methods of taking open order or of changing rein, to give them some active instruction before lining them up again for a quiz and discussion on position and aids. This should be short and to the point but is an essential link in the chain of understanding schoolwork. The pupils must know how they should sit and why and how they influence their horses; this should be carried out quickly but without impatience.

- The candidate should rejoice rather than be depressed if the pupils are of a novice standard for this will give him a wonderful opportunity to teach them to get the basic rules right and to inspire them with his teaching. However, enthusiasm must not run riot – do not go too fast in any direction!

- If there are one or two major riding faults which are obviously well established, such as looking down and sliding out, the ride should be lined up quickly, to the halt, in order that the candidate can give a brief mini-demonstration of the two faults, backed up by an explanation of their bad effect on the horse and their correction.

- The pupils must be encouraged to think more and more of their horses, whether they are straight, in a good form and how they move. These class lessons must never deteriorate into a queue, plodding nose to tail along an egg-shaped ditch.

- If the riders are more capable, being nearly all of Stage III standard, they should be tested and taught a variety of school figures and exercises and helped to improve the horses as they ride them better – and better.

- The challenge should be, "Here are six riders. Meet the challenge with sensible enthusiasm and get them all riding *forward* in a good form, with an obvious improvement and enjoyment – keep it safe – and show us your skills."

Lesson on the flat (35 minutes each)

(Not a flat lesson – that is just what it must not be!)

Each candidate will have a pupil to teach for a private or solo lesson on the flat. Both candidates and their pupils will share a dressage arena; all must work with consideration for each other.

The pupil wishes to compete in a dressage test at Elementary level in two months' time, he wishes to be assessed together with his horse, to work to improvement and to be set homework.

The candidate must be prepared to answer questions on simple changes of leg, counter-canter and shoulder-in if his lesson has not progressed to these movements through having had to make too many basic corrections in order to improve the pupil's riding and the horse's form. It would be a major error to ask for shoulder-in before the horse carries his rider in a correct manner, for a horse cannot be expected to work with a bend, in collection, until he has the training and the muscles necessary for such a transformation.

NOTES
• First, the candidate should check the tack and question the pupil briefly concerning his riding standard and experience and those of his horse. He should show a kindly and sincere interest not only in the information but also in the pupil himself.
• He should ask the rider to show him his horse. If the pupil is fairly inexperienced then the candidate should ask him to walk, trot and canter to either hand and to fit in several transitions. If the pupil is more experienced he can be asked to include some lengthening and shortening of strides at trot, counter-canter and some easy lateral work.

Both levels of pupil should be requested to work to a clear pattern, to think and feel how their horses are going and neither to rush nor to take too long. Each should be told, "Ride in for three or four minutes and let me watch your horse." This will put the rider at ease, though of course the candidate will observe the rider just as closely as he will the horse – but that is his secret!
• The next stage will depend on how the horse went during the first stage.

If the horse did not go well initially, the candidate should ask the pupil to analyse the problem and then ask permission of the pupil to ride the horse. The candidate will then be able to feel the difficulty for himself as this will make it easier for him to make an improvement.

If the horse went well in a good form, with no glaring faults, then the candidate should tell his pupil that it was good and he should ask his pupil what he felt could have been a little better and if there are any movements which he finds difficult to ride in the Elementary test. "Please show me."

When the problems have been demonstrated, the candidate should question the pupil, discuss the problem, ask if he may ride the horse, assess him quickly and formulate a plan for the next stage of the lesson.
• No candidate should ever run out of material for this lesson. He must ensure that the rider's position, balance and influences are good, that the horse goes forward, in a good form on the bit, is balanced, is calm and not tense or constrained and that he accepts the rider's aids, has a consistent rhythm and a regularity of footfall in all his gaits, with sufficient impulsion and that the rider does not mistake speed for impulsion.

'Well done!'

I do hope he is pleased...

'Too brusque.'

Oops! — I hope I can hold it...

Oh dear!
<u>No</u> preparations.
(Rider must learn to ride.)

I wish he would warn me before he slams on the brakes.

<u>Riding to the halt</u> ~ WELL and BADLY.

If the horse is incorrect, then the rider must be at fault: his seat, his balance and his aids must be carefully scrutinised and corrected. They may then be given some easy exercises to ride, to improve and test their performance, such as:
• Ride a correct 20 metre circle on the left rein at working trot; then a 10 metre circle at a shortened working trot or collected trot, return to the 20 metre circle and halt on the open side; turn right on the forehand, forward at working trot and repeat the whole exercise to the right, finishing with a turn on the forehand to the left, working trot and forward to halt.
• Forward in working trot, turn down the centre line and at X halt, immobility, salute; proceed at working trot and track left; left incline at medium trot; and repeat – track right next time.

EXAMPLES OF WORK FOR DRESSAGE LESSON.

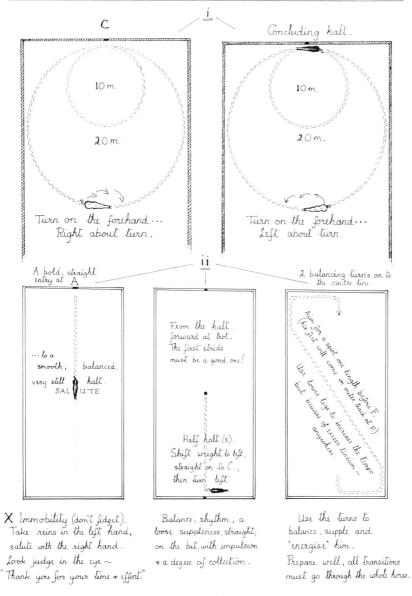

C

i

Concluding halt.

10 m.

20 m.

Turn on the forehand...
Right about turn.

10 m.

20 m.

Turn on the forehand...
Left about turn.

ii

A bold, straight
entry at A

2 balancing turns on to
the centre line.

...to a
smooth, balanced,
very still halt.
SALUTE

From the halt,
forward at trot.
The first stride
must be a good one!

Half halt (s).
Shift weight to left,
straight on to C.,
then turn left

Aim for a spot one length before F.
(the feet will come on outer track at F)

Use loose legs to increase the tempo
but beware of excess tension —
anywhere.

X Immobility (don't fidget).
Take reins in the left hand,
salute with the right hand.
Look judge in the eye ~
"Thank you for your time & effort."

Balance, rhythm, a
loose suppleness, straight,
on the bit, with impulsion
& a degree of collection.

Use the turns to
balance, supple and
'energise' him.
Prepare well, all transitions
must go through the whole horse.

- Use any school figures you like to show direct but smooth transitions between the two gaits, working canter and medium walk.
- Use the arena to show your work to improve counter-canter.
- Prepare him with some leg-yielding and then ride 5 to 10 metres in shoulder-in, where you like.

All these little tasks set a challenge and encourage the pupil to use his own initiative, to feel and think for himself and he will soon reveal the quality of his training to date, and will provide plenty of material for the remainder of the lesson. Make mental notes of the pupil's work and of your corrections so that you can incorporate them into your summing up, and can relate suitable exercises into your plan for his homework.

The jumping lesson (18 minutes each)

Candidates will be briefed that their pupil is due to compete in a local, informal Riding Club competition at the end of the week and that he has come for a last minute "polish up".

NOTES

Safety rules must be carefully observed and checked:
- The field gate must be shut and the surrounding fencing adequate.
- The pupil must be suitably clothed.
- The saddlery must be suitable, sound and secure.
- The fences must be well built – no false ground-lines or airy, flimsy poles.
- No jump-cups should be left empty above poles or uprights, or lying about on the ground, other than under a wing or on the foot of an upright.
- The rider must be sufficiently competent to control the horse on which he is mounted.

The candidates can be a great help to each other during this lesson: two pairs of hands can re-organise fences twice as quickly as one pair. Here is another opportunity for candidates to show their training, efficiency, maturity and manner. The candidate acting as assistant must be involved rather than ignored: he must be positioned with direction rather than left standing about, in the way.
- Normally a course of small fences will be set up in the jumping paddock. It should include a variety of uprights, spreads and at least one double.
- Candidates must understand that the examiners will be looking for good teaching of correct technique rather than the jumping of higher fences, especially if the footing is hard or heavy. The horses will have several lessons each and no horse must be lamed during the day. Fences should not be raised above 1.10 metres.
- This is a short lesson. Providing the candidate has a positive approach, is well-trained, has had experience and has a plan, he will have plenty of time in which to effect an improvement.
- He should check that the fences are satisfactory for his requirement. He should not waste time with unnecessary "scene-shifting", but if the ground is poached in front of any fence, he should ask if he might move the fence to better footing before starting his lesson.

- He must know the correct measurements or distances between fences and must always check the distance between related fences for himself.
- The candidate should always set the fences low to start with, 0.6 metres is high enough. Refusals are demoralising and non-productive.
- Candidates should not waste time setting out rows of ground poles, this takes too long and achieves little that is relevant to the task in hand which is, in this case, the weekend's competition.
- The candidate should ask the pupil if he has any particular problems when jumping fences with his horse. Whatever the answer he should then ask the pupil to select two fences and to ride his horse over one fence at a time, on both reins. "I would like to see your horse jump." That statement will set the scene for the remainder of the lesson.
- The candidate must be quick to spot the rider's shortcomings and must be equally quick to lead him into an encouraging and progressive lesson for improvement. Together they must get the basics right.
- The candidate should work to a "potted plan" of introductory work, the upright fence, the spread fence, the double, and then put them all together as a small course with one change of direction.

Sample Problems

RIDER FAULTS

Weakness of nerve; balance; timing; co-ordination; technique – for example, any one or all of the nine phases of the jump, badly ridden; experience.

These faults must be looked for, assessed and corrected. Unless the rider is right, the horse cannot jump in a good and fluent style.

HORSE FAULTS

Always due to bad or hurried training, combined with faulty riding.

Refusing

Look for the cause, and remove it! (Unless it is the rider or the fence itself!)

Teach the pupil to turn his horse back on his tracks whenever he refuses in a training session. The pupil must be warned against doing this or showing his horse the fence when riding in a competition. Either would result in elimination. The purpose of this is solely for schooling the horse.

Teach the pupil never to use his whip as he turns away – or in temper – but to use it once, firmly, just behind his leg on the side towards which the horse refused as he re-starts towards the fence.

If the horse refuses more than once, quickly tread in the divots and lower the fence (removing empty cups), making it small enough to ensure that he will jump it next time.

Teach the pupil to be quick and generous with his reward. Let them negotiate the lowered fence twice before raising it.

TRAINING OVER FENCES.

"I would like to watch you and your horse jump any three of these fences."

What fun! She sounds O.K.

Later!

HELPING WITH A PROBLEM.

(Lowered fence)

"Correct him by turning him back to the right. (When training, remember)."

"As you re-present him, if necessary, use your whip behind your left leg and approach slightly from the left."

Be quick and quiet with the rebuilding of the fence – do not do it while the horse and rider are standing watching. Tell the latter you are going to raise the fence while he practises a few trot, halt, trot transitions round the fences to make his horse even more responsive to the forward-driving aids, tell him that you will call as soon as the fence is ready, and that he must then ride the horse into it just as well as he did last time and he will succeed.

If the refusal was at any part of a double, each fence must be lowered and taken individually, then the two lowered fences must be jumped as a double before the fences are raised.

Remember that if the fences are lowered the distance between them may have to be shortened.

Rushing

Again, find the cause: this is usually a bad habit. The horse must be taught that the rider is far more pleased with him if he keeps a calm head and a steady rhythm when he is jumping.

Tell the pupil to trot in and out of the fences using plenty of small circles around and in front of them. He must use these circles and many transitions, together with patting and praise to reassure the horse, to keep him steady and to improve his form while a few of the most suitable fences are lowered. It is best to select fences which are of simple construction, facing away from the home stables or the field gate, and which stand on their own, on level or slightly rising ground. They should not face the paddock's perimeter fence if this is even remotely jumpable.

Having prepared the fences, the pupil should be told to walk his horse very calmly towards the first, easiest fence, to halt facing it and to reward the horse for standing still as he looks at the little fence from a distance of 3 to 5 metres. He should then walk and trot quietly forward and over the fence, after which he should be brought to a halt as soon and as smoothly as possible, and be rewarded again for standing absolutely still. That these halts are both still and prolonged is important in order to instil obedience and calmness into the horse and to allow him plenty of time to understand the simple requirement.

The pupil may then be told to repeat exactly the same routine over the other lowered fences. He must halt after each fence as soon as he can without being feeble or rough. He should be reminded to be very quick and generous with his rewarding and to hold the halt for at least twenty seconds before moving on to the next fence.

When this preliminary stage has been completed, the fences should be raised so that he rides his horse over two halves of a course with a halt in the middle. As it is most important that the rider stays happy and calm it is helpful to himself and his horse if he speaks aloud as he rides the course. His voice and its tone will provide the instructor with a clear indication of his pupil's mood, rhythm and co-ordination.

At the close of the lesson the candidate should remind the pupil of the slow, preliminary stage and he should be advised to use it every day before the competition and to return to it frequently in order finally to cure his horse's nervous habit of rushing. It must be explained that it will take time for the horse to understand this new procedure and for his confidence to be established.

Jumping flat

The horse does not bascule or round his back as he jumps, he does not use his body to the best advantage and often knocks down the fence. He should not be blamed for being careless, it is his style which is wrong and the fault is most usually caused by incorrect training or riding; he may have been raced or his rider may override him, hurling him at his fences – they may both be very tense.

CIRCLES AND A LOW, SPREAD FENCE.

Combining dressage and jumping ~ for the mutual benefit of both.

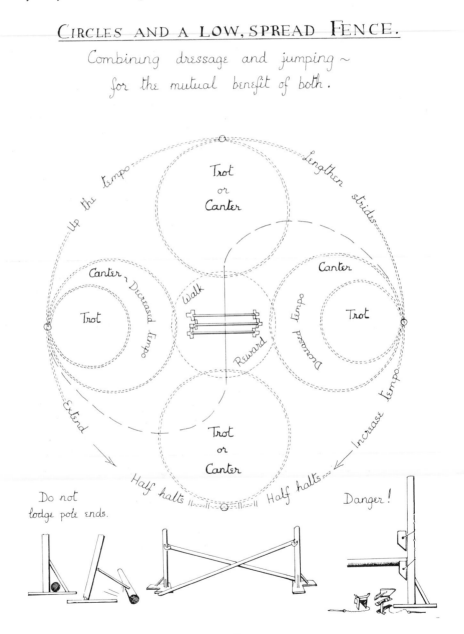

The candidate must watch, feel and analyse the cause. Any rider fault must be corrected. He should select a single low spread fence, and tell his pupil to ride a 20 metre circle, at trot first round the fence and then move its track to include the fence.

The rider should make several half-halts during the circles to steady and balance himself and his horse. He should approach the fence at a slow trot, remembering but not over-rushing his forward-driving aids and being very careful to allow the horse full freedom of his head and neck over the fence.

Purposely the candidate will not have decreed whether the rider circles left or right – the choice is his, and then, if the horse lands with the outside legs leading the rider's balance is proved to have been badly at fault.

Jumping on a circle is an invaluable testing exercise for all riders and horses – only if the rider is using his weight aid correctly to lead the horse on to the circle track as he lands will the horse land with the correct legs leading. The horse will prove the rider's balance and technique either to be correct or at fault. Jumping on a circle will also improve the style of both partners.

Riding to a halt between fences will also help the horse to engage his hindlegs under him, so that he jumps off his hocks with an improved bascule.

Putting in a short stride

This fault – also known as "propping" into the fence – may be caused by faulty training or riding, or it may be due to pain. For example, sore feet, forelegs, back or mouth, he may be tired or unfit or the horse may be a cobby type who is rather idle and just likes to jump in that way!

Providing that pain is not the cause, the candidate should use a combination of fences to help the rider and his horse to find and keep a rhythm. He should use the first fence as a placing fence for the second "out" fence which should be a spread.

The pupil must be encouraged to keep his own rhythm and his forward-driving aids consistent during all nine phases of the jump. He should keep the horse in an active, short working canter and he should say aloud, "Canter, canter, canter", all the way along the track and particularly before and between the two fences. If he has weak or fading lower legs then he should be told to say, "Legs, legs, legs", as a constant reminder.

Next the pupil should be told to use the same technique over three or four fences, starting with the double.

If the horse is idle by nature and does not respond readily to the leg aids then he should be sharpened up by several direct transitions, walk to trot, halt, trot, walk, canter and so on – these must not be rough, nor must the horse be "puffed" before he is asked to jump three or four more fences, or he will be even less inclined to jump freely and well.

As before, the horse should be rewarded with patting and a halt every time he does well.

Standing-off

Novice riders find standing-off, or taking off too soon as it is also known, before the fence a particularly un-nerving fault. Horses which jump in this way are usually long-striding, bold horses whose training has been rushed or is insufficient.

PLACING POLES AND FENCES ~ USE WITH CARE !
They must be set out at the most suitable distance for the horse.

<u>Distance guide lines</u> :- *shortest for small ponies, novice or nervous riders, low fences and when the approach is ridden at trot.*
Lengthen distances for larger horses, bold riders, higher/wider fences and canter approaches.

<u>Ponies</u> ~ Short people take short strides.

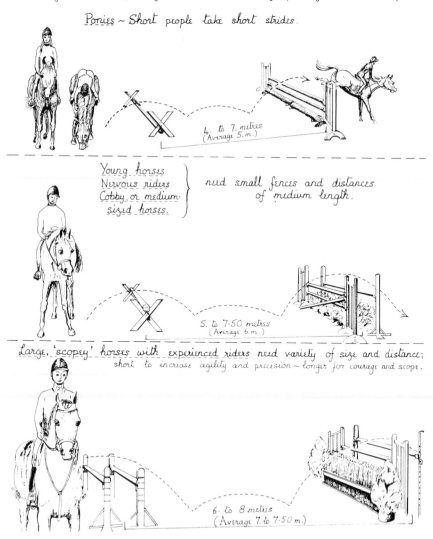

4 to 7 metres
(Average 5.m.)

<u>Young horses</u>
<u>Nervous riders</u>   } *need small fences and distances*
<u>Cobby, or medium-</u>   *of medium length.*
<u>sized horses.</u>

5 to 7·50 metres
(Average 6.m.)

<u>Large, 'scopey' horses</u> with experienced riders need variety of size and distance; *short to increase agility and precision ~ longer for courage and scope.*

6 to 8 metres
(Average 7 to 7·50 m.)

A ground pole should be used to encourage the horse to stretch the ligamentum nuchae at the top of his neck, to round his back, and to concentrate on his co-ordination and footwork. The pupil should be asked first to ride over the pole lying on the ground, and then to trot over it when it is placed 2.5 to 3 metres in front of a low fence. A ground pole used at this distance will organise the horse's feet on to the right place for him to take off over the fence and to make a safe and easy jump.

The candidate must watch the horse carefully to see that the pole is placed just right for this particular horse: a few centimetres further away from or nearer to the fence may make a difference to the comfort of the take-off. He must also watch the rider closely.

To approach the fence at canter, it is easier for a novice rider if the placing pole is moved back to a distance of 5 to 5.5 metres from the fence.

Ground poles used in this manner can be extremely useful tools for developing the co-ordination and style of riders and horses. However, the "operator" must be well trained, proved and practical in their use before he uses them in a lesson or an examination. Placing poles can be time-consuming in a short lesson and if the poles are placed incorrectly they can be injurious or dangerous.

When the rider and his horse are asked to jump a series or course of fences, the candidate must remind his pupil to keep his horse securely between leg and hand, to contain his form with the hindlegs well engaged, and to maintain a consistent rhythm throughout. He should be encouraged to say, "Canter, canter, canter," aloud as he rides the course when he is practising at home but not during a competition.

Jumping to the left or to the right

This fault may be varied or consistent, as may be the case. If the horse wavers to one side over one fence and to the opposite side over the next fence it is indicative of a faulty, unwieldy rider-burden; either his seat, his aids or his approach to the fences may be at fault. The rider may be over-facing his horse or he may be indeterminate in his riding of a good track; he may have a loose seat and upset his own and his horse's balance by sliding out to the left and/or to the right, or he may override the horse causing him to lose balance, rhythm and confidence. The track chosen may have been crooked or it may not even have been considered. The fences may be too big for the horse's present athletic ability.

Whatever the cause, the rider's faults must be corrected and he and his horse may be improved by using well-sited and constructed fences combined with leading-in poles to invite the rider and the horse to the centre of the fence. This will train them both to seek and establish a straight jump over a fence.

Initially a pair of ground poles may be placed on the ground on each side of the intended approach phase, exactly at right angles to the fence. A second pair of poles should be set as a slanting, inverted V on the take-off side of a low fence. This fence should be negotiated several times and the

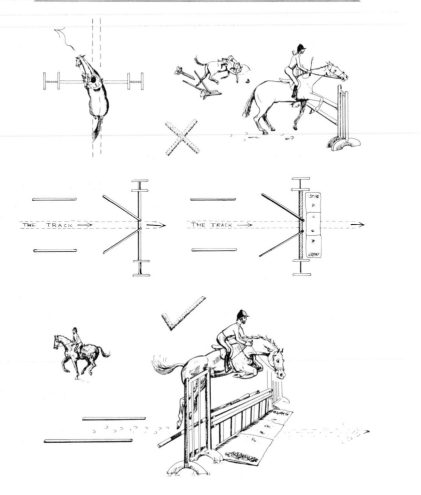

horse rewarded, before it is raised slightly, if both horse and rider are ready for this. Then the first pair of poles may be removed from the ground where they have been indicating the approach and may be used to form leading-in poles, an inverted V on the next fence to be jumped.

The horse may have formed a habit of twisting his forelegs out to one side due to bad riding – a crooked or unbalanced seat or heavy, harsh rein aids obstructing the free play of the horse's head and neck. Defective conformation or soundness, or an ill-fitting saddle also may contribute to this fault in the horse's jumping technique but by far the most common cause is the rider.

The candidate should correct the rider and encourage the horse to improve his technique. A small spread fence with leading-in poles on the take-off side will be useful and, if available, the addition of two soft objects of some sort, laid on either side of the track on the landing side will help to improve his pupils' style. The objects should provide two patches of contrasting colour and texture to the footing of the track; they should be of a soft material such as paper or fertilizer bag, weighted with a handful of soil, as there must be no risk of injury to horse or rider should they land on them by mistake. These latter additions will encourage the horse to look at and over the fence, to stretch his head and neck forward between the "foreign bodies". The instructor must use his commonsense and use and show discretion. If the horse is nervous and spooky, the objects must not have too alarming an appearance nor must they be too close together, for under no circumstances must they cause the horse to refuse to jump the fence.

As with all corrections of this nature the candidate must demonstrate a sensible blending of patience to establish confidence and of calculated initiative to inspire a marked improvement in the partnership's performance.

The lunge lesson

This lesson is divided into two parts, practical and theoretical: the latter includes lungeing techniques, accident procedures and basic first aid as well as the preparation of rider and horse for novice competitions.

Although in the earlier Assistant Instructor's examination candidates will have passed the test of lungeing a quiet horse for exercise and of giving a first lungeing lesson, in Phase (d) of this examination, candidates' prowess is tested much more closely and to a greater depth. The examiners must be satisfied that the candidate is capable of giving a good lunge lesson to a rider of Stage III standard. The lesson must be of real value, improving the pupil's seat, equestrian education, influence and feel. The instructor must also prove himself to be efficient in his handling of the equipment and competent in his management of the lunge horse, his pupil, the lesson format and content. Quite a tall order, when you come to think of it!

NOTES

The preparation for this section is often far too skimped, with the sad result that the candidate cannot satisfy the examiners and thus he fails not only this phase but the whole of the Intermediate Teaching examination.

Book 1 supplied full details of balancing, suppling and corrective exercises for riders and of lungeing technique which should be studied and revised regularly.

The practical part

The routine of the lunge lesson can be itemised in eight points:

(i)   Preliminary assessments and inspections must be short but thorough. Under normal circumstances on his home ground the instructor will know the lunge horse with whom he gives a lunge lesson. Even if the horse is unknown, at a Pony Club camp for instance, or a Riding Club

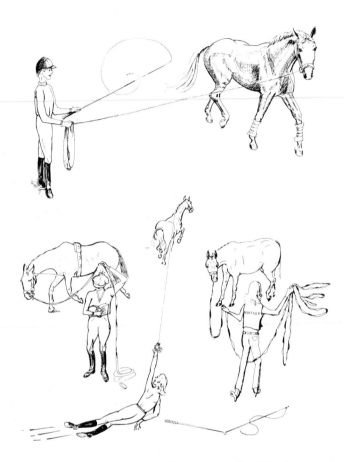

instructional day, the instructor will have watched the horse's behaviour, form and movement in the ride or he will be less restricted in his working in, getting-to-know-you time before the start of the lesson itself.

For this examination the situation is different: to save time in a full programme, the centre is detailed to provide horses which are "used to their job and well worked in". Therefore the candidate would be quite within his rights if he were to ask the horse's handler some pertinent questions before taking over from him. For example:

"Has the lunge horse any fads, fancies or foibles?"

"Is he 100 per cent level?" (Some lunge horses develop a habit of intermittent unlevelness which is an evasion rather than a technical unsoundness.)

"Is he better when worked to the left or right?"

"Is he usually lunged in side reins or not?"

If any of the horse's legs are not clothed in protective boots or bandages the candidate should ask, "Is this in order?"

These questions and their answers will serve as a useful guide and will save valuable minutes and can be asked during the preliminary inspection of the horse's tack and equipment.

(ii) See that the lunge area's footing and fencing are good. This does not mean that you have to emulate Dr. Watson or Hercule Poirot in treading the entire area searching for a rock, a rabbit hole, a projecting nail, a swinging gate or a broken fence – just one good, all-embracing look will do!

(iii) Meet the pupil, exchange names and discover his hopes and ambitions for the lesson. Lay the foundations for a good rapport. During this time, tactfully check that his clothing is serviceable, neat and comfortable and that it conforms to the rules of safety. A hard hat and smooth-soled boots or shoes which fit well are "musts". A plain shirt or jersey is infinitely preferable to a jacket; the latter may be more orthodox and smart but definitely it detracts from the value of a lunge lesson for it conceals the position and movements of the various parts of the rider's body.

(iv) Lunge the horse without the rider, first explaining to the rider that you are going to lunge the horse for a minute or two in order to settle him, to see how he moves and how he reacts, whether he is sluggish, responsive or nervous, and to establish a common wavelength so that the horse will understand and obey your commands.

Encourage the pupil to watch the horse as he works: the pupil must not be ignored, this is part of his lesson.

The candidate's handling of the equipment must be extremely neat and efficient before he presents himself for this examination – a cocktail of loops of lunge-line, a dropped whip, a loose horse or a fallen pupil are all serious mistakes, none of which should be seen at an examination of this standard.

The first candidate to lunge the horse should lunge him free initially and then the side reins may be fitted if they are required, before he is lunged to the other hand.

The aim of this stage is to get the horse lungeing well on a circle of between 15 to 18 metres. If he is sluggish and does not go forward well on the circle track, the line should be shortened to decrease the circle. As he comes within reach he should be given one sharp "sting-hit" in the hip-thigh area of his hindleg after which he will stay out on the circle track and will work well: he will now respect the whip and the lunger wielding it.

As soon as the horse is lungeing well he should be halted and rewarded. The side reins, if worn, should be unclipped from the bit and fastened to each other over the withers or on to the Ds on the front of the saddle.

(v) The pupil mounts, assisted by the candidate. While the pupil takes and adjusts his stirrups, checks the girth and takes up his reins, the candidate should watch his methods carefully to see if he is self-taught, careless or well-trained.

(vi)   Confirmation of the aids: "Thought, weight, legs, rein aids and voice". If the pupil can produce that list in the correct order, the candidate may be justified in feeling exhilarated by the discovery that the pupil has started already to be a thinking rider. Quickly he should get him on the move and discover more. But a *warning note!* All the foregoing procedures could easily fill half an hour or they could be accomplished in four minutes. This latter period of time is quite long enough either for the purpose of the examination or on any other occasion. In both cases the essential priority must be that the pupil should spend the bulk of his lesson thinking, feeling and being improved as he is being lunged. As with all lessons the greatest percentage of the time must be spent actively – in *doing*, feeling and thinking.

(vii)   To get the rider on the move, ask him to put the horse on the aids in a good form, to walk forward on a 15 to 18 metre circle and then to ride him at working trot while horse and rider make each other's acquaintance.

Explain that you want him to analyse the horse and his way of going for a few minutes.

This short appraising, acquainting and analysing period at the beginning of a lunge lesson is often omitted. I have heard even quite experienced instructors make this error: they put up the rider, remove stirrups and reins, clip on quite tight side reins, tell the pupil that he, the instructor, will be entirely responsible for controlling the horse while the pupil concentrates solely on his position and the exercises and forgets about the horse.

How wrong and sad is this practice. The horse wears a resigned or resentful expression under his cavesson, and his trot deteriorates on the tramline circle track. The instructor issues a stream of directions and corrections punctuated by an increasing number of whip cracks. The rider tries so hard to follow instructions that he is soon aching all over, and he thinks, "It must have been a brilliant lesson." But it is doubtful that it was even a good lesson, for to be so the pupil must be encouraged to think and to reason, to make corrections, to do a few exercises to aid those corrections and to feel all the time the effect those corrections have on the way the horse goes.

(Our cavalry forebears were more considerate of their horses than are some of their modern counterparts. In former days wooden horses were especially built for pupils to sit on whilst carrying out balancing, suppling and fittening exercises and learning polo, sword and lance drill to spare the live horses from drudgery and injury. Surely all instructors should aim to keep their horses lively, interested and with ever-improving form and gaits, whilst giving them a prolonged and happy life.)

The candidate now should tell the pupil he may walk whenever he wishes, if he has discovered enough for his assessment, if he needs a rest or if he is ready to relinquish his stirrups and reins.

Sit to the left, in balance.
Keep the 'puppet-strings' taut.
Relax your right knee. Hips level.
Think walk, grow tall
and forward to
WALK

EARLY LESSONS ~ 'magic'.
Think left; sit left; thumb left and he
will turn left ~ you try it...

The beginner learns the feel, the thrill,
and the correct technique.

LATER ~ a correct seat attained...
subtle, invisible influences...

THINKING

right shoulder
and left thumb
lead forehand~

(as seen
by trained,
'X-ray'
eyes.)

A lowered heel and knee shift weight
to left, 'puppet-strings' keep pelvis level.

During this brief period at walk, trot and halt the candidate will have been able to make a preliminary assessment regarding the pupil's seat and aids and the horse will have accepted the rider. They should discuss and make initial alterations and the side reins should be clipped on to the bit if they are needed. The side reins should not be too tight; often their weight alone is sufficient to indicate a good form whereas tight side reins will restrict the free play and use of the horse's musculature, neck, back and limbs and will make him resent the work.

(viii) The real "meat" of the lunge lesson now commences. Its content will depend on the rider's initial request and his present standard.

Although the lesson will be more effective if the pupil rides without reins and stirrups, he should not be deprived of their use if he is at all apprehensive. If the rider is nervous he will be stiff and stiffness is one of the worst of all rider faults. The nervous pupil should be asked to say when he feels safe enough to do some work without reins and stirrups – perhaps during the last five minutes. However, most pupils will volunteer to ride without stirrups and/or reins and this will be most advantageous to both the pupil and the candidate.

If the rider has various faults in his posture or seat when riding these must be corrected. Now the rider must be told to concentrate on feeling for and making corrections while the instructor organises the horse.

The most common rider faults are:
- Not thinking – either with or for the horse.
- Underdeveloped senses of balance and/or rhythm.
- Seat sliding to the outside: a common and major fault found in most riders of every standard, a fault which is often exaggerated by being lunged.
- Stiffness anywhere – poise "yes", excess tension "no"!
- Seat bones bumping, unlevel, or not let down on to the saddle.
- Hips crooked, unlevel or the pelvis tipped forwards or backwards; the axis of the hips not matching that of the horse's hips.
- Head carriage faulty: looking down, tilted to one side, or the chin jutting forward.
- Shoulders rounded, pulled up or unlevel, their axis not matching that of the horse's shoulders.
- Unsteady arms, not carried correctly from the back of the shoulders, thus upper limbs lacking elasticity, revealed by elbows sticking out and backs of hands uppermost, jostling hands interrupting the required smoothness of the rein aids.
- Lower legs lacking suppleness, stability and vigour.
- Inner hand creeping in towards the withers – a bad fault which interrupts the "elastic band" on the inner of the horse's central line.

Many exercises for correcting rider faults and for improving balance, suppleness and confidence have been described fully in Book 1, so they will not be listed again here. Suffice it to say that while exercises can be extremely beneficial they must not be rattled through in a rather hectic, thoughtless manner. Each case must be accorded the relevant exercise to cure the fault – a head-turning exercise will help to eradicate stiffness in the neck or spine, but it will do little to help toes which stick out!

A lunge lesson can be exciting and improving but it can also be extremely boring if the instructor lacks trained skill, imagination and enthusiasm. The instructor must inspire his pupil to maximum endeavour for improvement; he must also show that he has tact and a high regard for safety, that he teaches his pupil to be more aware of the horse and his movement, and that although he stirs the rider to make definite corrections to his seat, he is improved and elated rather than stiff and exhausted at the end of the lesson.

The theoretical part

This will include, for example, lungeing or lesson procedures, preparing a pupil for a novice competition.

If the candidate has a good knowledge of the contents of Book 1 and a thorough, practical understanding of the theory and the routines he will be well-equipped for this part of the examination. He must respond readily and clearly to all the questions put to him and provide clear evidence of his training and of practical experience.

The rules for accident procedure and first aid are revised by the medical authorities periodically so it is as well to obtain and learn from the latest leaflet as distributed by the B.H.S.

Preparing a pupil for a novice competition

This could cover an extremely wide field because, of course, there are, to name just a few, classes for novice show ponies, hacks and hunters, as well as hunter trials, team chases, dressage events, horse trials, show jumping classes, added to which each category has its own set of rules.

• The rule book: the pupil must obtain one, read it and make a note of any query he may have or action he must take. This he must discuss with you, his trainer.
• Unwritten rules: the "done" thing, or there again, those things which are *never* done, but none of which can be found in a rule book. Most are founded on commonsense, safety, courtesy or tradition and are handed on by instructors or parents to each succeeding generation.
• Procedures and methods to improve performance. This is where the Intermediate Instructor can genuinely provide some help to a pupil anxious to compete at novice level without disgracing himself – or his instructor.

The candidate should prepare and have up his sleeve, so to speak, four or five lists each containing what he considers to be the ten or twelve more important advisory notes for his pupil to learn before he competes. All should be preceded by, "Read and abide by the rules in the (appropriate) Rule Book."

Also, "Be sure that you and your horse are registered, have chosen the right class and made out your entry form and fee correctly. Discover the location of the show or competition, write out full details of the exact route, and work out how much time you will need to get there."

JUMPING DITCHES AND WATER.

Love, patient understanding and intelligence must prevail.

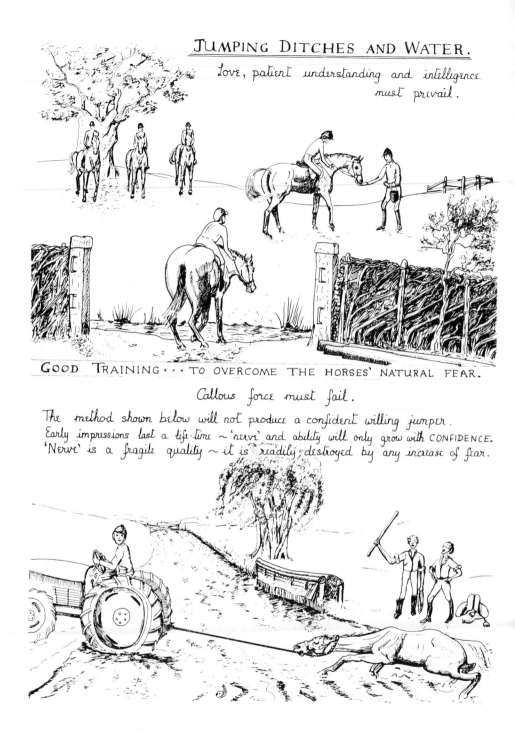

GOOD TRAINING··· TO OVERCOME THE HORSES' NATURAL FEAR.

Callous force must fail.

The method shown below will not produce a confident willing jumper.
Early impressions last a life-time ~ 'nerve' and ability will only grow with CONFIDENCE.
'Nerve' is a fragile quality ~ it is readily destroyed by any increase of fear.

Suggested headings:
Advice on competing in a show class.
Advice on competing in a hunter trial.
Advice on competing in a dressage test.
Advice on competing in a show jumping competition.
Advice on competing in a horse trial.

General advice

The kind of information which would be helpful to your pupil, and required by the examiner, can be presented as twelve items to keep in mind:

(i) Be prepared for a long day and bring water and food for you and your horse.

(ii) Arrive in plenty of time. Find a suitable place to park or to tie up your horse.

(iii) Report to the secretary's tent or horsebox. Collect your number, find out the whereabouts of your arena or course – there may be a map of the latter.

Check programmes and start times – there may have been some last minute changes. Ask for clear directions to the stables if you are staying overnight.

Locate the loos and a water tap. *Never* let your horse drink from a water trough other than at home. Troughs harbour dangerous germs such as those which cause coughs, strangles, equine 'flu – and so on.

Enquire if there is to be a prize-giving; if the event is supported by sponsors, it behoves competitors to support the sponsors!

(iv) Walk the course – cross-country or show jumping. Imagine you are your horse as you select the best track – between and over the fences. Study every fence most carefully before you reach it. Look from afar for a fluent line, the approach, to where the fence looks inviting to the landing and the line to the next fence. Then walk up to the fence and look at it closely – it may not be what you thought it was! Be prepared to adjust your ideas and your line of approach. Look to see if there is an easy alternative which may suit your horse better and which route is best for him where fences are related, for example, an in and out or double.

Make a halt exactly half-way round and "say" the first half of the course to instil it firmly into your memory; when you have finished walking the course – through the finishing flags, remember – repeat the whole course, fence by fence, together with any obligatory turning flags, to make quite certain you are course perfect.

Identify the arena for your dressage class and watch a test or two while you are walking your horse around. Note the entrance to the arena – some are obscure and you do not want to have to dash like a competitor in musical chairs searching for the way in! Note also which way the centre line runs and at which ends are A and C, the latter = the judge (friendly of course!). It is important to orientate yourself with the arena when you are working in.

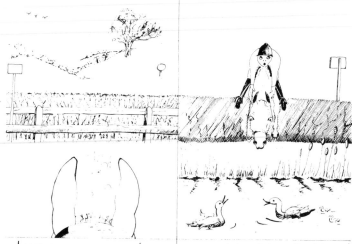

Imagine you are your horse.......may not be what you thought it was!

(v)   Prepare to ride in. This may be done in less formal attire but it should none the less be neat and safe – suitable for riding, not for the beach!

Walk your horse around quietly to inspect and accept his new surroundings. Young horses are often very anxious and quite naturally so: they should be reassured not reprimanded, for the latter will only make them more nervous. If there is a chilly wind blowing, it is best to leave a rug on over his loins, under your seat and over your knees, and he may be taken at a quiet trot to keep him warm.

As soon as the horse has settled, he should be given some easy suppling work. This work must be good for both your sakes; it should not be too demanding but all movements such as transitions, turns on the forehand, halts, canter departs must be well ridden as must the school figures you ride.

Remember that work on the flat is necessary if you are preparing for dressage, cross-country or show jumping. Prepare your gymnast well! If you are both about to jump a course of fences, your horse should be given some practice to get his eye in and his muscles warmed up. Start over a low fence and build up to a bigger upright and a spread. Do not give him too much jumping or he will be sickened or tired before he starts the actual competition.

(vi)   Give your horse a break. If time allows remove the horse's bridle, loosen his girths and let him have a short drink. If he is not due to perform for an hour and is not going cross-country he may be given five to fifteen minutes of hay or grass. Then put finishing touches to your tack, your horse and your clothing.

(vii)   Get your horse and yourself ready. You should both look as neat and tidy as you possibly can. His bit, buckles and stirrups, and all three pairs of feet should be shining.

Remember to put your number on your arm, or in the middle of your back and the ends of the tapes should be carefully hidden away.

If you are showing or riding a dressage test, push your saddle back before tightening your girths. If you are jumping, remember your surcingle and breastplace, and fit suitable studs.

Put all your kit away tidily. It is a help if those items you will require on return such as the headcollar and water bucket, are put away last. Lock your vehicle.

(viii) Report to the start steward. Check which two horses precede you so that you are ready to go to the start without being called for – the steward should not have to search for any competitor. Check all your saddlery finally at least five minutes before you are due to start.

Ride in again quietly but purposefully until it is your turn.

Note what sort of a noise your dressage judge makes: he or she may hoot, whistle or ring a bell. You must enter at A as soon as the signal has been given.

(ix) The test or round. The whole performance must be fluent. Balance, rhythm, suppleness, impulsion, timing, accuracy, are all factors which are important whether riding on the flat or over fences.

The start and the finish must both be ridden well.

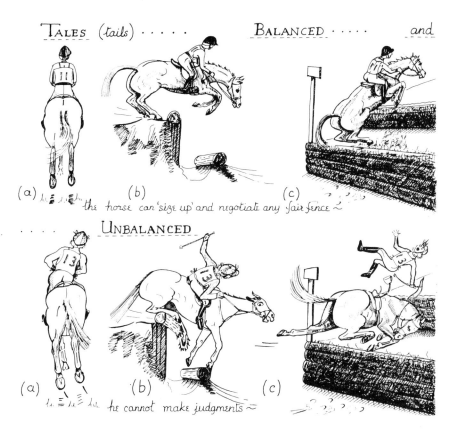

TALES (tails) · · · · ·   BALANCED · · · · ·   and

(a)   (b)   (c)

the horse can 'size up' and negotiate any fair fence ~

· · · ·   UNBALANCED

(a)   (b)   (c)

he cannot make judgments ~

(x)   On completion of the test or round, competitors should remove themselves from the area in which they have been competing, quietly and reasonably quickly; they should not loiter, coffee-house or disturb any other competitor who is about to start or who is already competing.

(xi)   See to the horse's needs: after his tack has been removed he should be sponged down, dried off and if cold he should be rugged up before he is given a drink and is fed. If the day is hot he should be hand-grazed for half an hour if such a facility exists.

He must be checked for injuries and to see if his shoes are all right. His studs should be removed and the stud-holes plugged. His tack should be wiped before it is stored neatly away – it is particularly slovenly to take bridles home with the bits uncleaned.

Tie up the horse, offer him another drink and give him a haynet while you check the score-board.

(xii)   Before you go home, thank the organiser. He and his team have been planning and toiling for months in order to give you this one day's fun, and they will still have all the clearing up to do afterwards.

Attend the prize-giving ceremony if there is one. Take the trouble to tidy yourself up for this: sponsors, organisers and judges always look well turned out, competitors should have the courtesy to do the same.

Check the exit to the ground, it may differ from the entrance and the driver of a Landrover which is trying to get out through the gate where everyone else is coming in can be the most unpopular person of the day!

Check your vehicle: that the trailer's legs are raised and secure, that the coupling, brakes and lights are connected and working as they should.

Drive or ride carefully home.

NOTE

It is always extremely helpful to a pupil who is new to the game if he can be guided and advised by his instructor at his first competition.

The five-minute lecture and discussion on stable management

Each candidate will be asked to give a five-minute lecture on a simple aspect of basic stable management as if they were briefing inexperienced yard-workers or students preparing for the B.H.S. Assistant Instructor's examination or tests of a similar standard.

There is a special emphasis on the subjects being simple and straight-forward, the object being to give the candidate the opportunity to show his ability to teach general horse-care procedures and routines to trainees, to ensure that all duties and tasks will be well carried out and that the yard will be run efficiently.

The "captive audience" for these short lectures will be students or pupils of the appropriate standard, provided by the centre: thus the lecture situation is a genuine one.

After the lectures have been delivered, the examiners will lead a discussion on other stable management subjects. The approach to this will be basic rather than deep, with the examiners looking for sound, practical

314

general knowledge on the care of horses in the stable, at grass, in work and at rest.

NOTE

Prepare!

Although the subject on which you are to speak will have been given to you in advance, on the day of the examination, a candidate would be ill-advised to rely only on this short time for his research, note-making and general preparation. In fact, he will be lucky if his jangling nerves allow him any time to remember salient facts, sort them into a logical order and commit them to paper. How much better if beforehand he has revised his earlier stable management notes and while so doing he has made a series of précis on each subject on a postcard, ready to use as a basis for a five-minute lecture at any time – at Pony Club camp or to his own students at the drop of a hat.

A student-instructor will often ask, "Could we do the lectures, some-time?", as though they could be coached fully on Phase (f) in one hour. To that student I would advise the instructor to say, "Of course, why don't you make a start this evening?" Self-motivation, again, must come to the fore: each individual must compile his own notes for his personal learning and future teaching. This is work which no one else can do for him.

A Sample List of Notes and Précis

These are listed in alphabetical order for quick reference:

Ageing horses by their teeth, and other signs.
Bandages: types, methods, dangers.
Bedding: types, methods, precautions.
Bits and bitting: types and principles.
Boots: types, methods and care.
Breeds and types: most common . . . in one sense but definitely not in the other.
Bridles: types, fitting and care.
Clipping: machines, types and maintenance.
Clipping: ponies, horses, types, methods.
Clothing, horse: types, method and maintenance.
Clothing, human: for safety and efficiency.
Condition and conditioning for different types of work.
Conformation.
Gadgets: types, fitting – their purported use in the hands of an expert – rarely if ever!
Galloping: for fittening.
Games: instructional.
Gates: opening, closing and fastening.
Grass-kept horses and ponies: care of.

Grass liveries: reception and attention.
Grassland management.
Grooming: objects, methods, kit and care.
Handling: in stables and out, training, objects and methods (including leading in hand and loose schooling).
Hay: types, grasses, production, storage.
Halter and headcollar fitting: types, tying up.
Identification: sex, size, age, colour, markings.
Insurance: accident, clients' personal, horses, equipment, saddlery and vehicles.
Knots: reef, clove-hitch, sheet-bend and slip, quick-release and granny knots, fastening, bandages, string, cord and rope.
Lameness: recognising, locating, testing, treatment.
Lungeing: equipment, uses, fitting, handling, technique, methods.
Manure: management and disposal.
Medicine cupboard's contents.
Minor ailments: keep it minor!
Parasites: types and controls.
Plaiting: see Trimming.
Poulticing.
Ride and lead: usual procedures, plus encouraging both horses to go in a good form.
Roughing off and turning out to grass.
Routines: of every sort! For example, morning, mid-day, evening stables, cleaning tack; before and after competitions; before and after hunting, point-to-point etc.
Rugs and blankets: types, fitting, uses and methods.
Saddles and saddlery: types, fitting, methods.
Safety precautions: handling horses, equipment, machinery; in stables, riding, during lessons; riding indoors, out of doors and on the road.
Shoeing: see Feet.
Signs: of good health, off-colour, loss of condition and fever. Also signs of azoturia, broken wind, colic, laminitis, lymphangitis, tooth trouble, worms, etc.
Stable construction and fittings: keep to the basics for your précis card and notes but start planning and compiling additional work in preparation for the Senior Instructor's Stable Manager's Certificate.
Teeth: formation, location, types, changing size, shape and markings, indicating horse's age.
Temperature: when and how to take and chart, together with pulse and respiration.
Travelling: preparations and procedures, including loading problems.
Trimming and plaiting.
Ventilation: see Stable Construction.
Winter care: stabled, at grass, and precautions for severe weather conditions.

Examples of five-minute lecture subjects

- Give an introductory talk to new students or yard workers.
- "A horse is due to arrive tomorrow for grass livery. You will be away. Brief your deputy and students or yard workers on the procedure to follow before, during and after its arrival". This subject may be varied by the substitution of a stabled livery, a three-year-old, a load of hay, straw, horseage, etc., or a visit from the veterinary surgeon, the farrier or the parents of a prospective pupil.
- Maintenance subjects: daily or weekly routines; fire precautions; vermin control; upkeep of buildings through the seasons; paddocks; indoor/outdoor schooling areas; setting fair; yard duties of a skeleton staff on a non-operational day.
- Riding school procedures: meeting and welcoming pupils; before, during and after the lesson; road safety; rules for riding in company; briefing pupils taking B.H.S. Horsemanship or Pony Club H Test next day.
- The care of horses requiring special attention, those who are infectious or contagious, elderly, with a mild but chronic wind-problem, with stable vices, and so on.

These few instances, together with the preceding list should provide plenty of food for thought as well as a sturdy foundation on which potential candidates can base their homework.

Practice

Book I provides advice on improving voice production and usage when lecturing. For progress, confidence and perfection, a list of reminders follows:

PREPARE
- Short notes beneath underlined headings.
- Introduction.
- Facts.
- Conclusions.
- Question.

BREATHE
Self discipline for confidence, good posture – no "nerves".

POSITIVE THINKING
Teach – with sincerity.

MANNER
This must be lively and kindly, with perhaps a hint of urgency.

PROJECT
- Every lecture must make a suitable impact.
- Speak clearly – not too quickly.

- Emphasise – each fact.
- Vary – pitch and tone.

PAUSE

From time to time to allow assimilation and reflection.

ILLUSTRATE

If relevant, a quick, clear sketch on the blackboard can be of real value, as can prepared, large-scale diagrams.

QUESTION TIME

If the lecture has been interesting there should be at least one question or comment from the audience. Let that be the challenge!

The results

At the end of the day the Chief Examiner gives out the results in two separate lists: those who have passed followed by those who have failed.

This can be another character-developing occasion for a horseman. The candidate must forewarn himself beforehand that there is every possibility that his name will be on the second, the fail list, for it only takes one major slip in any one of the six sections or a collection of minor mistakes to show the examiners that the candidate is not yet up to the standard required.

It is imperative to look at this final part of the examination day as objectively as possible so that it is educational, whatever the result may be. I am certain that most candidates manage a more positive approach if they regard the whole day as an interesting and valuable equestrian experience at the end of which they will receive an unbiased and true appraisal of their standards in the many spheres of horsemanship which are covered by the examination. If they pass, it is a bonus but if they fail it is not a disaster and they must take full advantage of the constructive criticism offered by the Chief Examiner and his expert team.

If your name is not included on the list of those who have passed you must face the fact that you have failed. It is demoralising and unnecessarily depressing for all concerned if you don't take the verdict with a "stiff upper lip" like a true sportsman. Discipline yourself: don't allow negative thoughts to creep in and cloud your mind. Think positive! You will gain far more from the examination if you accept the result and the accompanying comments with good grace; it is not so very difficult to create a desire to learn of and from your mistakes, to improve your own performance and to avoid repeating the same errors when next you sit the same examination. The examiners are experienced, practical horsemen who are ready and willing to give advice, providing you are obviously receptive.

Take your personal notebook with you for the final summing-up and write down every piece of guidance you are given. If you do not capture these pointers now they will fade beyond recall before you have com-

318

pleted your journey home. If you pass one, two, three, four or even five sections of the Intermediate Teaching Examination it is easy but dangerous to be complacent about these sections in your future preparations, no section is "in the bag" until the whole examination is accorded a *pass*.

If however, you are one of the successful candidates, whose name was included on the first list – those who have satisfied the examiners in all phases of the examination – you will have every reason to be happy and content as you look forward to taking on the challenge of the next steps up the ladder.

The Ladder of Responsibility

The passing of an examination to a higher level can be an exhilarating experience but it can also be the cause of two "major ailments" to the successful candidate. He may have a swollen head or a prideful heart, both of which can stifle the will to learn more and to make further improvements. Readers, do be warned!

Although now you may know a little of the art of horsemanship, you can never reach the goal unless you remain humble enough to learn more – and more, from every horse you ride, pupil you teach, course you attend, candidate or competitor you evaluate and from every thought and feeling you experience.

Go out and ... *think* as you ride, teach, judge and observe, train your eyes, your mind and your perception. The more help you give to others the more you yourself will be helped along the fascinating bridleways of *horsemanship*.

Looking to the Future

There are many steps still to be climbed in order to qualify as an experienced horseman and before sitting the more senior instructors' examinations. Adventurous staircases lead in numerous directions – training horses, teaching pupils, competing, judging, coaching and examining, each facet complementing the others, and all having individual problems to be surmounted with due consideration and recording. Whilst the following months and years are being filled with vital research, practical experience and achievement, time and funds must be allocated for further studies and lessons.

Excellence is an esteemed goal which is rarely attained. No horseman can afford to neglect his own performance; if he is not corrected and improved at regular intervals inevitably his technique and style will deteriorate. On the contrary all horsemen must seek further education. They must continue to think and feel, and feel and think, with ever-increasing sensitivity and perception. Their rewards will be rich as their success rates soar, their contentment waxes and they earn the reputation of being top-class riders for whom all horses go happily – in good form.